Film History and National Cinema

STUDIES IN IRISH FILM SERIES

1   *National Cinema and Beyond*
    Kevin Rockett, Trinity College, Dublin and John Hill, University of Ulster,
    editors

2   *Film History and National Cinema*
    John Hill, University of Ulster and Kevin Rockett, Trinity College, Dublin,
    editors

FILM HISTORY
AND NATIONAL CINEMA

Studies in Irish Film 2

John Hill & Kevin Rockett
EDITORS

FOUR COURTS PRESS

Set in 10.5 on 12.5 point Ehrhardt for
FOUR COURTS PRESS LTD
7 Malpas Street, Dublin 8, Ireland
e-mail: info@four-courts-press.ie
http://www.four-courts-press.ie
and in North America by
FOUR COURTS PRESS
c/o ISBS, 920 N.E. 58th Avenue, Suite 300, Portland, OR 97213.

ISBN 1–85182–924–5 hbk
ISBN 1–85182–953–9 pbk

Printed in England
by Antony Rowe Ltd, Chippenham, Wilts.

Contents

ACKNOWLEDGMENTS   7

INTRODUCTION   9
John Hill and Kevin Rockett

PART 1: FILM STUDIES: 'THE GLOBAL' AND 'THE LOCAL'

On the future of parochialism: globalization, *Young and Dangerous IV*
   and Cinema Studies in Tuen Mun   17
Meaghan Morris

Representing Okinawa: contesting images in contemporary
   Japanese cinema   37
Mika Ko

The conquering heritage of British Cinema Studies and the
   'Celtic Fringe'   47
Sarah Neely

Musical and mythical patterns in Paul Thomas Anderson's *Magnolia*   57
Danijela Kulezic-Wilson

PART 2: FILM HISTORY AND HISTORY IN FILM

'Spleen of a cabinet minister at work': exhibiting X-rays and the
   cinematograph in Ireland, 1896   69
Denis Condon

Theorizing Irish animation: heritage, enterprise and critical practice   79
Maeve Connolly

Halas and Batchelor: animation, propaganda and *Animal Farm*   90
Elizabeth Coulter-Smith

Cathal Black's *Korea*   97
Emilie Pine

Escape from Fantasy Ireland: Martin Duffy's *The Boy from Mercury*   106
Pádraic Whyte

6 *Contents*

PART 3: FILM, REPRESENTATION AND IDEOLOGY

From feminism to post-feminism: Pat Murphy's love story *Nora*   117
Dióg O'Connell

The Snapper: a contemporary crisis pregnancy?   129
Dervila Layden

'Ebony saint' or 'demon black'? Racial stereotypes in Jim Sheridan's
    In America   143
Beth Newhall

Revisioning vision in the Bloody Sunday films   154
Ellen E. Sweeney

NOTES ON CONTRIBUTORS   165

INDEX   167

Acknowledgments

Special thanks to the Higher Education Authority North South Programme for Collaborative Research for providing financial assistance for the publication. Thanks to Carol Kyle, Janet Mackle, Robert Porter and Sally Quinn at the University of Ulster for their assistance with the organization of the Irish Postgraduate Film Research Seminar at the University of Ulster in April 2004. Thanks also to Martin McLoone of the University of Ulster and Paula Quigley of Trinity College Dublin, for chairing sessions. Thanks to Antoinette Prout of the Irish Film Institute in sourcing cover film still, and to Fox Searchlight Pictures for use of image.

Introduction

JOHN HILL & KEVIN ROCKETT

The Irish Postgraduate Film Research Seminar is a joint venture between Trinity College Dublin, and the University of Ulster at Coleraine designed to promote original research in the area of Irish cinema and to encourage the training and development of young researchers working in an Irish context. Since 2003, the Seminar has been supported by the Higher Education Authority's North South Programme for Collaborative Research which has made possible the provision of three postgraduate studentships, special training events and the publication of the Seminar proceedings. The first seminar took place at Trinity College in 2003 and led to the publication of *National Cinema and Beyond: Studies in Irish Film I* in 2004. The second seminar occurred at the University of Ulster on the Portrush campus in 2004 and the current volume grows out of that event.

FILM STUDIES: THE GLOBAL AND THE LOCAL

Although a key ambition of the Seminar has been to promote new research in the area of Irish cinema, it has been recognized from the start that such work cannot be conducted in isolation from developments elsewhere. Irish cinema may provide a specialist area of study but it is also one that is informed by and itself informs more general debates about film. These include discussion of the increasingly globalized character of both film production and reception, the future of national cinemas in a global context, the relations between film and various forms of cultural identity and the emergence of distinctive aesthetic forms in response to the changing conditions of film production and distribution. It is therefore fitting that the volume begins with a wide-ranging discussion of the relations between the 'local' and the 'global' by the distinguished Australian scholar, Meaghan Morris. Taking as her topic, the 'future of the parochial', Morris seeks to rescue the idea of 'parochialism' from its identification with inward-looking backwardness. For her, parochialism is better understood as 'a complex disposition' that 'provides an angle from which to consider issues of cultural impact and change under globalization in a concrete way'. Using the example of the Hong Kong film *Young and Dangerous IV: 97*, and drawing upon her own experiences of teaching cultural studies in Tuen Mun in the new Territories of the Hong Kong

9

Special Administrative Region (HKSAR), Morris identifies how parochial-ism – or an emotional investment in place – may possess a multi-layered dynamism that complicates any simple opposition between 'backward' parochialism and 'progressive' internationalism.

A resistance to spurious 'internationalism' is also evident in Mika Ko's study of the representation of Okinawa in contemporary cinema. Taking as her start-ing-point, the recent 'Okinawa boom' within Japan, Ko indicates how the rep-resentation of Okinawa as a 'loveable other' in popular Japanese films bypasses the socio-political predicaments characteristic of contemporary Okinawa. By focusing on the Okinawan director Takamine Go's experimental film *Tsuru-Henry* (1999), she shows how the film mobilizes a complex notion of Okinawan identity that rejects both the 'cosmetic multiculturalism' of contemporary Japanese ideology and the 'essentialism' of nationalist discourse.

Identifying the dominant image of Okinawa in terms of a 'festive paradise' in which singing, dancing and drinking are the prevailing activities, Ko notes the similarity with historic representations of the Irish. In her discussion of the heritage film, Sarah Neely also observes how the cinematic representation of Scotland and Ireland has been involved in the construction of tourist imagery aimed at the international audience. However, while the conventions of the her-itage film may cultivate the picturesque, Neely indicates how heritage debates have been primarily associated with English heritage and how this becomes com-plicated in the context of the 'Celtic' countries. In particular, she suggests how Scottish and Irish cinema have been drawn to child-centred narratives that fore-ground an 'alternative heritage'. By highlighting the unstable point-of-view of the child, she suggests, these films have the potential 'to expose contradictions within the meta-narratives of national cinema' and subvert dominant concep-tions of the nation. This is also an argument developed by Pádraic Whyte in his discussion of *The Boy from Mercury* (1996). Indicating how the young Harry Cronin functions as an allegory of the Irish nation, he suggests how the film moves beyond the nostalgic construction of childhood to provide a critique of the ideological burdens weighing down on the present.

Whereas Neely and Whyte seek to retrieve the local meanings contained within apparently universal stories of childhood, Danijela Kulezic-Wilson moves in the other direction by suggesting how the mythic is embedded in Paul Thomas Anderson's complex drama of contemporary US lives, *Magnolia* (1999). Focusing on the film's use of music, Kulezic-Wilson suggests how this is responsible for the creation of patterns that invest the film with a mythic mode of perception. Like Ko, Kulezic-Wilson is one of a number of scholars based in Ireland working on topics that are not themselves specifically Irish in character. In this respect, Film Studies in Ireland is not confined to Irish topics just as Irish Film Studies itself is carried on both inside and outside of Ireland (as the work of Neely and Ellen Sweeney indicates). The eclecticism of the current volume therefore not only reflects the diverse character of film research in Ireland but also suggests some of the productive ways in which 'global' and 'local' perspectives may interact.

Part Two of the book is more directly concerned with Irish film history and analysis. New forms of research into early cinema have been responsible for opening up debates about the emergence of cinema and how this is to be understood. Denis Condon's research has been focused on Irish cinema before 1921 and, in his contribution to this volume, he examines the early commercialization and popularization of the X-ray and the Cinematograph. Condon reveals how newspapers fuelled the public imagination when X-ray images were discovered and then demonstrated in Ireland in 1896, only to be rapidly superseded by the more flexible and varied cinematograph. While the latter found its important role in medical science, the cinematograph was to go on to become Ireland's most popular entertainment within a generation.

Maeve Connolly also opens up another aspect of the history of Irish film production in her pioneering article on the history of Irish animation. Tracing the limited history of Irish animation before the 1970s, Connolly suggests some frameworks in which recent animation practice might be understood. In doing so, she identifies two main trajectories, one rooted in the commercial initiatives of the 1980s, the other with links to a history of avant-garde practice. Like Neely, she identifies the pull of the heritage industry and its encouragement of imagery reliant upon sanitized versions of the past. However, she also identifies a strand of more self-reflexive animation practice critical of heritage discourse and more alert to the complexities of contemporary Irish experience. In doing so, Connolly also indicates how certain strands of Irish animation have evaded its prevailing associations with childhood and sentimental forms of entertainment. This point is also pursued by Elizabeth Coulter-Smith in her discussion of the career of the animators John Halas and Joy Batchelor whom she argues were responsible for the development – in Britain – of a form of informational or propagandistic animation aimed at the adult audience. Taking the animated version of *Animal Farm* (1954) as her case-study, she indicates how this work departs from the mainstream tradition of Disney.

Representations of the past, and their relationship to the present, are also explored in the essays by Emilie Pine and Pádraic Whyte. Pine focuses on Cathal Black's *Korea* (1995) which is concerned with the legacy of the Irish civil war, itself a rare topic in Irish cinema. Set in the early 1950s, as the modernization of Irish society began to develop, the film explores the social tensions of the period in a way that presages the upheavals of the 1990s. Whyte's essay deals with Martin Duffy's *The Boy from Mercury* (1996) set in the Ireland of the early 1960s in which a young boy finds release in Flash Gordon films and the fantasy that he is from the planet Mercury. This serves as a means of dealing with the painful loss of his father and the oppressive conditions in which he finds himself. In both cases, Pine and Whyte identify how the films avoid the nostalgia for the past characteristic of the heritage film (criticized by other contributors) as well as the fatalism of political melodrama in which characters become the victims of the tyranny of the past. Both films, it is suggested, are 'histories of the present' involving forward-looking narratives in which the return to the past becomes the means for an escape from the hold that it exerts.

FILM, REPRESENTATION AND IDEOLOGY

While the relationship of Irish film to Irish history and ideas of the nation remains a continuing interest for film researchers, the critique of 'essentialist' notions of the nation has inevitably led to a focus on other forms of cultural identification within the nation. Given the historical dominance of men within Irish society, and a lengthy tradition of feminist film analysis, the representation of gender within Irish film continues to be a major area of concern. Continuing the theme of representations of the past, Dióg O'Connell analyses the representation of James Joyce and Nora Barnacle in Pat Murphy's *Nora* (2000). While the film has been seen in some quarters as a retreat from the feminist experimentation of *Maeve* (1981) and *Anne Devlin* (1984), O'Connell argues that the film successfully evades the conventions of the mainstream love story and the heritage film. The film, she suggests, is best understood as a 'post-feminist' work in which the relationship between Joyce and Nora is dramatized in terms of a liberal-humanist discourse of equality.

Dervila Layden's analysis of *The Snapper* (1993), however, is less sanguine about the 'post-feminist' gains wrought by changes in the Irish nuclear family in recent years. Focusing on the trauma of the pregnant single mother, Layden detects an advance from earlier representations of pregnancy contained in *Reefer and the Model* (1987) and *Hush-a-Bye Baby* (1989) but is keen to emphasize the continuing social discrimination against single mothers. Partly reading the film as a social document, Layden highlights the changing role of the father in the film and the strength of the single mother but suggests that Ireland's pregnancy narratives continue to be beset by the experience of trauma.

If the analyses of O'Connell and Layden grow out of a feminist concern with the representation of gender in Irish society, Beth Newhall's chapter deals with the representation of race and ethnicity. As a result of the huge influx of migrant workers from eastern Europe, Africa and Asia during the 'Celtic Tiger' boom, the ethnic character of Irish society has changed dramatically. While these new realities have yet to figure significantly in Irish film, Jim Sheridan's partly autobiographical *In America* (2002), dealing with an Irish family's move to New York, appears to offer a timely meditation upon issues of migration and cultural identity. However, while the film may appear to offer a sympathetic portrait of multiculturalism, Newhall argues that this is not the case (echoing Ko's arguments concerning the 'cosmetic' nature of Japanese multiculturalism). Drawing on the work of Ella Shohat and Robert Stam, Newhall demonstrates how the film's portrait of Mateo corresponds to well-worn stereotypes of the African 'other' resulting from the imperialist conquest of Africa in the eighteenth and nineteenth centuries. It is all the more ironic, therefore, that a filmmaker whose career has been marked by sympathetic portrayals of disability (*My Left Foot*) and English judicial and police prejudice (*In the Name of the Father*), should (unconsciously) adopt some of imperialism's racist paradigms.

The volume concludes with Ellen Sweeney's discussion of the Bloody Sunday films, the only essay this year to deal with the North. Like other contributors to the book, Sweeney is interested in the relationship of the film image to historical memory. However, her focus is less on the manner in which these films challenge official accounts of events than the raising of questions concerning the very possibility of representing traumatic memory. Drawing on ideas taken from Gilles Deleuze, Sweeney examines the interplay of 'subjective' and 'objective' point-of-view in *Bloody Sunday* (2002) and *Sunday* (2002), indicating how each in their different ways problematize the 'totalizing gaze' of the British state. In this way, Sweeney seeks not only to reveal the implicit ideologies at work in film texts but also the ways in which the formal language of film may be seen to embed particular perspectives.

As with the previous volume, much of the writing here represents work-in-progress, the thinking-through of research questions and analytical issues involved in the study of Irish and international cinema. As the Irish Postgraduate Film Research Seminar proceeds, and further work is undertaken, so we hope that both Film Studies in Ireland and Irish Film Studies will continue to open up new areas of investigation and debate.

Part 1: Film Studies: 'The Global' and 'The Local'

On the future of parochialism: globalization, *Young and Dangerous IV*, and Cinema Studies in Tuen Mun

MEAGHAN MORRIS

In the critical rhetoric of culture today we are always tripping over problems of spatial framing and distinction. Not only do we have the 'local', the 'region-al', the 'national' and the 'international' to contend with but their 'trans-', 'intra-', and 'infra-' dimensions as well; for example, there are intra-national regions ('rural and regional Australia' means anywhere beyond the big cities), and supra-national regions ('Australia in the region' generally means 'East Asia and the Pacific'). 'Borders' and 'boundaries' are everywhere, although in the specialized geography of cultural theory they tend to serve not as bar-riers but as bridges for 'crossing' a rising tide of 'flows'. Globalization as it unsettles old colonial geographies is widely held responsible for this shifting and floating of categories, and, coming to the island of Ireland as I do from my home in Australia via a working life in Hong Kong, I do not propose to contest this.

My theme is a stubbornly earth-bound or binding force that is a worry in all three of these literally 'insular' (island-based, water-bound) places: parochial-ism, most simply defined by *The Macquarie Dictionary* as a 'narrowness of interest or view'. The word is of Christian origin, 'pertaining to a parish', but those of my Chinese students who have no experience of parishes understand its connotations easily with reference to the village or its urban projections, the housing estate and the district. In the negativity surrounding the idea of parochialism there is a legacy of evangelizing, bureaucratic modernism, a thing about the darkness of peasant life and below that the need (by creating parish-es) to keep the pagan in the peasant at bay; unease with the parochial and indeed the capacity to imagine parochialism always belongs to the ones with wider horizons.

Parochialism is a blighted *affective* condition and in this it differs from insularity, a way of knowing and handling the world. Insularity has an epis-temological strength that may command a certain respect: I once saw a rugby league team in Sydney admiringly described as 'the proud and insular Bulldogs'. However, when a coach's move from a top Sydney club to one based in a 'friendly and parochial' North Queensland town is described as suiting him well, the same syntactic construction becomes just a touch condescending. Another attitude surfaced in a recent spat in the AFL (Australian Football League, sponsors of a mutant form of Rules football with its heartland in Victoria) when the coach of the Brisbane Lions slammed the 'rampant', 'home-town parochialism' of the national organizers in Melbourne.[1] No hint of a compliment there: in a shifting world, insularity provides a base or a grounding but parochialism is a *lapse*, an emotionally backward way of inhabiting the spatial frames of the present.

Increasingly conflated with a spatial impermeability and cultural imperviousness to capital, historical back-sliding has economic costs today and this is one reason why parochialism is so often seen as a worry, especially in insular places with other kinds of competitive disadvantage to overcome. Unless we, too, are rampant parochialists – an attitude that the forced mobility of academic as of other kinds of labour increasingly makes hard to sustain – teachers worry about parochialism in students; it narrows their future as well as their present. The brutal simplicity of this struck me when I moved to Hong Kong and had to buy a whole new everyday life: in the big electronics store where sales earn a commission, the charming young man who could surmount the agony of using sociable English took my order every time. Henri Lefebvre saw a service economy and a culture of customer-oriented personalities arriving in the 1960s, but the intensity of the pressure placed by globalization on our emotional capacity to handle cultural strangers skilfully for hours on end has since become extreme – rising first, no doubt, in 'global cities' and metropolitan centres but eventually spreading, with waves of migratory capital and labour, to rural and once isolated areas as well.[2]

Yet as my football examples serve to suggest, most people still participate in parochial circuits of affect and belonging: family, sport, and, since it is possible to inhabit institutions and professions or trades in parochial ways, the distribution of employment (and lack of it) are just three of the forces that work to keep us grounded and emotionally bounded. In the frameworks of value internal to Australia I have been a parochial person most of my life, although it is a cosmopolitan feint to admit this; I experience national belonging through Sydney and north-eastern New South Wales, approaching the rest of the continent as foreign ('a nice place to visit' but 'how could anyone live there?'). My parochialism has roots in a tenacious family culture of living in close proximity – an immigrant peasant and working class way of life severely eroded over the past thirty years and now tinged with sentimentality for those who have left it behind – but it has blossomed in the airy self-absorption

1 Richard Hinds, 'The name of the game's national, so it's time for Victoria to let go', *Sydney Morning Herald* (7 September 2004), p. 36. In fact the article points out that 'the AFL has gone much further than any of its major competitors in [Rugby] league, union and soccer to establish a viable and truly national competition'.   2 Henri Lefebvre, *The practice of everyday life* trans. Steven F. Rendall (Berkeley and London, 1984, orig. 1962).

of elite cultural life in Australia's premier city. As all those who live in 'second tier cities' know, a high metropolitan parochialism can be truly dense in its failure to conceive of its own restricted nature; the parochialisms of Paris and New York are in this respect exemplary.

From the outset, then, it should be clear that I approach parochialism not as an unequivocally bad object that must be eradicated (I doubt that it can be) but as a complex disposition of variable significance which provides an *angle* from which to consider issues of cultural impact and change under globaliza-tion in a concrete way. To think about parochialism involves taking inhabi-tant perspectives into account along with the migratory and mobile, tracing the sediments of culture as well as the flows, and remembering that parochial-ism itself is a portable way of dwelling; in the highly charged value conflicts that can arise in multicultural societies, my cultural 'baggage' may be your social 'burden' and vice versa.[3] My focus here, however, is on low-level issues arising in universities and other cultural industries, such as the cinema, that are obliged to cope with an 'export' imperative. These issues interest me as a film teacher because I still see education as a way of constituting grounds for hope, and cinema as a mode of pedagogy that is all the more effective at spreading what Donald Horne calls 'hypotheses about existence' for being casually attended, lax about whether we get it or not and, for the most part, pleasurable enough to teach us in our dreams.[4]

RUNAWAY GLOBALIZATION

Let me begin with a fieldwork anecdote. A few years ago I left Sydney for Hong Kong and Lingnan University, a small liberal arts environment situat-ed neither on Hong Kong Island nor in Kowloon, the two areas that in media representation anchor a global image of Hong Kong as a city, but in Tuen Mun, a semi-rural, rapidly urbanizing area in the outer western New Territories of the Hong Kong Special Administrative Region (HKSAR) of China, some fifteen minutes drive from the mainland border. I had worked in Asian cultural studies networks for years, and in Hong Kong I hoped to evade the exhaustion and disillusion pervading the Australian university system: the distribution of overwork to some and casualization to others, the lunatic piles of paperwork, the rising barriers dividing a research career from under-graduate teaching. Within a couple of years, I found that I had migrated to an earlier phase of the same process; when the University Grants Committee

3 See Meaghan Morris and Brett de Bary (eds), *'Race' panic and the memory of migration*, vol 2 of *Traces: A Multilingual Journal of Cultural Theory and Translation* (Hong Kong, Tokyo, Seoul and Nanjing, 2001).   4 Donald Horne, *The public culture: the triumph of industrialism* (London and Sydney, 1986), p. 4.

of Hong Kong released its Sutherland report on Higher Education in Hong Kong in 2002, its policy scenarios of 'excellence' transported me back to 1987 and the Dawkins reform in Australia.[5] We are wary these days of unfolding historicist time-lines along which some places are ahead of others. However, those old colonial maps support the newer circuits of trade remarkably well: Lord Sutherland is Vice-Chancellor of the University of Edinburgh, and John Dawkins (Australia's education minister in the Labour government of the time) took his ideas from Thatcher's Britain.

Of course, there are always local inflections of context and uptake that sustain differentiation as the same scenario unfolds from place to place, although on the ground this is not necessarily an unmitigated good thing. Take the international refereed journal (IRJ), the tyranny of which was one thing I had wanted to escape. When I left Australia, the distribution of a chunk of funding and thus of quality of life to teachers and of hope and opportunity to students depended on the capacity of an academic 'unit' to churn out articles ('product' or 'McArticles' might be more appropriate terms) for these largely unread repositories of the parochialism of sometimes British, usually American, blind reviewers. An IRJ is ill-suited in cultural domains of enquiry to its mission of monitoring quality; not only do reviewers often lack the background to assess the *significance* of work formulated in contexts that differ from their own (a problem of cross-cultural reading with which writers who possess more than parochial aspirations should, I believe, strive to cope) but they must answer on the basis of ignorance a usually obligatory question: 'has the author made reference to the relevant literature on this topic?'. When making decisions about relevance most of us suffer in some degree from a 'narrowness of interest or view', but a blind reviewer has the added disadvantage of not knowing what materials circulate as significant for scholars in an unidentified elsewhere.

The more extreme stories from the 1990s of political correctness in American academic publishing should be understood in this context, which is one of globally unequal terms of trade in the publishing industry itself. All those true and untrue tales of manuscripts rejected for ignoring work by women and minority scholars that might not exist in a given area or historical period attest to our public knowledge that the 'relevant literature' question is a canon-forming exercise that has more to do now with solidarity-enforcement than with diversification, let alone with evidential and other scholarly criteria of pertinence. Loading up texts from around the world with bibliographies featuring names from the North American academy, English-language pub-

---

5 J.S. Dawkins, *The challenge for higher education in Australia* (Canberra, 1987), *Higher education: a policy discussion paper* (Canberra, 1987), and *Higher education: a policy statement* (Canberra, 1987); and Stewart R. Sutherland, *Higher education in Hong Kong* (Hong Kong, 2002).

lishing transnationally distributes an Anglo-American social politics: less often remarked on is that this process ultimately shapes the lucrative business of textbook production and sales. No doubt about it, we discover fine works of scholarship this way. The production of their universal *relevance*, however, has less to do with quality than with the expectation of Anglo-American reviewers to be always at home in the scholarly world, and with their publishers' creation of a market across that world.

The operations of this kind of empowered, institutional parochialism do most damage when they foster a second-guessing phenomenon whereby new generations of scholars take it for granted that the first thing you do when you aspire to publish is to assemble a mental 'box' from materials canonical across the Atlantic. Right now, this assumption is not evenly distributed across the English-using world: Ireland and India retain publishing economies in which, respectively, an 'insular' and a national mode of address remain viable. When the Atlantic mode of address locks in, however, it swiftly corrodes our capacity to address our social communities with any immediacy – especially if our disposable time for writing more than once or twice a year is shrinking in the name of budget stringency and educational reform. Language itself becomes a distancing medium when writing for IRJs, even for Australians (who are usually fluent in English at university level). The precise definition of this or that cultural fact is suddenly *rendered* parochial, a patch of Aussie local colour to be highlighted in scare quotes and laden with a gloss, or bleached away by some blandly global phrase, a hilariously wrong Americanism or a blob of theory jargon.[6]

Imagine, then, the situation of Cantonese-speaking Chinese scholars in Hong Kong who must deal with all this *also* by shifting their intellectual production into a second language (one which is not, contrary to legend, widely used by ordinary Hong Kong people) and another script as well. As the IRJ regime locks in firmly to the humanities in the wake of the Sutherland report – through contract renewal processes and performance-based promotion, plus plans to upgrade the Research Assessment Exercise (RAE) to British levels of intensity – the negotiation of formidable problems of linguistic and cultural translation on an everyday basis becomes a condition of my colleagues' survival as university employees. However, this structural marginalization of the Chinese language and thus of local community concerns is not driven by any simple ethnic or national binary: journals in Chinese are scorned in Hong Kong Business and Social Science circles precisely because they are rarely refereed, and little sympathy accrues to Chinese humanists from compatriots in other faculties. Exception is made for literary scholars in the Chinese Department, yet by some alchemy it seems sensible in this system for anyone

6 I develop this argument in 'Afterthoughts on Australianism', *Cultural Studies* 6:3 (1992), pp 468–75.

writing about, say, TV dramas made in Cantonese or Mandarin, or subtitled in Chinese and watched in Hong Kong, to address their work in the first instance to Western English-readers who may never see the texts or care what issues they raise.

A drastic shift of affective positioning (that is, in how it feels to be a scholar) is entailed by this imperative to write always in translation for a remote and purely professional readership, a shift tricky to execute in a field like cultural studies which claims to valorize local practices and community involvement and which attracts, in the Hong Kong context, experienced social activists. Yet the sanctions for not making the shift are clear and, in an industrial culture favouring fixed-term contracts over tenure, they are unnegotiable for most academic staff. One obvious solution would be the creation of more Chinese refereed journals. However, at this point of innovation a specialized notion of the *international* context blocks linguistic pluralism in research publication; under the IRJ regime (as would-be editors soon discover), 'international' narrowly means the Northern Anglo-sphere.

This brings me back to Australia. When I left, Australian-based publications were deemed national and second-tier, while anything from Britain and the USA was international by definition; a corollary of this is that even the most 'rampantly home-town' work of a parochially British scholar is international wherever it appears. In Hong Kong today, I am asked to discourage staff from publishing work not only in Hong Kong but in 'obscure' journals from Taiwan or mainland China – a distribution of reputational brilliance and shadow that is actively parochializing texts that millions of people may read. Running away, I find that globalization runs through me; I have a whole new level of insight about what it means to be an agent of imperialism now that it is *my* job to help colleagues submit their work to an IRJ.

PAROCHIAL POWER-WALK

Another of my reasons for moving to Hong Kong was somewhat less naïve. The realization that I could learn more about Australian culture by living in an Asian society came with an embarrassing moment in 1992 when I gave a paper in Taipei carefully explaining the persistence of an aesthetics of the Sublime in what I took to be, in that context, an exotic white Australian fear of being 'swamped' by a vast population from Asia – only to be gently told that Taiwan people of course have their own 'sublime' of invasion from the mainland, including indigenous legends centuries old.[7] The flush of disbelief at one's

---

7 This discussion is appended to my 'White Panic, or *Mad Max* and the Sublime', in Kuan-Hsing Chen (ed.) *Trajectories: inter-Asia cultural studies* (London and New York, 1998), pp 239–62.

own educated lack of imagination that fills moments like these with amazement also brings a recognition and suspension of parochialism – the affective intensity of which is indeed a cognitive limitation when it blocks our capacity to imagine affinities with a more or less neighbouring island.

For all that, parochialism as an emotional investment in place has an energy that makes it a positive resource in some contexts. Many of these are bellicose, and yet, more subtly, shifts of perception and feeling occur when that 'narrow' vision turns outward to find its gaze returned in kind; violence is not the only possible outcome when parochialisms meet each other. An old expression of other potentials is the ethnographic comedy of errors, running from seventeenth century European picaresque novels and eighteenth century philosophical tales of thinking travellers (a genre renewed for TV in 1972 by the David Carradine series, *Kung Fu*), to popular films about culture shock featuring peasants (Bruce Lee in *Way of the Dragon*) or other primitive figures (Paul Hogan in *Crocodile Dundee*) negotiating a city, or urbanites lost in places they have mistaken for the wild (Jackie Chan in *Who Am I?*). Arguably, the identification processes so often mobilized by popular narrative arts offer manifold opportunities to feel empathy with other people's parochialism, even as they invite us to enjoy their cultural mistakes. Certainly, the enduring popularity of place-based TV dramas – *Melrose Place, Beverly Hills 92010, The O.C.* (USA), *Coronation Street, Eastenders* (UK), *Number 96, Bellbird, Neighbours* (Australia), *Under the Lion Rock* (Hong Kong) and *Meteor Garden* (Taiwan) are a few canonical examples – suggests that the 'parish' is a widely *translatable* framework for exploring the volatility of bounded everyday lives, a pleasure tweaked towards surrealism by reality TV.

Perhaps the most intense reflection on parochial living today is provided by urban crime and gangster fiction.[8] Alongside classical crime capitals such as London, Los Angeles and Chicago, or Tokyo, Shanghai and Hong Kong, city after city in recent decades has found a novelist, a TV series or a film to unfold for a wider world its stories of 'turf' inherited and disputed, of shadow hierarchies of power assuring its administration, of the lairs and pathways of its gangs and serial killers, and of lives passed deep within the confines of its neighbourhoods and streets. Crime stories offer a line of flight from the global urban glamour-scape to the grim parts of cities such as Boston (Dennis Lehane), Edinburgh (Ian Rankin) or Montreal (Kathy Reichs), and to the functional basements, back-rooms and offices of aspirational suburbs (New Jersey in *The Sopranos*). In this expansion of the terrain for parochial myth there is a hint of that quest for authenticity that tourism claims to fulfil, but any promise of recovery is illusory: few popular cultural genres today are more

---

8 Thanks to Markus Reisenleitner; see 'The American Traveling Detective and the Exotic City: *Pépé Le Moko, Macao* and *The Third Man*' in S. Ingram, M. Reisenleitner and C. Szabó-Knotik (eds), *Ports of call: Central European and North American culture/s in motion* (Frankfurt, 2004), pp 259–68.

explicit than crime fiction about the grip of globalization on urban social economies and in the most restricted lives.

The credit sequence of Andrew Lau Wai-keung's film *Young and Dangerous IV: 97* (HK, 1997) is an exhilarating condensation of this power of parochial energies to affirm the tenacity and *flair* of place, while using the 'narrow view' as a way of seeing clearly the rules of engagement set by a wider world. As the fourth in a series of six Hong Kong 'triad youth' films made between 1996, the year in which the first three films appeared, and 2000, by which time three more films and thirteen spin-offs including a 'prequel' had also appeared, *Young and Dangerous IV* could presume a local audience familiar not only with its settings and streetscapes but with a cast of characters played, as a web-site on the series notes, by 'just about everybody' in Hong Kong.[9] However, its opening shots of a group of men walking along the external corridor of an elevated floor in a housing estate are intelligible to just about anybody; these men are striding with purpose, and they move like they own the place.

Restricted perspective in this sequence is a compositional principle. We see, in fact, very little and the sense of a controlled, collective 'power walk' just a shade of restraint away from a swagger or a strut is produced by the rhythmic editing of *glimpses* to the pulse of a theme song performed by the two male stars of the film, Ekin Cheng Yee-kin and Jordan Chan Siu-chun. After a chorally exclamatory production company credit for BoB & Partners, another is overlaid for four seconds by a low metallic growl which loudens to roar like the MGM lion for two seconds of black leader;[10] then a drum-and-bass prelude irrupts and the image sequence begins with an abrupt assertion in medium close-up, angled as though we are peeking upward from the side, of an oncoming cluster of dark shoes and trousers moving rapidly past the waste bins and pipes along a corridor wall. We hardly have time to register that the shoes are shiny and the trousers sharp when we cut to a credit, held fractionally longer, announcing in red and white on black that the Executive Producer is Raymond Chow.

The two-second pattern resumes when a reverse shot gives us an on-the-move view, hand-held from the position of a leader of the pack, along a narrow walkway cramped between railings on the left and the security grilles and utilities pipes of small flats on the right; ahead and to the left of us looms another wall crammed with balconies and windows, closing us in to the housing estate while establishing height from the ground. From this point on, the

9 'Young and Dangerous: the series', http://www.chinesecinemas.org/young.html; accessed 16/05/2005. Alongside credits and reviews by Shelly Kraicer, this site offers a list ('The Triad Boyz phenomenon') of the spin-offs from the series.   10 The second production credit is for Everwide (H.K) Limited. The BoB partners include the company linked to Wong Jing, the commercial genius of Hong Kong cinema, a prolific writer-director-producer, and 'perhaps one of the best filmmakers of all time' according to his Internet Movie Database biographers: http://www.imdb.com/name/nm0939147/bio

shot/credit/reverse shot visual pattern is held to a 'three times two-seconds' temporal rhythm (2:2:2) and a 4:4 musical beat. Sharp chords rising across the credit for producer Manfred Wong (Man Jun) promise the imminent arrival of melody, with the tension maintained across a closer, tighter shot of those relentlessly approaching feet. As the driving rock duet begins at the end of another credit, we catch vivid signs of life going on in the gloom – bright towels over the railing, red decorations on a door – and then shift to the rear of the group to see the heads and shoulders moving in front of us sway slightly to the beat. This densely inhabited vertical village is, unmistakably, 'turf', and the rest of the sequence elaborates its properties: potential menace (those shoes made for walking end up almost in our face); openness to insiders (the camera swerves briefly to peer into the apartment of a woman in a red dress); and an unavoidable level of abstract communal involvement (the last external shot of the power-walk is from the point of view of a neighbour one floor across and above).

In less than two minutes, the walkway sequence sketches a 'whole way of life' organized around the dynamic between energy (of rhythm and movement) and restriction (of vision and space) that will figure as a *tension* between desire and order in the ensuing narrative about the struggle to secure a proper succession of power in a territorially organized triad or crime 'family' (the Hung Hing society). The dominant feeling in the sequence, however, is one of confident vitality and pride; the oscillation of the point of view between the near outside and the deep inside of what is as yet (for the viewer) a faceless gang combines with the pulse of the music to give their walk its distinctively parochial and macho introversion: there is a show (of force, of numbers, of style) but its exhibitionism is all about solidarity; whether these men are gangsters or cops they draw power from this environment and their display is expressive of this, not assumed to impress outsiders; here, these men *belong*.

As it turns out, they are Hung Hing boys gaily accompanying the groom, Dai Tin-yee (Michael Tse), to a wedding. When they stop at the door of a flat where 'KK' (Pinky Cheung) is waiting with friends and family, face after face becomes visible during the bridal threshold banter which follows – and a series fan can put a name to every single pair of shoes. This 'local' film knowledge is not necessary for getting the idea that these are *our* bad guys, and that this housing estate is home territory close to the beating heart of Hong Kong Cantonese popular life, but an intimacy with the past experiences of these characters in previous films helps to bind us in to a sense of history unfolding. This history will be traumatic: soon, Tin-yee will be killed and KK raped in a ploy by a villain from the rival Tung Sing family, and a bitter war of succession with ramifications stretching from Thailand to Tuen Mun will reach in to twist the lives of everyone standing at this threshold between a tiny flat and a walkway somewhere in Causeway Bay.

Hong Kong cinema excelled at elaborating triad mythology in the 1980s and 1990s, with some of its internationally now most famous films (such as those made by John Woo with Chow Yun Fat) appearing between the Sino-British Joint Declaration on the future of Hong Kong in 1984 and the handover of power from Britain to China in 1997. In these years, Hong Kong popular culture was marked by many anticipatory attempts 'to negotiate', as Stephen Ching-kiu Chan puts it in an essay on the *wuxia* or martial sword-play films of the time, 'some sort of renewed sense of identity for the local community after colonial rule'.[11] As Chan explains, most works from this period by such directors as Yuen Woo-ping, Tsui Hark, Ching Siu-tung, Wong Kar-wai, Stephen Chiau, Jeff Lau and Corey Yuen 'contain substantial local elements difficult to translate readily to a non-local viewer', and while the *wuxia* films may be overtly challenging to outsiders in this respect (Wong Kar-wai's *Ashes of Time* is a good example), it is not hard to see how the imaginary of a self-contained triad world could also explore in deeply coded and layered ways those dilemmas of cultural locality and identity that were so pressing for Hong Kong people in advance of 1997.[12]

On the surface, however, the *Young and Dangerous* films are very accessible. Initiated barely eighteen months before the event of the hand-over itself, the series was phenomenally popular with young people; accordingly, the romantic treatment of hoodlums as heroes and its allusions to the social actuality of triad involvement in schools (not to mention the film industry itself) created controversy.[13] So did its MTV style, its comic-book inspiration, its 'garish, neon aesthetic and its pretty-boy take on criminal enterprise'[14] – which led some critics to find it empty and cynical beside the more

---

11 Stephen Ching-kiu Chan, 'The fighting condition in Hong Kong cinema: local icons and cultural antidotes for the global popular' in M. Morris, S.-L. Li and S. C.-K. Chan (eds), *Hong Kong connections: transnational imagination in action cinema* (Hong Kong, forthcoming).   12 While seemingly contrasted by their respective 'period/costume' and 'contemporary/urban' settings, the *wuxia* and triad genres of Hong Kong cinema are profoundly linked by a cultural imaginary organized by the concept of *jianghu*, literally 'rivers and lakes' (a possible translation is 'badlands'). *Young and Dangerous* is a *jianghu* series, the Chinese title of the first film being rendered as *Guo huo zi zhi ren zai jiang hu*. *Jianghu* is a figure of a self-contained, chaotic and combative world 'out there', a world which is not 'home' and which, like the imaginary chivalric order of medieval European culture, has its own laws, ethics and social structure. See Stephen Ching-kiu Chan, 'Figures of hope and the filmic imaginary of *Jianghu* in contemporary Hong Kong cinema', *Cultural Studies* 15: 3/4 (2001), pp 486–514.   13 See David Bordwell's account of the Hong Kong opening of *Young and Dangerous IV* in *Planet Hong Kong: popular cinema and the art of entertainment* (Cambridge, MA., and London, 2000), pp 26–8; chapter four ('So Many Ways to Be Cops and Rascals') in Lisa Odham Stokes and Michael Hoover, *City on fire: Hong Kong cinema* (London and New York, 1999); and Wellson Chin Sing-wai's social realist film made in riposte to the series, *Street Kids Violence* (1999). Jeff Yang gives a succinct account of triad pressure on the Hong Kong film industry in the 1990s in *Once upon a time in China: a guide to Hong Kong, Taiwanese and Mainland Chinese cinema* (New York, 2003), pp 105–8.   14 Yang, p. 259.

glorious heroics of John Woo's films from the previous decade.[15] Most cinemas have temporal-threshold films remembered (like *A Clockwork Orange* and *Pulp Fiction*) for scandalizing the cinema with the new visual styles and socially confronting moods of youth or pop culture at any given time, but *Young and Dangerous* did this right on the edge of a momentous transformation in Hong Kong's worldly situation. From the outset, the series affirmed a changing order; with the Hung Hing society acting as an emblematic local community and a body politic modelled on a patriarchal clan, the films follow a group of friends led by charismatic Chan Ho-nam (Ekin Cheng) and his brash sidekick Chicken (Jordan Chan) as they undergo recruitment, training, testing, and consolidation to emerge – those who survive – as a new generation of leaders.

In the process, the series signalled not only a pragmatic recognition of the 'hand-over' fact but also the turn towards regional or pan-Asian networks of activity that would promise survival and reinvention to many Hong Kong-based filmmakers and cultural activists during the years after 1997 and the financial crises assailing the film industry and the Hong Kong economy at large. Indeed, in *Young and Dangerous IV: 97* (the Chinese title of which translates as *97 Wise Guys No War Cannot Be Won*) the event of Hong Kong's return to China in '97' registers as a condition which the Hung Hing leadership eagerly factor in to their financial planning. More pronounced in later films, as Ho-nam gathers wealth and power, this upwardly mobile, globalizing turn struck some critics as a failing: 'the sense of locality began to fade away'.[16] On the other hand, the *Young and Dangerous* series powerfully created an imaginary 'parish', a densely local, introverted world, with such vividness that anyone anywhere touched by parochial feeling might grasp the sense of attachment bordering on need that the characters feel towards the narrowly circumscribed places and thick communal relations that have shaped their lives – while at the same time asking ruthlessly what *future* their world allows these characters and on what terms their ways will survive.

The answers do not always remain in a parochial comfort-zone. Gangster fiction always exploits the drama of short-term lives, but time horizons in the *Young and Dangerous* films are foreshortened by more than acts of violence. Always returning to its bases in urban-popular Hong Kong, the series maps the long lines of business and family interests and of economic, political and personal influence rapidly linking the course of even minuscule

15 See Shelly Kraicer's dismissive account of *Young and Dangerous I*, and her later revision of this negative response in the light of the later films: http://www.chinesecinemas.org/young.html. 16 Chu Yiu-wai, 'Who Am I? Postcolonial Hong Kong Cinema in the Age of Global Capitalism' in E.M.K. Cheung and Chu Y.-W (eds), *Between home and world: a reader in Hong Kong cinema* (Hong Kong, 2004), p. 51. Chu's argument is more complex than I can indicate here, suggesting that the later films of the series fail to probe 'the in-between-ness' of local settings and global consumerism.

events in the heartlands to others taking place across the diaspora in Macau, Taiwan, Holland, Thailand, Japan and Malaysia, as well as over the border in mainland China. At one level, this transnational urban geography is a marketing ploy, articulating an export strategy for the *Young and Dangerous* enterprise itself; offering adventures abroad to audiences in Hong Kong, it mythologized Hong Kong and linked it to other cityscapes featured for overseas Chinese and foreign audiences. However, the series does not rest in an easy oscillation between the exotic and the domestic, diaspora and home. It also takes us out to Tuen Mun, an 'other' space *within* Hong Kong, where the future of gangster globalization is revealed as by no means hospitable to all forms of parochial life.

TAKING A TOUR OF TUEN MUN

Small communities have a tenacious capacity to differentiate themselves internally. I grew up in a country town with '2,381 people' (as we learned to recite at school) and no less than three 'no go' areas in which I never set foot as a child. Their boundaries were marked informally by a street-sign, a creek or a paddock, but these were barriers which few of us crossed. While one division was racial (the Aboriginal 'common') and another sectarian (flying stones made the convent school area risky for state school kids, and vice versa), the most mysterious to me now is the one that stigmatized half of the town as 'East End'. I have no idea what was supposed to be wrong with life 'over there', a mile away. Memories of British ways of inhabiting towns must have shaped this expression, but nothing by way of poverty, alcoholism, petty crime and abuse could not also be found around our 'West End' housing commission strip on land reclaimed from the Jam Tin Swamp.

   This little Australian geography is local (following the *Macquarie*, it pertains 'to a particular place') but I would call the hatreds that scarred it parochial in the sense that their 'narrowness' of focus on and *within* the local was cosmic, and all-consuming; we ignored the Greek and Chinese families who also lived in the town. Place is always relational, as Doreen Massey reminds us, and these divisions arose within a nation-building project enabled by the globe-encircling order of British imperialism, the currents of which carried sparks of hatred ('memories') to this particular valley and that mountain over there, where they flared up to consume the indigenous 'mattering maps'.[17] The portability of parochialism as a way of *living* the local derives from the same political economy that fosters cosmopolitanism, and there is nothing pre-ordained about parochialism's hold on

17 Doreen Massey, *Space, place and gender* (Cambridge, UK, 1994). The phrase 'mattering maps' is from Lawrence Grossberg.

hearts and minds; amnesia, indifference, withdrawal, a happy promiscuity, humane solidarity and, today, life-style consumerism are other viable ways of living *la vida loca*. Within a space of parochial feeling, however, observations like these have little traction. A strong parochialism has no 'outside'. Relations with other locales do not have to be denied, because their otherness does not matter.

Affective disengagement from the risks and rewards of reciprocal cultural trade is at the heart of parochialism as a 'problem' in globalization; just how much introversion can a local community concerned with survival afford to sustain these days? The future of parochialism is an explicit theme of *Young and Dangerous IV: 97*, in which Chicken opts to fight for the leadership of the Tuen Mun branch of Hung Hing against a local contender, 'Barbarian' (Chan Chi-fai). A forty minute drive from the bright lights of Causeway Bay, hours more if the traffic is jammed, the 'new town' of Tuen Mun is widely considered remote by Hong Kong Island people, and its towering public housing estates are as foreign to Chicken as the mountain country parks, old villages and lush foliage that surround them. Chicken is the most travelled and *débrouillard* of the younger 'triad boys', although the charm of his streetwise style of urbanity is that he changes slowly and learns the hard way; as the film begins, he is back from exile in Taiwan and acting as Chan Ho-nam's offsider in Causeway Bay. Barbarian is a village-based thug whose world is defined by Tuen Mun; brutish, inarticulate and stupid, he is an immediately recognizable stereotype of the backward rural cousin with the taint of the peasant, the 'mainlander'. The contrast between the two men extends to their political legitimacy claims: Chicken is an outsider in Tuen Mun but he has talent and experience; the incompetent Barbarian gets lost outside Tuen Mun, where he has roots, 'mates' and an inheritance claim through his murdered boss, Dinosaur.

This urban-rural, centre-periphery conflict between competitive meritocracy and an inept dynastic principle is fictively internal to Hong Kong, although it has an affective relevance to wider issues invoked by '97' as a signifier of repatriation ('Barbarian!' says Chicken reprovingly in a face-off where he is vastly outnumbered by his foe, 'we are a family!'). Since Barbarian is secretly advised by the Tung Sing provocateur, Lai Yiu-Yeung (Roy Cheung), a sadistic Mozart fan who has killed both Dinosaur and Chicken's friend Tin-yee, the film leaves no doubt about which side of the parochial face-off we take: Barbarian's incapacity and corruption exposes Hung Hing to infiltration. This negation of a 'backward' mode of parochialism is clearly established by contending stylistic statements. Taken on a tour of Tuen Mun Town Centre, Chicken sticks out like a sore thumb in his elegant black suit, cool shoes and dark, collarless T; the locals sport cheap white or coloured tops over sloppy chinos or jeans, and a shot downward emphasizes that some wear rubber thongs on their feet.[18] This ultimate sartorial vulgarity is the first thing we see of Barbarian himself as he arrives with a Rottweiler on a leash, and the camera pans upward to complete the picture of a walking Hong Kong fashion crime – ripped jeans, singlet, gold chain, fat pendant and a lurid blonde stripe in his hair.

Local knowledge is invited by the camera movement here. Lightened hair and thongs worn in public have connotations in Hong Kong of, respectively, criminality (flaunted or fantasized) and an uncouth lack of social respect; a colleague compares thongs in the classroom to slippers, a move hard for a Sydney girl to follow since you can't wear slippers in sand. Barbarian looks to me like an Australian sporting hero, give or take the gold chain, but as a Tuen Mun resident I see (and, in some ridiculous way, feel nettled by) the ethnographic force of that reiterated movement down to obsess, once again, about feet. Shoes mark social positioning and act as an index of personal *quality*; in another scene, the new Hung Hing boss Mr Chiang (Alex Man) rebukes the North Point leader, Fat Lai, for lack of class in baring his feet in a business environment. Indeed, Fat Lai has a treacherous streak that sees him exiled, in the end, to Albania, and those thongs forecast Barbarian's fate; he is at home in the Tuen Mun streets (as the well-shod Chicken was in the power walk at the beginning of the film), but an exclusively parochial base and an 'old school' grass roots style does not suffice to carry Tuen Mun (emblematically the most remote and backward of locales on the *Young and Dangerous* world map) into a prosperous future.

Without following this fascinating film too much further, it is worth noting that dispersed across the territorialized culture clash at its core is what I can only call a *bitching* discourse about critical details of fashion, style, verbal gesture and, in the case of Chicken's allergic reaction to Barbarian the first time they meet, exactly how many glasses of orange juice it is proper to consume at a banquet. Chinese social etiquette exceeds my understanding, and my referent for this needling (which begins at KK's flat, as 'the boys' tease each other about dressing up for the wedding) is the conformity-inducing parochialism of the girls' school yard, where it matters brutally whether your socks are showing by how many millimetres above the ankle, and where a hem-line must hang in relation to pelvis, thighs and knees. To call this refined style-policing 'feminine' is only to say that Barbarian's rather basic male fashion sense is hegemonic where I'm from, but certainly, in counter-point to the bellicose encounter of localized masculine codes in the Chicken-Barbarian face-off, there runs through the film an alternative parochialism of *fashioning* – both of selves (bodies and behaviours), and of consensus about the elements of an evolving Hong Kong style.

18 I owe my sense of the importance of clothing signifiers and the power of the link between the rural and the historically 'backward' in contemporary Chinese discourses of globalization to the work of my student, Ms Sit Tsui (Margaret Sit).

This more flexible practice of boundary maintenance has its cruel, intolerant moments but fashioning flourishes, unlike the gang war, in the variable moods and movements of everyday social life. Bound up with but not reducible to the pleasures and frustrations of consumption (a primary zone of Hong Kong popular culture across most socio-economic levels), the fashioning process works also through conversation, humour, verbal jousting and wit; transcending the contents of any style consensus, it thrives on change and happily incorporates ideas from beyond the parish, remodelling these for local purposes and tastes. This is a way of being parochial *and* cosmopolitan, of holding deep, narrow loyalties while enjoying wider perspectives, and a key bearer of this principle is Lam Suk-fan (Karen Mok Man-wai), Chicken's girlfriend and, as it happens, the British-educated daughter of a priest. Barbarian is too rigid and exclusive in his commitments to practice fashioning and, while he is capable of a mean trick or two, he has no idea how to bitch. Chicken bitches Barbarian about his hair and all that orange juice, but Barbarian's fight-back is limited to verbal and physical violence.

Ultimately, the new parochial game outlined by *Young and Dangerous IV: 97* revolves around acquiring the socio-cultural knowledge needed for expanding the business on a family networking principle (thinking local, acting global). Chicken's fitness to lead Tuen Mun is proved in the end by his readiness to learn, when he must, about strange places. On his tour of the pokey malls and teen gang haunts of Town Centre he asks economic questions, learning that there is no prostitution industry and that the locals make a living by 'smuggling of course, illegal immigrants and stealing cars'. In contrast, when Barbarian is taken to the city to see 'the prosperous side' he gripes about its remoteness, grinning happily when Fat Lai explains some capitalist basics ('different companies are making money at the same place and same time'). In a splendid finale, these contending approaches to place and locality stage a public debate in a hall packed with 'rascals': Barbarian plays to parochial sentiment, invoking local memory markers and a happier past with 'no outsiders', while Chicken appeals to parochial interests with a lecture on the operational knowledge needed to run Tuen Mun – teaching both the on-screen and off-screen audience that the area includes four hospitals, thirty-four schools, three police stations and over 600,000 people.

Certainly, sentiment is winning the crowd when the room explodes with revelations of treachery, and victory to Chicken is awarded not by popular vote as intended but by the gift of Mr Chiang, the wise new Hung Hing chief executive. Himself a hereditary leader as the brother of the family's founder, and a talented expatriate returning after twenty-five years as a businessman in Thailand, Chiang reconciles both kinds of parochial appeal: combining the sentimental authority of tradition and the pragmatic authority of worldly success, he could perhaps be seen as a wishful or optimistic model for the Hong Kong Chief Executive incoming in 1997, Tung Chee-hwa.[19] However, Chiang is just a background, stabilizing figure for the narrative and this kind of thin political allegory that wraps up the ending is not where the film's energies lie. The narrative work it does along the way with parochial feelings, rhythms of life and survival fears is rather more vital, I suspect, to its 'export' value as well as to its local popularity.

NEIGHBOURHOODS

Lingnan University has residential colleges and most students spend a year living mainly on campus in Tuen Mun. Some are local, but for those who come from housing estates in the urban area of Kowloon this residency appears at first as an exile to the ends of the earth. As a foreigner happily resident in Tuen Mun (with its sandy beaches, blue water and green grass just like home), I wonder about cultural boundaries that operate in time as well as in space – becoming more uncertain, the longer I stay, about how to place the cultural differences that undoubtedly operate in the classroom. I think less often about Australian assumptions and their historical constitution, and mercifully little about American identity categories; after years of being interpellated grandly as 'Western', my sense of eccentricity is diminished for now, and I have access to the luxury of puzzling about what is 'new' and what is not.

This is much less clear than common notions of cultural difference on the one hand and the effects of media globalization on the other might lead one to expect. Sometimes I am tempted to call our students 'post-media', in that on the whole they don't watch TV or go to the cinema when they first come to Lingnan, and we introduce them to these activities as I was first exposed at university to theatre and gallery-going. Few students read for pleasure; I did so in my youth, but that made me the neighbourhood freak. Mobile phones are pervasive, but not all cultural studies students arrive as big Internet users except for ICQ, a 'pen-pal' network which is, along with watching VCDs, the main PC-based function not colonized by their schooling. Asked about pastimes, most students will say 'hanging out with friends and family' and 'karaoke'; I'd have said the same, except that we played charades and climbed trees. The media products that arouse most interest on VCD are TV dramas from Japan, Taiwan and, lately, Korea, although everyone seems steeped in the 'hearsay' world of Cantonese radio and Chinese newspapers (neither of which do I ever see students actually using). Awareness of Hollywood and Western pop culture ranges from low to near zero, in part because of the narrow range of films in Hong Kong's pricey multiplexes, a low uptake of

---

19 The son of a wealthy entrepreneur appointed to the Hong Kong leadership by the central government in Beijing, Tung in fact lacked the fictional Mr Chiang's ability in business and politics; see http://en.wikipedia.org/wiki/Tung_Chee-Hwa

English-language programmes even on cable or satellite TV and the flow-on of this indifference in gossip media. Most students are engaged, however, by the vivid, fantastic, scandal-ridden legends of the struggling Canto-pop industry (which many local film stars inhabit), and passionate about the 'idols' created by the booming popular culture industries of East Asia.

Nevertheless, in the classroom the discourse of 'quality' firmly attaches to Hollywood, and most students insist when a course begins that Hong Kong films, past and present, are *bad*. I bitch about this with my colleagues, for whom it marks a generational difference in part, and I spend time elaborating the goodness of classic Hong Kong cinema with students bemused by such enthusiasm from a foreigner who can't understand Cantonese (while Tuen Mun shop assistants gently try without fail to dissuade me from buying 'Chinese movie', as though my inability to read characters has led me to make a mistake). This blanket dismissal of local films is uncanny to one raised in the 1950s on the 'badness' of Australian culture, a discourse undergoing a revival in film contexts now as the national cinema fades and star Australians move to Hollywood ('the good ones get away').[20] Yet this echo entails no simple or shared postcolonial cringe: far from effusing over the global successes of 'our Jackie', as Australians do for 'our Nic', Hong Kongers more often treat dismissively and in an aesthetically reasoned way the Hollywood work of their filmmakers, and, while Australia's national cinema has rarely enjoyed popularity, the disaffection of Hong Kong audiences with the average products of their cinema is relatively new.[21]

This jumble of issues is the stuff of lunch-time conversations and department meetings, where, enlivened with names, anecdotes and tales of pedagogical failure or success, it helps to form the rich parochial life of our programme – as such talk does in any collegial unit preoccupied with the 'interests and views' of small and precisely situated groups. In casual formulation, these concerns seem remote from 'cinema studies' understood as a practice presupposing not only a body of knowledge but a consensus about the importance of *debates* that rarely translate to my classroom, and often just get in the way. Wanting to encourage students to think imaginatively about film economics and policy, I find writings clogged with polemic against 'textual' approaches that have no referent for my students, and sarcasms that make no sense. Looking for texts to help students develop complex, interesting answers to the hard cross-cultural questions they ask ('but *why* does

20 A discussion with Helen Grace clarified this issue for me.   21 My point here is about classroom conversation, not film industry logics. However, one line of partial convergence between Hong Kong and Australia is that filmmakers in both places project a future based on co-productions with mainland China. For Australians this is largely a dream, which might or might not materialize in individual cases. For Hong Kongers, it is a complex present reality which is already reshaping the cinema and which has much wider cultural and political ramifications.

G.I. Jane love the American navy?' remains my all-time favourite), I find critiques presuming various answers and modelling attitudes to them ('because she is a dupe of patriarchy' fails to answer the question). Looking for pleasurable reading I fall asleep myself, or browse books from the 1960s with a public mode of address but parochially Western themes, and end up once again with Graeme Turner's *Film as Social Practice* – a textbook that unfailingly teaches but lets its reader breathe.

Like viable parishes and housing estates, academic programmes engaged with local communities have a strong sense of place and cultural distinctiveness, and they share this regardless of location. I would guess that many teachers of undergraduates will recognize my caricature of the textbook selection process, and the frustrations of 'fashioning' a course from bits and pieces of imported material pragmatically cut for local pertinence and comprehensibility – as well as the euphoria of sometimes seeing students make everything come together in miraculous ways of their own. Working with Anglophone cinema studies in Hong Kong adds new layers of difficulty and delight for me, but my problems of relating as a teacher to the *discipline* I draw on are not much different from those I have encountered in socio-culturally more diverse Australian classrooms in the past. They do differ greatly, however, from those of dealing with the position-taking anxieties and phantom 'turf' rivalries induced in students by the process of professional formation in American-style graduate schools – a process by which academic writing is shaped, and to which much of it is now devoted in ways which show up in chokingly narrow modes of address.[22]

As the distance widens between mass undergraduate teaching and research training (with responsibility for the former increasingly dumped on postgraduates themselves), the creative task of redefining what it means to transmit a discipline and the implications of this for its practice is necessarily being assumed, I think, in hitherto 'remote' or unlikely places. In the Hong Kong context, Lingnan University adopts what we might call (following the *Young and Dangerous* model) a cosmo-parochial mission; offering academically ordinary students a liberal arts education 'with Hong Kong characteristics', we insist that these characteristics include an 'international outlook' as well as an understanding of the Chinese national formation in which they now live. Tuen Mun may be the ends of the earth as viewed from Causeway Bay, but it is also the site of a unique educational experiment which includes the first stand-alone Cultural Studies department in the Chinese-speaking world. At the same time, as teaching in English to people whose grasp of the language is fragile spreads with the corporatization of universities across Asia and much

22 On the impact of cross-industrial pressures on academic publishing see Lindsay Waters, *Enemies of promise: publishing, perishing and the eclipse of scholarship* (Chicago, 2004).

of the post-colonial world, the Tuen Mun teaching condition is becoming a global norm.

I take an optimistic view of the potentials of this and I find theoretical reassurance in recent work of Anne Freadman's suggesting that we define culture through 'the number of languages available to individuals and the uses they make of them'.[23] She is not referring only to 'natural' languages, although as a teacher of French in Australia she frames her argument in 'The Culture Peddlers' with a critique of the curriculum planning assumption that 'a' language is coextensive with 'a' culture (learn French, cook a quiche). Pointing out that many cultures may inhabit or share a language (say, Chinese or English), and that cultural groupings can be local and highly exclusive of other people who speak 'the same language', she suggests that 'all cultures are constituted by their neighbourhoods, and the social agency of individuals is constituted by the plurality of borderlines that they live on'. In this perspective, I take it, the key issue to begin with is not simply one of crossing (or not crossing) borders but rather of understanding how people embedded in particular circumstances are living on *numerous* borders. Far from being an abstruse theoretical move to pluralize for pluralism's sake, both this model of social agency and the hierarchies of access that it helps to account for work as common sense in parochial knowledge systems: when two of those 'proud and insular Bulldogs' took opposing sides in an Australia-New Zealand test match, just days after the emotional blast of winning the 2004 NRL premiership together, no-one who cares about football had trouble deciphering the headline, 'It's Sonny v Willie', or grasping the instant switch from an 'intra-' to an 'inter'-national border game.[24] As teachers, I think, we try to mobilize this kind of knowledge in our students and increase their capacity both to 'switch' and to access more of the neighbourhoods available to them.

Transposing the constitution of culture from language to the organized but interconnecting domains and areas ('neighbourhoods') of everyday social practice further allows Freadman to situate her reflection on pedagogy not in the 'gaps' (as we so often say) between languages and cultures, but rather in 'the intercultural at the heart of culture itself': for example, in the jokes and parodies that all cultures use to represent themselves as though from an exterior, and the stories that parents use to acculturate their children. Teaching, for Freadman, is story-telling, and its function is to give students a way of apprehending things that are 'not yet' part of their culture. From this future-oriented model of pegagogy it follows for me that the fashioning of a curriculum

23 Anne Freadman, 'The culture peddlers', *Postcolonial Studies*, 4:3 (2001), pp 275–96.   24 James Hooper, 'It's Sonny v Willie: Clash of Bulldogs' heroes', *Daily Telegraph* (6 October, 2004), p. 84.

that might be up to the task of enhancing the social agency of students in the Tuen Muns of this world (whether in Hong Kong, Australia, the U.K. or Ireland or Britain) should not require students – or, indeed, teachers – to renounce parochialism in order to acquire 'an international outlook' . On the contrary, if the latter is not to be a simple projection of rampantly 'home-town' agendas imported from elsewhere, the first task is to deepen our knowledge of the former, rendering visible not only its boundaries but the complexities within – and work outwards from there.

Representing Okinawa: contesting images in contemporary Japanese cinema

MIKA KO

2002 marked the thirtieth anniversary of Okinawa's reversion to Japan. Despite the hopes of the Okinawan people, little has changed in the social and political situation of Okinawa in the past thirty years. The US military has continued to play a dominant role within Okinawa and progress towards demilitarization, the creation of a non-military civilian economy, and an improvement in democracy has been slow. While the economic and political problems of Okinawa have continued, there has nonetheless been something of an 'Okinawa boom' in mainland Japan since the mid-1990s. This has involved a significant growth of interest in Okinawa and Okinawan culture and an increasing consumption of Okinawan goods, cultural artefacts, and images of Okinawa. This has also been manifest in the growth in the number of films set in Okinawa.

The dominant media image of Okinawa to be found during this 'Okinawa boom' has been that of an exotic southern 'wonderland' typified by blue sky, blue sea, exotic flowers, and cheerful natives devoted to singing and drinking. To use the words of the Okinawan academic Tanaka Yasuhiro, Okinawa has been represented as an 'eternal festive space'.[1] Tanaka also points out that this festive image of Okinawa shares features with Yanagida Kunio's *Nanto-ron* (i.e. studies of the southern islands). Yanagida, one of Japan's most prominent folklorists and ethnographers, sees Okinawa as a storehouse of Japanese social forms – from religious beliefs to family rituals – that have been lost in Japan as the result of industrialization. Yanagida's view of Okinawa, or what has been described as '*Nanto*-ideology' (ideology of the Southern Islands) by Murai Osamu, played an influential role in shaping subsequent discourses on, and images of, Okinawa.[2] As Tanaka argues, '*Nanto*-ideology' has granted Okinawa 'a status of the privileged place, as a unique place for one's soul to go back, or, put differently, as a place to evoke one's nostalgic sentiment'.[3] In other words, representations of Okinawa are, in many cases, nothing more than representations of Japanese nostalgia for a utopian vision of its own pre-modernity.[4]

*In the article Japanese names are written in Japanese order with the surname first.   1 Tanaka Yasuhiro, 'The media representation of "Okinawa" and US/Japan hegemony', *Inter-Asia Cultural Studies*, 4:3 (2003), p. 421.   2 Murai Osamu, *Nanto ideorogi no hassei: Yanagida Kunio to shoku-minchishugi* (*The birth of Nanto ideology: Yanagida Kunio and colonialism*), (Tokyo, 2004).   3 Tanaka Yasuhiro, 'The media representation of "Okinawa" and US/Japan hegemony', p. 421.   4 In Japanese

It is also important to consider the political nature of the recent Okinawa boom. Tessa Morris-Suzuki argues that the cultural appropriation of Okinawa is a typical example of Japan's 'cosmetic multiculturalism'.⁵ Although there has been a recent trend in Japan in which cultural diversity is praised under the banner of multiculturalism, as the word 'cosmetic' suggests, Morris-Suzuki considers Japanese multiculturalism to be superficial and often no more than a disguised form of nationalism. While cultural diversity is praised and 'other' cultures become the object of economic consumption, this only serves to exemplify Japan's generosity towards, and capacity to accommodate, 'other' cultures. At the same time, claims for the political and economic rights of the bearers of these 'different' or 'other' cultures are typically ignored. It also goes without saying that there exists a rigid hierarchy between the dominant Japanese culture and 'other' cultures, since 'cosmetic multiculturalism' presumes a stable and superior position from which the dominant culture may generously 'accommodate' the culture of others. Moreover, by emphasizing the happy coexistence of different cultures, it neatly conceals the oppressive conditions imposed on minority groups, both in the present and the past. As Tanaka suggests, in relation to Okinawa, '[w]hile the nature and culture of Okinawan "festive space" is admired and consumed in media discourse, the underlying structure of contradictions and violence is obscured and forgotten'.⁶

It does not mean, however, that all the phenomena and cultural artefacts relating to Okinawa are simply absorbed into the Okinawa boom or cosmetic multiculturalism. As Morris-Suzuki argues, there is still a positive aspect to 'cosmetic multiculturalism' since it provides a space from which minority groups may assert themselves.⁷ As such, there may be potential to transform the 'festive' space constructed by the Okinawa boom into a critical space of interrogation, negotiation and resistance. For instance, in 2003, the Yamagata International Documentary Film Festival (YIDF) organized a special programme called *Okinawa – Nexus of Borders: Ryukyu Reflections* which featured films related to Okinawa. This special programme involved the screening of a variety of films (both feature and documentary) from the pre-war period to the present, including films about the battle of Okinawa, propaganda films made by the US military administration to glorify their role in Okinawa and diasporic films made by Okinawan Brazilians. In this way, the festival may be seen to have been made possible by the Okinawa boom but also to have used

cinema history, the representation of Okinawa through an ethnographic gaze may be found in Imamura Shohei's *Kamigami no hukaki yokubo* (*The profound desire of the Gods*, 1968). However, while Imamura's films used Okinawa to criticise Japanese capitalist modernity, images of Okinawa in the current Okinawa boom tend to service the capitalist consumer economy.   5 Tessa Morris-Suzuki, '"Posutokoroniarizmu" no imi wo megutte' ('Discussion over the meanings of "post-colonialism"'), *Gendai Shiso*, 29:9 (2001), p. 185.   6 Tanaka Yasuhiro, 'The media representation of "Okinawa" and US/Japan hegemony', p. 431.   7 Morris-Suzuki, '"Posutokoroniarizmu" no imi wo megutte', p. 186.

the boom as an opportunity to offer an interrogation and critique of its ideological character. Similarly, Takamine Go's films may also be read as a critique of the Okinawa boom and an explicit refusal of the cosmetic multiculturalism (of which it is a part).

This article examines, firstly, the festive image of Okinawa represented in
Nakae Yuji's *Nabi no koi* (aka *Nabi's Love,* 1999) and *Hotel Hibiscus* (2003)
and discusses how these representations are related to the cosmetic operation
of multiculturalism within Japan. The paper will then proceed to examine
Mugen Ryukyu Tsuru-Henry (aka *Tsuru-Henry,* 1999), directed by Takamine
Go, and consider how Takamine challenges, through diverse cinematic strategies, the dominant representations of Okinawa and, by doing so, Japan's cosmetic multiculturalism.

Aaron Gerow argues that most of the films set in Okinawa 'ultimately fail
to undermine either the nationalistic or the touristic containment of Okinawan
otherness'.[8] *Nabi's Love* and *Hotel Hibiscus* are no exceptions to this tendency. *Nabi's Love* was released in 1999 and proved a great success both in mainland Japan and Okinawa. It would be fair to say that, along with the popular
TV drama *Chura-san* in 2001, *Nabi's Love* was a key contributor to the
Okinawa boom. The director Nakae Yuji was born in Kyoto but he has lived
in Okinawa for more than twenty years since he went to Ryukyu University
as a student. Nakae has made five films, all of which are set in Okinawa.

Nabi's Love's official website describes the film as follows: 'You can't help
singing. You can't help falling in love. This movie is coming from the southern islands to make you happy'. As this would suggest, the film represents
Okinawa as a stereotypically exotic southern island or 'eternally festive space'.
Briefly, the narrative of *Nabi's Love* consists of two romances, involving the
film's main character Nanako and his grandmother Nabi. Nanako has quit her
job in Tokyo and returned to the small Okinawan island where her grandparents live. Although the film does not identify what has happened to Nanako
in Tokyo, it is implied that Nanako is escaping from Tokyo in order to find
emotional healing in Okinawa. In Okinawa, Nanako falls in love with
Fukunosuke, a young man from mainland Japan who happens to be staying
at Nanako's grandparents' house. Meanwhile, Nanako's grandmother Nabi,
who is nearly eighty years old and enjoying a happy life with her husband
Keitatsu, meets her old love Sanra. Nabi and Sanra fell in love sixty years
previously but they were forced to separate because of opposition from Nabi's
family. After their separation, Sanra left the island for Brazil while Nabi married Keitatsu. Reunited with Sanra after sixty years, Nabi leaves the island
with Sanra in the end of the film.

8 Aaron Gerow, 'From the national gaze to multiple gazes: representations of Okinawa in recent
Japanese cinema' in Laura Hein and Mark Selden (eds), *Islands of discontent* (Lanham, 2003), p.
282.

In order to create a 'festive' image, the film exhibits all the stereotypical 'signs' of Okinawa: blue sky, floating white clouds, beautiful sea, unspoiled landscape, Okinawan songs and locals who enjoy drinking and dancing. For instance, when Nanako and Nabi go out for a walk, they see a man wearing a mask standing on the street. As he sees Nabi and Nanako, he walks in front of them singing a traditional folk song with his sanshin guitar (an Okinawan three-string guitar). This Okinawan folk song is followed by Irish music when they arrive at the grocery owned by Reiko. Reiko is married to the Irishman O'Connor who plays the fiddle while some elderly locals dance. Here the stereotypical representation of the Okinawans' prediliction for singing and dancing is reinforced by the incorporation of an Irish character. Like the Okinawans, the Irish are commonly associated with singing, dancing and drinking. And, while it can be argued that there is something in common between Okinawa and Ireland in their historical experiences of outside domination and oppression, the film only draws attention to superficial and stereotypical similarities.

The coming together of various dominant discourses on Okinawa is evident in the final sequence which follows a scene in which Nanako and Fukunosuke embrace on the beach for the first time. The first half of the sequence basically consists of the relay singing of a traditional Okinawan folk love song by different characters. During the singing, Nanako tells her grandfather Keitatsu of her intention to remain in Okinawa with Fukunosuke. Keitatsu announces this to the people gathered in his garden and asks them to dance for good luck. Keitatsu starts singing and playing sanshin guitar and all his guests cheerfully dance for the rest of the sequence. Keitatsu's song and the accompanying dancing continue uninterrupted and there is only one cut during the sequence. However, as the camera moves through the dancers, we see Nanako and Fukunosuke sit on the verandah wearing Okinawan wedding costume. The camera then returns to the dancers but when it catches the couple on the verandah again, we see a grouping of Fukunosuke, a pregnant Nanako, their three children and Keitatsu. In this way, the sequence spans a period of five to ten years during which the Okinawan characters continue to sing and dance and, thus, give a concrete embodiment to the idea of Okinawa as an 'eternally festive place'. The sequence also manifests *Nanto*-ideology. The gathering of local people at Keitatsu's house, along with small details such as Fukunosuke carrying 'straw rice bags' and cooking rice by a fire in the garden, clearly suggest how life in Okinawa is seen to have been bypassed by modernity and to have retained the strong community bonds believed to be lost in the big cities of mainland Japan.

The stereotypes represented in *Nabi's Love* are not, of course, negative. However, in order to understand the current political situation in Okinawa, paying attention to what is *not* presented may be as important as (or sometimes more important than) what *is* presented. In other words, it is important to ask what is erased, or suppressed, by the foregrounding of images of Okinawa as a paradise. For instance, in *Nabi's Love*, the past only exists in Nabi's tragic love of sixty years before. Signs of Okinawa's tragic and chaotic history during this period, including the Battle of Okinawa at the end of World War Two, American occupation and the reversion to Japan, are all erased.

Nakae's *Hotel Hibiscus* is based on a *manga* comic of the same title. The story revolves around the ten-year-old girl Mieko and her 'international family' (as the film puts it) who are running the Hotel Hibisucus (which contains only one guest room!). Mieko lives in Naha, the capital of Okinawa, with her Okinawan parents, grandmother, sister and brother. The reason why they are called an 'international family' is that her sister Sachiko and brother Kenji are both mixed-race children by different fathers – Sachiko by a white American and Kenji by a black American. Like *Nabi's Love*, *Hotel Hibiscus* mobilizes tourist images of Okinawan landscape and stereotypical representations of the Okinawan people. However, unlike *Nabi's Love*, which is set in a small island within Okinawa, the US military presence is clearly incorporated into *Hotel Hibiscus*. One day, Mieko and two of her friends decide to look for *kijimuna*, Okinawan mythical sprites, in one of the US camps. While Mieko and her friends walk on the beach singing, there is a spectacular tracking shot of the beach and sky. At the end of the beach is a US military camp where Mieko and her friends crawl through a big hole in the fence. Although we hear the jets in the background, we do not see any fighters or runways inside the base. All that is presented is a plain field. Thus, while the tracking shot of the beautiful beach is followed by a sequence inside the military camp, the base is not seen as spoiling Okinawa's landscape or threatening the Okinawan people's daily lives. Rather, the camp is presented as a part of the landscape and as an unthreatening playground for children. Similarly, although once inside the camp, Mieko and two boys are caught by American soldiers, the soldiers are presented as friendly and unthreatening, particularly the character of George whom it transpires is the father of Kenji, Mieko's half-brother.

One day a letter from George arrives at the Hotel Hibisucus, indicating that he is in Okinawa and that he wants to see Kenji. All of Mieko's family, except for Kenji, visit George at the base. Mieko's mother hugs George, saying 'I missed you', and then introduces him to her husband (Mieko's father). Mieko's mother explains to George that Kenji is not with them and that he wants to be a boxer. While disappointed by Kenji's absence, George slips a bundle of notes into Mieko's mother's hand. Meanwhile, Kenji runs past the gate of the base without noticing his family and biological father. George runs parallel with him and shouts encouragement across the fence: 'Kenji, you are the champion!'.

What these scenes involving the US base present is an image of harmonious coexistence between Okinawa and the US military at odds with the reality of Okinawan life. Local people have strongly resented the existence of the bases, particularly since 1995 when a local school-girl of about Mieko's age was abducted and raped by three US servicemen. And while there are certainly mixed-race children in Okinawa as a result of liaisons between Okinawan women and American military personnel, it is common for US servicemen to avoid their paternal responsibilities. These are, however, problems that the film largely ignores through its representation of a happy 'international family', friendly and responsible US personnel and a military base which children may safely enter. Similarly, while the relationship between Mieko's father and George might hint at the strained relations between Okinawa and the US bases, Mieko's father greets George with a friendly smile and a 'Welcome to Okinawa!' As he makes a polite bow, his wig falls from his head, turning a scene of potential confrontation into a comical encounter devoid of political implications. Thus, while Okinawa may accommodate more than seventy per cent of US military bases in Japan, the film shows these bases to be benign and unthreatening. As such by foregrounding images of Okinawa as a 'paradise', *Hotel Hibiscus* presents a reassuring view of the US military presence which denies the social and political problems it generates and celebrates the contented 'internationalism' of the Okinawan people.

In Nakae's films, therefore, Okinawan cultures are confined within an image of an 'eternally festive space' or, as *Nanto*-ideology suggests, a space where Japanese nostalgia for its own pre-modernity may be projected. It must be noted, however, that the cultural containment offered by this frozen version of Okinawan culture also implies containment within the nation-state. For while the 'otherness' of Okinawa is celebrated, it is still packaged and enclosed as a part of 'Japanese' culture. As Tanaka suggests, Okinawan cultural difference is 'recognized as "the other within", not as "the other without"'.[9] In this way, Okinawa is re-defined within a framework of Japaneseness whereby the issue of US bases is absorbed into the rhetoric of Japanese responsibilities within the US-Japan global security partnership. In terms of this subsumption of 'the other within', the ending of *Hotel Hibiscus* is significant. Mieko makes a big banner to welcome her mother and sister back home from their trip to America and hangs the banner at the entrance to their house. On the white banner is written in Japanese 'Welcome back, mom' while a big red apple is drawn at the centre.[10] It is, of course, difficult not to associate a white banner containing a red circle at its centre with the Japanese national flag. Thus, when Mieko's mother and sister return home, this international family is, in effect, re-united under the flag of Japan (itself seen as an ally of the US). In doing so, the scene also offers a utopian vision of Japan as a multicultural and globalized country which belies the military, economic and political inequities involved in the current position of Okinawa.

9 Tanaka Yasuhiro, 'The media representation of "Okinawa" and US/Japan hegemony', p. 422.
10 The use of an apple is a kind of play on words. On the banner is written '*Okaeringo*' which is a combination of two words, *okaeri* (welcome back) and *ringo* (apple).

The 'Okinawa boom' is welcomed by Okinawans. The local tourist industry is happy to advertize the appeal of Okinawa as a place of 'comfort' and the Okinawan people appear to enjoy the popularity of their culture and islands amongst mainland Japanese. However, as Tanaka points out, there is also a sense in which the 'Okinawa boom' has encouraged Okinawans, almost without noticing it, to play the part of the 'lovable other' that has been constructed for them. As a result, the more that Okinawan people internalize a dominant paradigm of themselves, the more difficult it is to create their own mode of address, or occupy a position from where they can articulate their own subjectivity. Put differently, the more they end up serving Japan's cosmetic multiculturalism, the more Okinawa's socio-political predicaments remain hidden. In this respect, Nakae's *Nabi's Love* and *Hotel Hibiscus* seem to manifest, and contribute to, the cosmetic operation of Japanese multiculturalism inherent in the current Okinawa boom. In his films, Okinawa is enjoyed and consumed – offering comfort and reassurance rather than disturbance. Both *Nabi's Love* and *Hotel Hibiscus* 'play' Okinawa in the way that is desired and scripted by the dominant Japanese culture and enclose it within a Japanese national imaginary.

Takamine Go presents Okinawa in a different way. Takamine was born in Okinawa in 1948 but has lived on mainland Japan since the late 1960s. He has made eleven films including three feature films. With a few exceptions, almost all of the films are set in Okinawa. Commenting on the recent popularity of shooting films in Okinawa, Takamine has observed that '[m]ost of the films set in Okinawa flatter Okinawa, and in these films Okinawa plays Okinawa'.[11] As his remark suggests, Takamine's films refuse to portray Okinawa in a stereotypical way (as 'Okinawa'). I shall now examine how Takamine's feature film *Tsuru-Henry* explores the complex forms of Okinawan subjectivity and, by doing so, challenges Japan's cosmetic multiculturalism.[12]

Tsuru-Henry was shot with a digital camera. The story is set in Okinawa in the late 1960s before it reverted to Japan. However, as Aaron Gerow points out, it 'has less a story than a set of intermeshing texts'.[13] It is therefore difficult to describe the film's plot. In the simplest description, it is about Tsuru and Henry, a mother and son making a film from a script which Tsuru encountered by chance. Although the narrative of *Tsuru-Henry* is constructed around Tsuru and Henry, like a Russian doll, different stories keep coming out of each other. Apart from the central story of Tsuru and Henry, the film also focuses on James, the protagonist of the film that Tsuru and Henry are making, *Rab? no koi* (*Love's Love*). In *Love's Love*, James is a mixed-race child, the son of an Okinawan

11 Quoted in the online newspaper article '*Okinawa ni "kobinai" eiga*' ('The film which "does not flatter" Okinawa'), http://mytown.asahi.com/okinawa/news02.asp?c=18&kiji=246. 12 I would like to thank the director, Mr Takamine Go for providing me with a copy of *Tsuru-Henry* which is not currently commercially available. 13 Gerow, 'From the national gaze to multiple gazes', p. 298.

woman and a US high commissioner in Okinawa, who has had the memory of
his father erased by the US government. At one point in the film, James comments: 'I can't trust America which only regards Okinawa's military importance
as a keystone of the Pacific. Nor can I rely on Japan, so-called mother-land for
us. I am totally disgusted with the states which have mercilessly determined
who I am without ever consulting me'. His voice-over continues: 'I am not an
American. I am not a Japanese. I may not be an Okinawan. How long do I have
to keep going like this?' As this monologue suggests, James' predicaments function as an allegory of the embattled situation of Okinawa. In this respect, by
showing James's struggle to regain his memory and identity, the film *Tsuru-
Henry* is also investigating the complex forms of public memory and political
identity that articulate what is Okinawa.

   Love's Love, however, is not a fictional script existing only in *Tsuru-Henry*.
Takamine wrote the script of *Love's Love* four years before the production of
Tsuru-Henry, but gave up making the film because of lack of finance. *Tsuru-
Henry* and *Love's Love* are, in many ways, imbricated, fused with each other to
such an extent that the viewer of *Tsuru-Henry* is confused as to whether what
is on the screen is a part of *Tsuru-Henry* or of *Love's Love*. With such a deliberate narrative confusion, Takamine seems to refuse a simple narrativization of
Okinawa and Okinawan history. Rather than presenting Okinawa in a simple,
linear manner, what Takamine attempts to figure in his films is multi-layered
or hybrid historiography in which the past is always part of the present and stories are always parts of other stories. In other words, his narrative as well as his
aesthetic strategy seem to make it possible to illuminate and scrutinize Okinawa's
multi-layered and complicated cultural historical dynamics.

   As some critics have pointed out, one of the most striking characteristics
of the film is its collage style, which it presents in various ways. First of all,
Tsuru-Henry is a collage of different languages. Japanese, English, Okinawan,
Chinese, and even an Okinawan regional dialect are all used within the film
and the dialogue shifts from one language to another. Secondly, *Tsuru-Henry*
more generally is a collage of different types of text or media. It consists of
images shot with digital video, paintings, newsreel footage, cartoon drawings
and theatrical stagings. For instance, the sequence involving the children's
film making group is shown as a montage of several cartoon drawings. The
sequence involving James recalling his contribution to the anti-base riots and
questioning his own identity consists of a mixture of actual newsreel footage of
the Koza riot in 1970 and several shots including James. The end sequence
of *Love's Love* is also presented in the form of *rensa-geki* (or chain-drama), a
combination of theatrical performance and film projections.[14]

14 The *rensa-geki* was popular on mainland Japan in the 1910s. While it largely died out on
mainland Japan during the 1920s, it continued to be a popular form of performance in Okinawa
until the 1960s.

The simultaneous use of different sounds and images is another example of the collage techniques deployed in *Tsuru-Henry*. In the opening of the film, Tsuru sings a popular Okinawan folk love song 'Shirakumo-bushi' ('Song of the White Cloud'). Tsuru's song is overlapped with James' recitation of the song's lyric in English. This does not mean that Tsuru's song is being commented upon in James' narration as neither of them is accentuated. Rather, it is like a mixed chorus in which the two sound texts may not be perfectly consonant but nonetheless present a peculiar fusion. Later, 'Shirakumo-bushi' is sung again in the sequence in which Tsuru performs her live radio show at the US military's communications' facilities known as the Elephant Cage. This time, Tsuru's song is mixed with a Chinese version of the *Internationale* being broadcast on Radio Beijing and the US army's 'Today's Saigon Report', both of which are caught by the huge antenna of the Elephant Cage. Thus, what we hear is a strange mixture of Okinawan folksong, a communist revolutionary anthem, and a report on the Vietnam War. While Tsuru is played by one of Okinawa's most famous folk singers, the song is not fetishized but instead becomes a part of a complex collage of sound in which the differing elements comment on each other.

The Elephant Cage sequence not only presents a collage of sounds but also of the history of Okinawan struggle. In the sequence, there are several shots of the Elephant Cage both in long shot and close-up. The surrounding scenery of the Elephant Cage is an extensive sugar cane field. Needless to say, the Elephant Cage signifies 'occupier' while the surrounding landscape represents 'occupied' Okinawa. Although it has existed in Okinawa since 1962, the Elephant Cage is strongly associated with the Okinawans' anti-US military base movement from the mid-1990s onwards. In one shot, the flag is waving in the foreground of the screen. This flag was used by one of the women's anti-base protest in 1997. On the flag is written '1000 memories' which refers to the 1,000 base-related crimes committed against Okinawan women. Thus, while the film is set in pre-reversion Okinawa of the late 1960s, the sequence contains multiple temporalities and a broader history of Okinawa's struggle.

Like the sound collage, the visual images in *Tsuru-Henry* are often shown through superimposition, producing yet extra layers of fusion. One striking example of this occurs in the scene of James' first monologue. For two and a half minutes, he recounts his own personal history and loss of memory. During this monologue, however, the images on the screen do not match what he tells us. While the voice-over constructs a coherent narrative, the images on the screen do not appear to possess any clear spatial, temporal or narrative order, consisting of an apparently arbitrary montage of images of old photographs and pastel drawings, sky, the script of *Love's Love*, a gajumaru tree, the US high commissioner, manual gadgets and so on. In most cases, each image is already a form of collage with images laid over one another through double or triple exposure.

In order to understand how Takamine's cinematic strategy of collage challenges the conventional representation of Okinawa and, by doing so, Japan's cosmetic multiculturalism, the Okinawan notion of '*machibui*' is of help. '*Machibui*' is an Okinawan word for 'chaos' or 'tangle'. The director Takamine once observed that the key theme of *Tsuru-Henry* is the notion of '*machibui*' and that the cinematic strategy deployed in the film may be described as '*machibui*' realism.[15] Takamine explained that *machibui* is like an Okinawan gajumaru tree. The gajumaru tree grows throughout Okinawa and it appears in *Tsuru-Henry* several times. As the gajumaru tree grows, the mass of new roots descends from its branches, pushing into the ground and fusing into one thick trunk which supports the whole tree. As a result of its collage style and multi-layered form, *Tsuru-Henry* is like a gajumaru tree. Several story-lines, different languages, different media texts tangle and intermesh with each other like the roots of the gajumaru and are woven together to form the film's overall structure. Takamine seems to assume that Okinawan experiences cannot be generated or encapsulated by a linear narrative but should be interrogated through a tangle of intertwining layers of different texts, stories, images and sounds that mutually affect each other.

Even though Takamine describes himself as an Okinawan nationalist, his aesthetic strategy suggests that he does not subscribe to any utopian vision of an essentialist or unified notion of Okinawan identity. As Gerow suggests, his politics of collage not only frees Okinawa from dominant mainland definitions of 'Okinawaness', but also avoids the pitfalls of an essentialized self-definition of Okinawa.[16] At the same time, Takamine also resists presenting a hybrid identity – of being both Okinawan and Japanese – as some kind of utopian condition. Takamine seems to recognize that appealing to 'cultural hybridity' or 'hybrid identity' may easily end up serving cosmetic multiculturalism or Japanese nationalism masquerading as an appreciation of an 'other' culture. What Takamine tries to do instead is to present a figuration of Okinawan subjectivity through the metaphors of the gajumaru tree. But the specificity of an Okinawan subjectivity is not presented as an authentic Okinawan essence, but as a 'tangled web', a complex, gajumaru-tree-like structure with branches and roots that are not easily distinguished from each other. Okinawan subjectivity is therefore not to be found in terms of an image or in a unifying concept, nor in the absence of such a thing, but in the very manner of fragmentation in which the diverse elements are intertwined with each other. By way of the diverse formal strategies he employs and by his refusal of the dominant representation of Okinawa, Takamine also makes *Tsuru-Henry* an explicit refusal of cosmetic multiculturalism.

---

15 Takamine Go Interview '*Machibui no naka ni ikiru machibutta hitotachi* ('Confused people living in chaos'), http://www.jca.apc.org/~hujisawa/cinema/takamine.html.   16 Gerow, 'From the national gaze to multiple gazes', p. 303.

The conquering heritage of British Cinema Studies and the 'Celtic Fringe'

SARAH NEELY

Since Charles Barr's initial use of the term in 1986 to describe wartime literary adaptations aimed at the international market-place, the 'heritage' film has occupied a central place in British cinema studies. Citing Laurence Olivier's *Henry V* (1944) as an example, Barr also indicated how such films simultaneously reflect both 'then and now'.[1] When Andrew Higson adopted the term a few years later the relationship of the films to Thatcherite Britain was central to his analysis and eventual formulation of heritage as a genre.[2] These films seemed to say less about the 'then' depicted in nineteenth-century and early twentieth-century novels than they did about the political climate of the 1980s, a time when the National Trust's promotion of stately homes developed a symbiotic relationship with the film industry. Debates around heritage focused on the films' representation of a social elite at a time when unemployment had reached a crisis. While those films designated as 'heritage' were heavily criticized for their representation of Britain, the conception of heritage itself became firmly attached to this period, leading to questions concerning whether or not heritage offered a productive framework for the new cycle of films that followed the 1980s.

As time moves on and new contextual frameworks surface, the genre formulated around the earlier films jars awkwardly. Conceptions of heritage change, and different versions of the 'national' past have been offered on film and television. However, one of the dangers of the heritage label, as with all genre studies, is that new films do not fit neatly into the critical framework of the heritage debates and are therefore ignored. Higson takes up these issues in his recent book, charting the impact of transnational filmmaking on the 'heritage' film.[3] The focus, narrowed to 'English Heritage', avoids any confrontations with the British question. As far as class goes, Higson blames the films themselves for their narrow focus on 'monarchs, nobility, or aristocrats'

---

1 Charles Barr, 'Introduction: Amnesia and Schizophrenia', *All our yesterdays: ninety years of British cinema* (London, 1986), pp 1–30. 2 Andrew Higson, 'Re-presenting the national past: nostalgia and pastiche in the heritage film' in L. Friedman (ed.), *British cinema and Thatcherism: fires were started* (London, 1993), pp 109–29. 3 Andrew Higson, *English heritage, English cinema* (Oxford, 2003). Higson responded to criticisms of his notion of heritage in his earlier article 'The heritage film and British cinema', A. Higson (ed.), *Dissolving views: key writings on British cinema* (London, 1996), pp 232–49.

and, rather than widen his scope, he claims 'it is difficult to find films that step confidently away from the privileged classes'.[4] Even though films such as *Elizabeth* (Shekhar Kapur, 1998) and *Braveheart* (Mel Gibson, 1995) may signal the possibility of such a shift in focus, Higson identifies the new cycle of heritage films as 'cross-over' films characteristic of the industries' transatlantic rather than domestic crossing of borders.[5] Ultimately, Higson's categorizations seem to be based upon commercial success more than anything else.[6] Rather than focusing on identity and representation, this body of films appears to be defined by marketing and distribution.

Although Higson mentions the possibility for a study of heritage films with Ireland, Scotland and Wales as their subject matter, he maintains that borders must be drawn in order to 'prevent the book from spiralling out of control'.[7] Still, Higson makes fleeting mention of over a dozen films reflecting on the Irish, Scottish and Welsh past that could prove ripe for this type of analysis.[8] Certainly, even limiting a definition of heritage to films aligned with the *marketing* of heritage a wealth of texts present themselves.[9] The representation of Scotland, Ireland and Wales in 'heritage' films has, however, been the subject of criticism. As Ruth Barton argues in relation to Ireland:

> heritage films demonstrate the difficulty for a young national cinema of breaking with the dominant paradigms of representation that it has inherited, particularly within a mainstream environment. They specifically illustrate the interplay between tourism and representation within certain Irish cultural productions.[10]

Many of the debates around the 'Tartan Monster' in the 1980s have likewise involved a critique that such myths are either Victorian imposition or invention, constructed outside rather than within the nation. Yet despite the criticism of tartanry and pastoralism, their appearance in the promotion of Scotland and Ireland has hardly waned. While Ireland's tourist board continues to promote a rural 'Island of Memories', VisitScotland follows a similar approach, highlighting rugged landscapes and unspoilt natural beauty in its campaigns. Many of VisitScotland's promotions targeting the London Underground aim to whisk away frustrated commuters to a place that is seemingly untouched by everyday hassles.[11]

---

4 Higson, *English heritage, English cinema*, p. 26.   **5** Ibid., 260.   **6** Claire Monk has made this argument in her essay, 'The British Heritage-Film Debate Revisited' in C. Monk and A. Sargeant (eds), *British historical cinema* (London, 2002), pp 176–98.   **7** Higson, *English heritage, English cinema*, p. 4.   **8** Ibid., 26.   **9** Duncan Petrie argues how Higson's notion of heritage could apply to various adaptations and films engaging with the same images that have provided the face of Scotland's heritage industry in his book *Screening Scotland* (London, 2000), pp 69–70.   **10** Ruth Barton, *Irish national cinema* (London, 2004), p. 149.   **11** Highland Spring and VisitScotland joined forces in the summer of 2003, handing out bottles of water to travelers on the London

In Scotland, Ireland and Wales, tourist boards, local councils and film commissions have capitalized on the success of films featuring local areas as a backdrop. The Wales Screen Commission offers a 'Movie Map' similar to the British Tourist Authority's 'Movie Map' produced in 1998. In Scotland, Fort William and Lochaber organizations have run a 'Now You've Seen the Film' promotion. The leaflet, map, and website encourage tourists to explore the 'spectacular area' that has 'provided the backdrop for epic Hollywood movies', advising visitors on specific locations as well as clearly marked walks (such as 'The *Braveheart* Trail'). Similarly, the popularity of two BBC programmes – *Monarch of the Glen* and *Ballykissangel* – has also encouraged new ways of promoting the areas where they were filmed.

On the other hand, rather than limiting studies of heritage to commercial understandings, aligned with the heritage industry, a more wide-ranging definition of heritage could be offered. Higson initially defined the heritage film as involving 'the reproduction of literary texts, artefacts and landscapes which already have a privileged status within the accepted definition of national heritage [...and] the reconstruction of a historical moment which is assumed to be of national significance'.[12] Within this wider definition of heritage (i.e. adaptations, costume dramas or historical films), a wealth of material presents itself in Ireland, Scotland and Wales. *Ryan's Daughter* (David Lean, 1970), *Circle of Friends* (Pat O'Connor, 1995), *December Bride* (Thaddeus O'Sullivan, 1991), and *The Dead* (John Huston, 1987) are just a few examples of adaptations with Ireland as their subject matter. For a study of Scotland and the heritage film, several films, from versions of *Macbeth* to adaptations of Robert Louis Stevenson and Sir Walter Scott, could prove fruitful terrain. Historical or costume dramas of possible interest could include *Mrs. Brown* (John Madden, 1997) or *Regeneration* (Gillies MacKinnon, 1997). In Wales, the film most obviously falling under the heritage umbrella is *Hedd Wyn* (Paul Turner, 1992), but could also include *The Englishman who went up a hill but came down a mountain* (Christopher Monger, 1995), a film Martin McLoone has referred to as Welsh 'kailyardism'.[13]

However, moving even further from Higson's notion of heritage, Phil Powrie's identification of an 'alternative heritage' or 'rite of passage' film which illustrates working-class experience through the eyes of a child proves particularly relevant to recent filmmaking.[14] Whereas original notions of the heritage

---

underground. VisitScotland also devised the longest-ever advert for the London Underground, a panorama of Highland landscapes that ran the length of one platform. 12 Andrew Higson, *Waving the flag: constructing a national cinema in Britain* (Oxford, 1995), p. 27. 13 Martin McLoone, 'Internal decolonisation? British cinema in the Celtic Fringe' in R. Murphy (ed.), *The British cinema book* (London, 2000) p. 187. 14 Phil Powrie, 'On the threshold between past and present' in J. Ashby and A. Higson (eds), *British cinema, past and present* (London, 2000), pp 316–26.

film hinged on the films' look to a distant and stable past, many of the films emanating from Ireland and Scotland (and perhaps Wales) in the late twentieth and early twenty-first centuries focus on a more recent past and are often told through a child's narrative point-of-view. Throughout my PhD dissertation which looked at the adaptation of several contemporary Irish and Scottish works of literary fiction to film, several shared themes emerged. These included films such as *Venus Peter* (Ian Sellar, 1990) (which Powrie mentions in his analysis), but also *My Left Foot* (Jim Sheridan, 1989),[15] *Angela's Ashes* (Alan Parker, 1999), *Dreaming* (Mike Alexander, 1990), and *The Butcher Boy* (Neil Jordan, 1997).

Many, like Powrie's description of the 'rite of passage' film, involve a dedication to detail and perceived 'authenticity' that equals the alternative heritage film's 'bourgeois' counterpart. The story is generally told through the eyes of a child (primarily a boy). Instead of identifying the past as a secure place to which to escape, these films, through their alignment with a child, highlight a position of vulnerability. Voice-overs, further articulating point-of-view, are fragmented and marked by their incongruity with the events unfolding on screen and are frequently employed as a method of subverting traditional modes of discourse.[16] Along similar lines, the generally stable positioning of the 'woman at the window'[17] in the heritage film is subverted in these narratives. Rather than serving to emphasize a secure social positioning that the 'woman at the window' trope suggests, the window illustrates the problematic, often unstable, status of the child. This symbolic use of windows evokes the experiences of a child observing an adult world, but also seems to reflect class issues. Specifically, it dramatizes social exclusion. In these films, children, confined by adult society, are frequently framed through windows, further emphasizing their banishment from society and their fate to remain on the fringes looking in (or out).

Lynne Ramsay's film *Ratcatcher* (1999), a film set in Glasgow during a 1970s refuse workers' strike, is an obvious example. When the young protagonist, Jamie, ventures into the countryside he discovers a family home that is under construction. His positioning first inside the large window facing out onto a wide-open field and then later, once a pane of glass has been installed, outside the house, serves to illustrate his precarious relationship to the idealized domestic space. The trope of the window also provides provocative

15 Richard Dyer identified Jim Sheridan's *My Left Foot* as a 'heritage film' in 'Heritage Cinema in Europe' in J. Caughie and K. Rockett (eds), *Companion to British and Irish cinema* (London, 1996), pp 186–7.   16 Sarah Neely, 'Cultural ventriloquism: the voice-over in film adaptations of contemporary Irish and Scottish literature', in K. Rockett and J. Hill (eds) *National cinema and beyond: Studies in Irish Film 1* (Dublin, 2004), pp 125–34.   17 Julianne Pidduck, 'Of windows and country walks: frames of space and movement in 1990s Austen adaptations', *Screen*, 39: 4 (1998), pp 381–400.

metaphorical readings of Irish and Scottish national and cultural identities. For example, in *The Butcher Boy,* when Francie peers into the Nugents' window, either to watch their television or witness the domestic interaction between Philip and his mother, it is visually poignant. He is shown frequently throughout the film on the outside looking in (e.g. looking into the Nugents' house, or looking into the café). The occurrences in which he is 'inside' looking out, rather than illustrating his inclusion in society, serve to highlight his entrapment. It is also important to note that Mrs. Nugent, who has moved to the village from England, is seen by Francie as the primary source of his troubles. Later in the film, his exclusion from a stable domestic environment that his subject positioning in relation to the window illustrates is contrasted with his positioning in relation to the window of the industrial school. Here he is framed sitting leisurely in a chair in the Priest's room, daydreaming as he looks out of the window. It is one of the only times we see Francie secure, within a seat of power, perhaps hinting towards Francie's fate, and the older Francie Brady, from whom the voice-over and narration originates, locked into a lifetime of institutionalization. Towards the end of the narrative, in the film, when the young Francie's options and allies have dwindled to extinction, he uses a window as a slate upon which to note loved ones he has lost. Tracing his finger across the condensation on the window, he writes a list of names.

In many instances windows function as a melodramatic device, emphasizing the dynamics of the space situated between public and domestic thresholds, but they are also instrumental in evoking a certain degree of nostalgia. The relationship of the narrative to character and, ultimately the narrator, resembles a series of Chinese boxes (i.e. the young boy's observations of the community around him form one part of the story, while the narrator's more distanced look at the reality of childhood forms another).[18] Just as the voice-over represents Francie's positioning in society as a voice outside the immediate narrative, so the window denotes an isolation from what lies outside the narrative frame. Only diegetic sound is embedded in the image, a voice-over is somewhere outside.[19]

Studies of oral history have indicated the tendency to privilege the adult account over the child's, following a general assumption that while the child's history is likely to be narrowly focused, the adult's history will prove more representative of the shared experience of the collective. Although it is perhaps a generalization that only grown-ups think of people other than themselves, the child's history, perhaps more dedicated to the detail of personal

---

18 Edward Branigan likens the hierarchy of narration to a set of Chinese boxes, with each one representing a new frame of subjectivity and introducing a different relationship between subject and object. See his *Point of view in the cinema: a theory of narration and subjectivity in classical film* (Berlin, 1984), p. 2.   19 Michel Chion, *The voice in cinema,* trans. Claudia Gorbman (New York, 1999), p. 3.

experience, has the potential to expose contradictions within the meta-narratives of national cinema. If Higson's original critique of heritage identified the
films' efforts in terms of a conservative construction of the nation (and the
suppression of contradictions), perhaps the child-centred films, through their
mobilization of alternative narratives, might be looked at in terms of their
attempt to destabilize these earlier narratives of national identity.

According to Higson's notion of a national cinema, notions of heritage and
the national are inextricably tied. Arguing the case for cinema as a carrier of
the national, Higson defines it 'as one that draws on indigenous cultural traditions, [and] one that invokes and explores the nation's cultural heritage'.[20]
Higson's definition of the national signals the root of the complication. In relation to Britain, 'indigenous', or local – an antonym of national – functions on
several levels. All cinema draws on such traditions, but it is the act of con-
solidating and identifying a unifying source that is problematic.

The difficulty of representation and national culture exists across all art
forms. In 1936, Edwin Muir argued the case for a unified Scots language and
warned that Scots dialect was only capable of representing Scotland 'in bits
and patches', as 'divided' rather than as a whole. Muir feared that dialect
would condemn Scotland to 'remain a mere collection of districts'.[21] More
recently and optimistically, Willy Maley has argued for the advantage of dis-
junctive representation, reasoning that 'Scotland is best laid out in schemes
rather than gathered under one national heading'.[22] Maley's remarks are typical of more general arguments concerning the representation of Scotland and
the acceptance of Scotland's plural identities.[23] Ireland shares this change.
Gerry Smyth in his study of contemporary Irish fiction writes that 'it is perhaps no longer possible to offer a single artistic vision of the nation'.[24]

In short, the heritage label poses two key problems. Firstly, the general
limitations of the genre have involved a focus on a particular type of
'Englishness' rather than 'Britishness' or anything else for that matter. This
means films depicting a variety of representations of national identity are
ignored – Irish, Scottish, Welsh, but also across other cultural, social and class
lines. However, additional problems arise when applying the heritage framework to Ireland, Scotland and Wales because of the complicated nature of
'British' national identity that the heritage label poses.

20 Andrew Higson, 'The instability of the national' in J. Ashby and A. Higson (eds), *British
cinema, past and present* (London, 2000), p. 36.   21 Edwin Muir, *Scott and Scotland* (London,
1936), p. 71.   22 Willy Maley, 'Subversion and scurrility in Irvine Welsh's shorter fiction', in
D. Cavanagh and T. Kirk (eds), *Subversion and scurrility: popular discourse in Europe from 1500
to the present* (London, 2000), p. 191.   23 See, for instance, Douglas Gifford, 'Imagining
Scotlands: the return to mythology in modern Scottish fiction' in S. Hagemann (ed.), *Studies in
Scottish fiction: 1945 to the present* (Frankfurt, 1996), pp 17–49.   24 Gerry Smyth, 'Roddy Doyle
and the new Irish fiction', *The novel and the nation: studies in the new Irish fiction* (London, 1997),
p. 67.

Although not in reference to child-centred narratives, John Hill has noted how the more traditional notion of heritage film in Ireland functions rather differently from its British counterpart. Referring specifically to *The Dawning* (Robert Knights, 1988) and *Fools of Fortune* (Pat O'Connor, 1990) – two films based on Irish novels and shot in Ireland but nevertheless still considered as part of the 'Brit Lit' phenomenon – Hill highlights the complexities involved in applying the framework of the English heritage film to films reflecting on the past in Ireland. Unlike its English counterpart, these films resist representations of a past hermetically sealed off from the present, one that is easily revisited with nostalgia that such a safe distance affords. Hill explains:

> Ireland in the 1920s, especially during the War of Independence, is much less readily available as an object of nostalgia than the comparable period in England. The past, in this respect, is so obviously characterized by violence and social tension that it is clearly difficult to project it as any kind of golden age.[25]

Where the past in the English heritage film, representative of stability, is a comforting place to which to escape, the past in the Irish heritage film offers no such refuge. Instead, Hill argues, the past is not sealed off from the present, or, as the title suggests: 'The past is always there in the present'. The temporary escape from contemporary problems that traditional notions of heritage cinema promise, is not possible. Barton has also noted Irish films' departure from British films' ambivalent relationship to history, that of a past functioning 'as little more than background information and [...] seldom if ever problematized'.[26] In these films, the metaphoric symbol for the 'Nation' – the large country house – Barton explains 'is both alien to the landscape and under constant threat, of decay and attack'.[27]

As Powrie's formulation of the 'rite of passage' films illustrates, the childhood narratives exist in films about England as well as Ireland, Scotland and Wales. Powrie's designation of an 'alternative heritage', like the films he writes about, challenges notions of heritage narrowly constructed around the national identity of the privileged classes. However, the prevalence of the childhood narratives in Ireland and Scotland flag up further issues regarding their complicated relationship to England. The child in many of these films marks out the narratives as framed by their 'otherness' – a depiction that could be read as a general metaphor for 'Celtic' representation and its meaning constructed around its difference from England.[28]

25 John Hill, '"The past is always there in the present": *Fools of fortune* and the heritage film', in J. MacKillop (ed.), *Contemporary Irish cinema: from* The Quiet Man *to* Dancing at Lughnasa (New York, 1999), p. 30. 26 Barton, *Irish national cinema*, p. 135. 27 Ibid., 136. 28 David McCrone, Angela Morris, and Richard Kiely, *Scotland – the brand: the making of Scottish*

Although Ruth Barton criticizes the employment of child-centred narratives in Irish cinema as signalling a 'failure to break with the paradigms of
colonial representation with its infantilizing tendencies',[29] many of the films
referred to in this article resist such nostalgic readings and instead emphasize
the arduous friction between past and present and an inability to break with the
past. Neither the past or the present offers a place of refuge, nor is the division between the two clear. For instance, in *The Butcher Boy*, the voice-over
retracing the events that land Francie bandaged from head-to-toe – the first
image we have of him – begins: 'when I was a young lad, twenty or thirty or
forty years ago'. Rather than establish a clearly defined point in history, the
narrative begins as it will continue, with an uncertain narration, disrupting
any perceived stability of the narrative past. John Hill highlights a similar confusion of time in *Fools of Fortune*, a film also jumping back and forth across
time, resulting in feelings of disorientation that Hill explains 'undermines any
sense of the past's "separateness"'[30] – a key characteristic of the heritage films
associated with the body of films Higson identifies as 'heritage'.

The Butcher Boy is also an example of the child-centred narratives that
'plunder' heritage representations, but without the 'impartial regard' that
Barton identifies with other filmmakers.[31] On the one hand, the film treads on
similar ground to other types of heritage films, drawing from a wealth of
iconography and familiar landscape tropes. However, as Emer and Kevin
Rockett argue, while 'this magic realist perfection is also common to the
numerous heritage-type films that were produced during the 1980s and 1990s,
it is clearly of a different order, with the latter privileging nostalgia over ironic
or critical engagement'.[32] Referring specifically to the scene where a picturesque
loch is annihilated by an atomic bomb, Rockett and Rockett argue it to be 'one
of the most subversive images within Irish cinema. In that single moment, the
dominant representation of the Irish landscape is destroyed and its mythic
constructed nature revealed'.[33] The iconic landscape is literally and metaphor-
ically blown apart, representing the collision of a 'mythic past', a past that is
imagined or imposed rather than possessed, with a turbulent present. Rockett
and Rockett compare the scene to similar depictions in David Lynch's films,
pointing to the 'pleasure in its perfection and stylization' that 'nonetheless,
suggests a blackness, a disease or a violence at its core'.[34] A similar comparison
may be made with *Trainspotting* (Danny Boyle, 1996) or *Morvern Callar* (Lynne
Ramsay, 2002). In the infamous 'It's shite being Scottish' scene, a scene
Murray Smith has referred to as 'ironic heritage'[35], nostalgic shots more familiar to films such as *Rob Roy* and *Braveheart* are forbidden their sheltered dis-

heritage (Edinburgh, 1995), p. 57.   **29** Barton, *Irish national cinema*, p. 150–1.   **30** Hill, '"The
past is always there in the present"', p. 31.   **31** Barton, *Irish national cinema*, p. 150–1.   **32**
Emer Rockett and Kevin Rockett, *Neil Jordan: exploring boundaries* (Dublin, 2003), p. 193.   **33**
Ibid., 192.   **34** Ibid., 193.   **35** Murray Smith, *Trainspotting* (London, 2002), p. 25.

tance from the past and are, instead, forced to face up to its uneasy relationship to post-industrial Scotland. In *Morvern Callar*, like Lynch, Ramsay hints at the evil leaking beneath the surface of the assumed mundaneness of the 'everyday'. Not dissimilar to Lynch's subversions of idealized cinematic depictions of suburbia, highland hilltop views are spoiled by interruptions of the abject.[36] Throughout the film, scenic shots of misty moors and highland heather are literally crawling: bugs are everywhere, even infesting a carrot at the hyper-clean supermarket where Morvern works. The picturesque landscapes are further fragmented by Morvern's burial of her boyfriend as she disposes of the body parts at random points across the highland terrain.

These films relationship with the landscape is questioning. Rather than assuming the representations of the heritage landscape as an inheritance, the films highlight their characters disjointed relationship to it. Heritage assumes something is possessed, that something is owned rather than imposed. This is what is problematized in many of these contemporary narratives. In the 'It's shite being Scottish' scene, like the nuclear annihilation of Francie Brady's loch, what is worked through is the incompatibility of its characters and the world around them and its exported and preserved representations.

'History is written by those that have hanged heroes', says Robert the Bruce in the opening voice-over of the Mel Gibson's 1995 Hollywood blockbuster, a film that would become the poster-child for the Scottish National Party. Like all great heritage films, authenticity proved pertinent. Critics fumed over its historical accuracy, but as David McCrone pointed out, *'Braveheart* might have been bad history, but it made good politics'.[37] While it is certain there is such a thing as bad politics, it is not as easily convincing that there is ever a 'good' history. A large part of the debate raged around the historical truth of a film scripted by an American (of Scottish extraction) who became interested in Wallace when he stumbled upon his statue as a tourist in Scotland, and directed by an Australian-American actor most famous for his performance as a futuristic hero in *Mad Max* (George Miller, 1979). What the argument revealed was the tendency to believe that there is, in fact, an authoritative history.[38]

In all fairness, Andrew Higson has argued that there is no such thing as an authoritative heritage. In 1996, he maintained that although 'the typical heritage film projects a particular image of the national past ... there are other images of the national past circulating in other recent British films' – films he

36 A more in-depth comparative analysis between *Morvern Callar* and David Lynch's *Blue Velvet* may be found in Sarah Neely, 'Adapting to change in contemporary Irish and Scottish culture: fiction to film' (PhD thesis, University of Glasgow, 2003).   37 David McCrone, 'Tomorrow's ancestors: nationalism, identity and history', in Edward J. Cowan and Richard J. Finlay (eds), *Scottish history: the power of the past* (Edinburgh, 2002), p. 258.   38 For a more detailed account of this debate see Willy Maley, *'Braveheart:* Raising the stakes of history', *Irish Review,* 22 (1998), pp 67–79.

later suggests 'offer a version of heritage'.[39] Phil Powrie resists such a catego-
rization and instead defines the 'rite of passage' films as a third category of
historical cinema, alongside the heritage film and the biopic. He explains that
the films 'are not "versions of heritage"' as Higson would have it. They are,
rather, distinctly 'alternative', because ... they focus on and frequently aes-
theticize the working class or the lower middle class rather than the upper
middle class of "bourgeois heritage"'.[40] Although the distinction between the
films is evident, denoting one set of films as an alternative to another suggests
the sort of hierarchy that is being contested, a structure that is evident when
Higson suggests that these other versions of heritage 'are not generally graced
with the name "heritage film" ... precisely because they don't offer this same
vision of the national past'.[41] What lies at the base of the argument is whose
'vision of the national past' is to inform notions of heritage. The danger of
the conquering heritage is that, like the conquering hero, only one 'version'
of the story is privileged.

39 Higson, 'The heritage film and British cinema', pp 235–6.   40 Powrie, 'On the threshold
between past and present', p. 317.   41 Andrew Higson, 'The heritage film and British cinema',
p. 235.

Musical and mythical patterns in:
Paul Thomas Anderson's *Magnolia*

The human perception of reality is defined by the Gestalt principles of pattern-making. Our mind organizes seemingly unconnected visual, auditory and temporal perceptual data into units that link together into comprehensible wholes. Our need to organize perceptive stimuli into patterns is so pronounced that, according to Gestalt laws, we make units and accents even when there are none; we even perceive the ticking of a clock through patterns of strong and weak beats although they are all the same.

If it were not for its ability to adapt itself to the world through the Gestalt perception of pattern-making, the mind would be overwhelmed by a profusion of perceptive stimuli and would experience only chaos. The organization of chaos into patterns is something that brings unstructured things closer to our understanding, makes them recognizable, open for experience. Moreover, as Anthony Storr[1] remarks, this disposition towards pattern-making is active at every conceivable level in our mental hierarchy, influencing not only the simplest auditory and visual perception but also the comprehension of the most complex intellectual concepts. It has been employed in the creation of philosophical and belief systems. It defines the way we understand the world and also, unsurprisingly, how we construct and perceive art.

Artistic expression usually originates in the unstructured realms of intuition, feeling and sensation. The articulation of artistic ideas and feelings from their presumably chaotic origins into communicable forms is made possible by the ability of the mind to give them structure through the establishment of formal patterns. The use of patterns also facilitates the establishment of rhythmic relations among formal constituents, which generally enhances the accessibility of a work's content. The pattern-making is unimaginable without the use of repetition. As the repetition of what has been experienced before gives to Proust's hero of *Recherche du temps perdu* 'the substance to consciousness',[2] so does repetition in an art form help in the creation of patterns that bring the sensuous and the intellectual, the perceptual and the cognitive aspects of art together.

---

1 Anthony Storr, *Music and the mind* (London, 1997), p. 168.   2 Genevieve Lloyd, *Being in time: selves and narrators in philosophy and literature* (London, 1993), p. 141.

Music and film are similar in the way that they both use repetition and other patterns to create communicable form, to establish rhythmic relations among its constituents and to emphasize certain aspects of content. In addition, in both of these arts, the employment of patterns creates structures that echo mythical ones. I will use the example of Paul Thomas Anderson's film *Magnolia* (1999) to show how both mythical and musical attributes can be conjured up in film by the use of patterns and how this procedure itself reveals the connection between music and film on both analogous and interactive levels.

PATTERNS IN MUSIC AND FILM

All music forms are based on patterns of some kind, although only patterns in Western music are by definition hierarchical, which means that they are usually arranged in such a way as to create more complex structures than they are themselves. Forms of Western music are built on micro-networks of patterns articulated as motifs and phrases, while their large-scale structures are based on macro-patterns of sections and movements or, in serial music, on the combinations of serially organized parameters. Micro-patterns rely on co-dependent relationships between pitch and duration that are, together with harmony, the primary parameters of pattern-forming. If one of these parameters is changed noticeably, the pattern also changes, while changes in register, dynamic, tempo or instrumentation do not influence the recognition of the familiar pattern.

The principles of pattern organization on both micro- and macro-levels in music are determined by the rules and conventions of a particular style. Conventional forms resulting from these patterns have naturally undergone numerous adjustments and 'make-overs' throughout the history of Western music. However, the same principles of communicable form may be found in the most primitive binary and ternary musical forms as well as the most complex ones – the principles of creating rhythms of tension and release, alternating sections of density and sparseness and acknowledging the rhythm of formal expectation and anticipation.

In film, the process of creating patterns is generally located in the realm of narrative structure. Bordwell reminds us that 'narrational patterning is a major part of the process by which we grasp films as more or less coherent wholes'. The basic pattern is represented by the fabula (story), which 'perceivers of narratives create through assumptions and inferences. It is the developing result of picking up narrative cues, applying schemata, framing and testing hypotheses'.[3]

3 'The viewer builds the fabula on the basis of prototype schemata (identifiable types of persons, actions, locales, etc.), template schemata (principally the "canonic" story), and procedural schemata (a search for appropriate motivations and relations of causality, time, and space).' David Bordwell, *Narration in the fiction film* (London, 1997), p. 49.

At the same time, the intention to emphasize certain aspects of a narrative or generate an affective response to it may result in the conscious construction of a 'rhythmical' macro-form in a film that also involves patterning in the editing and the creation of the *mise-en-scène*. The reasons for this kind of rhythmical patterning are varied, and again they are usually created to fulfil certain demands of narrative or the intentions of a director, editor or writer to convey a certain kind of message. Nevertheless, these rhythms of patterning are governed by the same rules of macro-form that are active in music; namely they follow the same principles of alternating sections of tension and release, conflict and resolution, anticipation and its fulfilment.

The subject of patterning in an art form inevitably evokes the procedures typical of structuralist analysis. Although my approach does not originate in structuralism but formal music analysis, this methodology of linguistic and poetic analysis suggests itself as a natural accomplice. It brings us indirectly to the question of how patterns of music and film relate to myth, since the answer to that question originates in the ideas and work of the anthropologist and proponent of structuralism, Claude Lévi-Strauss.

MYTHIC PATTERNS

The idea of a relation between music and myth is an old one. Wagner believed that the structure of myths is so 'musical' that it can be revealed through the analysis of a musical score. Claude Lévi-Strauss's statement that 'music presents mythic structure in an almost pure state' is based on his assertion that both music and myth share some defining features. According to him, the fundamental cyclicism of myths is epitomized in music in the use of repetition and reprise. More importantly, they both share the ability to transcend articulate expression and the nature of their temporality. Both music and myth communicate messages larger than themselves and both are instruments for the obliteration of time, according to Lévi-Strauss. Myth is able to overcome the contradiction between historical, enacted time and a permanent constant, while music turns irreversible time devoted to listening into a 'synchronic totality, enclosed within itself. Because of the internal organization of the musical work, the act of listening to it immobilizes passing time'.[4]

In film, mythical aspects are usually introduced through narrative and 'enacted' through the 'cyclical-temporal motion' in a story, which, as in music, is accomplished through the repetition of the same pattern. This is a device typical of a mythical approach to storytelling in which human life is regarded not as a linear segment enclosed between birth and death, but as a con-

---

4 Claude Lévi-Strauss, *The raw and the cooked: introduction to the science of mythology* (London, 1970), p. 16.

stantly recurrent cycle. This cyclical structure enables characters and events from a story to outgrow the causal or historical determinations of a particular time and space and to assume a paradigmatic function that embodies universal characteristics of human nature.

Take, for example, the cases of Milcho Manchevski's film *Before the Rain* (1994) and Christopher Nolan's *Memento* (2000). These two films could not be more different in their choice of subject-matter, approach to storytelling and method of aesthetic realization, yet their stories share cyclical-temporal motion and the ideas that this conveys. *Before the Rain* tells the story of nationalistic intolerance and revenge in remote villages of the former Yugoslavia, while *Memento* uses the thriller genre to tell the story – backwards – about a man who is seeking to avenge the death of his wife. Despite their differences, both films exhibit the same theme of revenge and both employ circular structures in which the end of the movie becomes its new beginning, suggesting the ceaseless repetition of human weaknesses and sins, such as intolerance and the thirst for vengeance.

Lévi-Strauss' comments about the connections between music and myth on the one hand, and the ideas about mythical aspects of film on the other, inspired Royal S. Brown to suggest that the presence of music in film may evoke a mythic mode of perception. Brown says that this can be accomplished simply by music's ability to associate certain characters or narrative situations with particular musical themes or motifs, which can help create an 'intra-paradigmatic structure for a given filmic narrative, whereas the use of certain musical typologies, such as the waltz rhythm to suggest love, can imply extra-textual paradigms'.[5]

Brown's observation offers an additional perspective to the comparison between music and film in terms of their relationship to myth and mythic patterning. It makes it clear that the question of how film relates to music through its 'mythical' macro-patterns can be investigated both 'externally', by viewing the general framework of a film's patterns, and 'internally', by focusing on the role music performs within that framework. I will use both these approaches on the example of Paul Thomas Anderson's film *Magnolia* to examine how structural patterning in film can evoke both mythical and musical powers within it and how these mythical and musical aspects of patterning facilitate the understanding of a film's meaning.

---

5 Brown does, however, acknowledge that the presence of music in film may have the opposite function as well, by turning the paradigmatic implications of a given sign into a single symbol which can be 'read' only a single way, thus contributing to an 'unhealthy' tendency of mainstream film towards overexplication of meaning and the encouragement of the passivity of the viewer. Royal S. Brown, *Overtones and undertones* (Berkeley and Los Angeles, 1994), pp 8–11.

PATTERNS OF 'MAGNOLIA'

In order to be comparable to music in the way Lévi-Straus suggests, film has to develop a 'mythic narrative', which is mostly realized through the paradigmatic structure of its patterns. The films *Before the Rain* and *Memento* have been cited as examples of cyclical motion in a story which, by creating a circular narrative, suggests the ceaseless repetition of a pattern epitomized in a complete film. A different example of cyclical motion may be found in stories that are themselves based on the repetition of the same pattern throughout the film. In Federico Fellini's *Casanova* (1976), for example, the relationships are always of the same sort and, as Yvette Biró notices, they follow the same pattern: 'the gestures of approach, desire, and disgust are regulated by a single inner tendency – be it blessing or a curse'.[6]

This model of repetition can be substituted with an alternative approach, as it usually is in contemporary literature, so that the experiences of one character are not continuously 'repeated', but may be doubled or even multiplied by the parallel stories of different characters. This device stems from the earliest literary forms, Greek dramas and myths, and has been used, for instance, in Aldous Huxley's novel *Point Counter Point* (1928), where the duplication of situations and characters, and the interweaving of themes with repetitions and minor variations, act as one of the means of generalizing the novel's idea. This approach was brought almost to an extreme by Paul Thomas Anderson in his film *Magnolia*, which juggles nine main characters and interweaves nine distinct storylines connected through similarities of situation and emotion. A loose connection between all the storylines is provided by the film's title that refers to the name of the street running through the San Fernando Valley, 'a place without distinguishing features or final destination [...] an indeterminate space of multiple overlapping soap operas'.[7]

Magnolia presents us with two dysfunctional families, both headed by powerful men who were or are still connected with a TV quiz-show for brilliant kids. Both these men are dying and each of them is leaving an estranged, emotionally damaged child and a wife with substance abuse problems. The duplication of plot-lines is augmented by two additional shattered lives – kids who were or are stars of the eponymous quiz-show. There are also two characters – a policeman and a male nurse – who act as the agents of forgiveness. The fact that these two men are able to bring some relief to other characters through their innocence and the simple goodness of their actions underlines the core of the film's existential quest and brings out its central question: what can be forgiven or, more precisely, is it possible to forgive fathers for sins committed against their own children?

6 Yvette Biró, *Profane mythology: the savage mind of cinema* (Bloomington, 1982), p. 123.   7 Leslie Dick, '*Magnolia*', *Sight and Sound* (April, 2000), p. 56.

As if to prepare us for the striking concurrences between his characters and storylines, Anderson starts the film with a prologue that informs us about some 'real-life' cases of extraordinary coincidences. One of these stories is also quoted in Paul Auster's novel, *The Invention of Solitude* (1982). Deeply fascinated by these 'rhyming' coincidences in life, Auster writes:

> Just as two physical objects, when brought into proximity of each other, give off electromagnetic forces that not only effect the molecular structure of each but the space between them as well, so it is that two (or more) rhyming events set up a connection in the world, adding one more synapse to be routed through the vast plenum of experience.
>
> These connections are commonplace in literary works...but one tends not to see them in the world – for the world is too big and one's life is too small. It is only at those rare moments when one happens to glimpse a rhyme in the world that the mind can leap out of itself and serve as a bridge for things across time and space, across seeing and memory.[8]

Judging by the criteria proposed by Lévi-Strauss, *Magnolia*'s rhyming narrative exudes a strong enough mythical resonance to be comparable to forms of music. What makes this case even more interesting is Anderson's declaration that central to the film's structure is the music of singer-songwriter Aimee Mann, which is meant to provide a unifying voice for all of the plots and characters. The same function is also carried out by Jon Brion's orchestral score that appears between Mann's songs, underlying most of the action and supplying a melancholy sonic foundation for all strands of the plot. Both Brion's score and Mann's songs permeate the structure of this film from inside and outside, offering the blueprint of their own patterns to the film on both micro- and macro-levels.

The orchestral score consists of three distinct musical materials that successively underlie big chunks of narrative. The first one is used as a background for the part described in the DVD chapters as 'light showers', which introduces the dynamic of tragic family relationships and rhyming connections between different characters and their interactions. The second one spreads out from the chapter 'family picnic' to 'meltdown', where a Barber-like adagio is transformed into a mournful waltz that gives momentum to the dissolution of all the apparently 'regular' personal and family facades. All three materials are based on the continuous repetition of their basic formal constructs that are themselves built on short, repetitive phrases. Wrapped around different characters and threads of the action, Brion's music provides lengthy film sequences with a unique sonic aura, while its cyclical character enhances the sense of

8 Paul Auster, *The invention of solitude* (London and Boston, 1982), p. 161.

recurrence in connection with the events on the screen. Nevertheless, even though justified formally and conceptually, the continuous presence of orchestral music bestows an additional affective layer upon events already charged with high emotional and dramatic intensity, thus occasionally producing the effect of oversaturation.

Dramaturgically more effective is the employment of Aimee Mann's songs that frame the film in the opening and closing credits and envelop it from the inside when used as diegetic music. One song is particularly symbolic of how music lends its own patterns to the film, providing it with mythic overtones. The song 'Wise Up' initiates the sequence which not only symbolically but also formally emphasizes the bonds between all characters. After the numerous moments of intense emotional pain that all the protagonists are experiencing, one of them, sitting in her apartment alone, starts singing along with Mann's song, which is heard playing in the background. Successive lines are then picked up by other characters isolated in their own cocoons of pain and loneliness, so that the song becomes the most effective demonstration of the characters' connectedness.

This was a risky manoeuvre on the director's part, one which made some critics scoff and others wince, partly because of its sentimentality and the fact that at one point even the character lying on his death bed starts singing, making it look almost like a scene from a *Monty Python* show. But most of all, this sequence provoked heated discussion and comments because it used an approach which is unheard of in the context of a film narrative that ultimately relies on the conventions of classical storytelling. However, the whole structure of Anderson's film relies on a string of extraordinary coincidences and, as was stated at the very beginning of the film's unusual 'prologue', so does life. One of them is this sequence in which all of the main characters, located in different parts of the town, 'share a moment' through a song.

A similar moment happens in *Almost Famous* (2000) when its characters start singing along to a song of Elton John, which director Cameron Crowe also uses to cut from face to face and show the spirit of (at least temporary) connectedness between his protagonists. But an important difference here is that in Crowe's film all the protagonists are sitting on the same bus, sharing the unity of the same time and space in the scene. Crowe's explanation is simple: he says that music can achieve in film in just a few moments what scenes and scenes of dialogue cannot. Crowe's comment actually refers to one aspect of film music's influence on film that Royal S. Brown omits to mention when he discusses its ability to evoke a mythic mode of perception, although one might claim that it is actually the most important one – its affective power.

In his book *Myths to Live By*, Joseph Campbell quotes John Perry's definition of the living mythological symbol as an 'affect image', which is an image that 'hits one where it counts'. It is not addressed to the brain. It speaks directly to the 'feeling system' and immediately elicits a response, 'like the answer of a musical string to another equally tuned'.⁹ This probably explains why music has such a powerful influence in evoking a 'mythic mode of perception' in films in general, and why Paul Thomas Anderson wanted it in this sequence. It is the point of intersection formally, as it brings all the characters and stories together. At the same time it is also the point where the tones of the intense emotional drama that had been building up until then suddenly become substituted with a moment of calmness and quiet grief. Nevertheless, having been placed somewhere around two thirds of the way through the movie, this sequence stands as its 'golden section', where most of *Magnolia*'s sense of pain and despair accumulates. It is also interesting that after this sequence all the accompanying music stops, apart from the short, cadence-like orchestral segment that underscores the moment when the events take a turn towards the coda. In the context of a structure based on duplicated patterns and rhyming characters and relationships, the 'Wise Up' sequence is that point in the film which, thanks to the music, reveals the deepest insight into the undercurrent of all-encompassing pain that connects those who had betrayed or had been betrayed by those whom they trusted the most, investing their pain with an aura of universal consistency. Thus, when it starts raining frogs at the end, it does feel like a response of heaven to a plague of ceaseless and endlessly multiplied suffering.

Magnolia's coda brings resolution through acts of forgiveness and reconciliation between some of its characters. The unspoken traumas of a daughter's childhood abuse are finally acknowledged by her mother; a son comes to say goodbye to his dying father who deserted him and his sick mother; the former whiz-kid's attempt to commit a crime is foiled by a forgiving police-officer; and the present whiz-kid stands up for the first time, at least symbolically, to his over-ambitious, not very caring father. On the other hand, the mythic aspect of the narrative, which refers to the 'constant in human sufferings', as Joyce would call it, is addressed again by the employment of another Aimee Mann song that flows from the last scene into the ensuing closing credits. Like 'Wise Up' earlier, the song 'Save Me' is a genuine part of the film that, through its lyrics, corresponds to the mythic aspects of the film's narrative, while its subdued melancholic musical style proves to be the most powerful device for plucking those strings that arouse an affective response to its mythical messages.

The case of Paul Thomas Anderson's *Magnolia* confirms that the macro-rhythm of patterns not only involves aspects of structure or our psychological or affective involvement with it, but also deeply affects our understanding of a film's meaning. In the same way that the Gestalt laws of perception and principles of pattern-making transform the chaotic world of perceptive stimuli into a familiar vision of reality, so the formal patterns of music and film

9 Joseph Campbell, *Myths to live by* (London, 1985). p. 70.

convey specific content through their structure, creating accessible works of art. And similar to the way in which the hierarchical nature of our disposition for pattern-making facilitates our ability to comprehend more complex intellectual concepts, certain ways of film structuring are able to translate the particular into the broader realm of the mythical. In *Magnolia,* the structure of rhyming plots, events and characters serves a double function similar to that of mythology itself. On one hand, it addresses the issue of the inevitability of individual death and the suffering that precedes it, while its duplicated patterns underline its repetitive nature; on the other hand, the insistence on the mirroring of extraordinary coincidences in the plot, and the tone of light detachment in the prologue and epilogue, help *Magnolia* to frame its intense exploration of grief with the comforting air of story-telling. *Magnolia*'s title might ironically play with the possibility that the film's duplicated patterns and characters overwhelmed by grief and misfortune reveal nothing more than a world of 'multiple overlapping soap operas', but its examination of revealed pain is too persistent and intense to allow us to take this possibility seriously. Rather, in the spirit of myth-telling, *Magnolia* reminds us over and over again that the human capacity for inflicting pain and suffering is infinite, but so is its capacity for forgiveness.

The example of *Magnolia* also shoes how the constitution of mythical patterns in film can be deeply influenced by music. Jon Brion's orchestral score provides the film with the unifying agent for numerous characters and storylines while formally underpinning the idea of recurrence through the repetition of its own patterns. On the other hand, the recurrence of Aimee Mann's songs throughout the film bestows the rhythm of musical patterning upon its large-scale form, while her music permeates its structure from inside too, connecting all the characters symbolically and literally in the 'Wise Up' sequence. *Magnolia* thus forms a relationship with music in both analogous and interactive ways. Besides employing music as a form of structuring and patterning, it also uses music to address the mythical aspects of its own patterns and, in doing so, reveal it as 'mythic structure in an almost pure state'.

Part 2: Film History and History in Film

'Spleen of a cabinet minister at work': exhibiting X-rays and the cinematograph in Ireland, 1896[1]

DENIS CONDON

The kinematograph, the bicycle, electric tramcars, labour-saving contrivances, etc, are not susceptible to poetic treatment, but are, in fact themselves poetry, not without a kind of suggestiveness, of a scientific age, with which the poetry of Greek and Hebrew tradition vainly endeavours to vie. It is no wonder that an age which has achieved this concrete type of poetry should be content with an attitude of simple politeness towards those dreamers who walk with their heads in a cloud of vision [...] The epics of the present are the steam engine and the dynamo, its lyrics the kinematograph, phonograph, etc., and these bear with them the hearts of men as the Iliad and the Odyssey of former days uplifted the youth of antiquity, or as the old English ballad expressed the mind of a nation in its childhood.

John Eglinton published these comments in his debate on Irish national literature with visionary poet W.B. Yeats in the *Daily Express* in 1898.[2] 'This message was apparently lost on Yeats', comments Luke Gibbons, 'for whom even the neon lights on O'Connell Street were signs of Armageddon'.[3] Eglinton's message that in an age of technological marvels people merely indulge poets was lost in many senses: lost as one minor and relatively undeveloped element of his argument; lost in the irony that it occurs in the course of a vigorous debate on literature; lost to a widely held belief in the importance of poets to the history of the period; and largely lost to Irish cultural studies as the words of a minor character in his engagement with a major canonical figure. The appearance of the moving-picture projector among the technologies that 'b[ore] with them the hearts of men' in 1898, however, holds particular interest for Irish film history. What was the cinematograph's relationship with its first

1 Research for this paper was made possible by funding from the Irish Research Council for the Humanities and Social Sciences.   2 The quote here comes from a selection of their exchanges, along with contributions from George Russell and William Larminie, that appeared in book form as *Literary ideals in Ireland* (Dublin, 1899), pp 42–3.   3 Luke Gibbons, 'Montage, modernity and the city', *Irish Review*, 10 (Spring 1991), p. 1.

Irish audiences? Was it only or primarily as a machine that the device engaged these audiences and, if so, at what point did the early cinema's opaqueness as novel technology give way to a transparency that shifted the focus to the image on the screen? While early film shows appear to have been popular, what place did they occupy in the Irish imaginary?

The year 1896 provides a useful starting point for a discussion of the reception of early cinema in Ireland. When one looks at contemporary newspapers for evidence of the terms in which the first film shows were presented to the newspaper-reading community, one finds that in 1896 the Irish public received far more information on X-rays, or early radiography, than of early cinematography. Both of these new visual technologies were presented first and foremost as scientific novelties worthy of a popular audience, but while X-rays became increasingly affiliated with medical science, cinematography became predominantly an entertainment medium.

From a technical point of view, the first successful public exhibition of projected moving pictures in Dublin was at the Cyclopia charity fete on the Ballsbridge show grounds of the Royal Dublin Society between 19 and 25 May 1896.[4] A show the previous month at the Star Theatre of Varieties, while commercially successful in the numbers attracted, did not meet the expectations of at least some members of its audience. A reviewer with the *Irish Daily Independent* commented that

> a little disappointment was experienced in connection with the display of the cinematographie [sic]. This instrument is undoubtedly capable of accomplishing great things, but it seemed to be out of order, and the pictures which it showed were much below the level of excellence which the kinetoscope or the zoopractiscope [sic] have already showed to music hall audiences.[5]

The *Irish Times*' reviewer made similar comments but added that the audience 'regarded the exhibition with interest, and applauded it'.[6] The manager of the Star, Dan Lowrey, noted in the theatre's engagement book that there was '[n]ot enough light on the pictures'.[7]

---

4 For details of the films shown, see *Irish Daily Independent* 21 and 22 May 1896. Unless otherwise indicated, subsequent newspaper accounts are from 1896. Similar disappointment was expressed at the first exhibition of the cinematograph in Edinburgh; see *Scotsman*, 14 April, reprinted in Colin Harding and Simon Popple, *In the kingdom of shadows: a companion to early cinema* (London, Madison and Teaneck, 1996), p. 12.   5 *Irish Daily Independent*, 22 April. The names of moving-picture devices are frequently misspelled in newspapers, and they will be retained in their original form below. Similarly, foreign words are often reproduced without their diacritics. Wilhelm Röntgen's name, for example, which appears variously as Röntgen, Rontgen, and Roentgen, will be reproduced in the standard form in the text but retained unstandardized in quotes.   6 *Irish Times*, 22 April.   7 Cited in Eugene Watters and Matthew Murtagh, *Infinite*

The exhibition of Robert Paul's animatographe projector at Cyclopia met with widespread approval in a context in which it could be compared direct-ly with other state-of-the-art novelties. Among the biggest attractions of this large annual fete, patrons could stroll around the mock-up Dutch village; ride the water chute, switchback railways, and merry-go-rounds; ascend in a hot-air balloon; and attend the Cafe Chantant, the Pembroke Concerts, and the Olympia Variety Entertainment. Other moving-picture and projected visual novelties vied for attention with the animatographe. A kinetoscope synchro-nized to a phonograph showed a 'champion high-kicker perform[ing] a vigor-ous and graceful dance to the accompaniment of an orchestra'.[8] Projection on a spectacular scale issued from the lantern tower:

> From this, as soon as the darkness had come over the land, numerous lantern slides were projected on to an immense linen screen, some 30 feet-square, at a distance of fully 150 feet. It is said that the screen is the largest one of the kind ever used in Ireland, and one can easily credit the statement. A display of the kind, on account of its rarity, is one of much interest, and that of last night attracted very general attention.[9]

While impressed, the *Dublin Evening Mail* reviewer expressed reservations because '[m]ixed with the slides dealing with subjects of general interest were many others which partook of the nature of advertizements, and were calcu-lated to make the spectator feel that he was being more or less imposed on'.[10]

Even in this dazzling company, the animatographe stood out. Reporting on the first day of the fete, the *Irish Times* revealed that the projector showed 'many life-like "living photographs"' and that 'their rapid succession and dexterous manipulation produced a most pleasing illusion'.[11] The *Independent* recorded that by the end of the second day the 'animatograph was so well patronized that an extra performance was given a little before 10 o'clock'.[12] By the third day, the *Independent* attempted to explain enthusiasm for the new device:

> From the first exhibition yesterday the animatograph drew large crowds of patrons. This is certainly, of the many things worth seeing at Cyclopia, one of the most entertaining. It is more so than the kine-toscope, for it shows the figures life size, and so imparts additional realism to the pictures.[13]

If cinematography was the most favoured visual attraction at Cyclopia, another spectacle had a far tighter grasp of the public imagination, at least as

varieties: Dan Lowrey's Music Hall, 1879–97 (Dublin, 1975), p. 166. 8 'Cyclopia: a big atten-dance', *Irish Daily Independent*, 21 May. 9 'Cyclopia Fete', *Dublin Evening Mail*, 21 May. 10 Ibid. 11 *Irish Times*, 20 May. 12 *Daily Independent*, 21 May. 13 *Daily Independent*, 22 May.

far as the daily newspapers reflect this. Among Cyclopia's well-patronized
scientific attractions was one that had beaten cinematography to the title of
the 'new photography', X-rays. As a souvenir of the fete, '[m]any had the
skeletons of the hand photographed under the new process'.[14] The relatively
small amount of press coverage given to X-rays at Cyclopia is in stark contrast
to the abundance of stories devoted to them in Irish newspapers in the first
half of the year, far more than those dedicated to the development of moving
pictures.

Wilhelm Röntgen's discovery was first publicized by the Viennese popular
press on 5 January 1896, and appeared in the following morning's London *Daily
Chronicle*.[15] The first Irish account of what was variously described as the new
photography, the new light and, even oxymoronically, invisible light seems to
have appeared in the *Dublin Evening Mail* on 10 January. Because many of the
public exhibitions in Ireland were conducted within a scientific paradigm and
so attempted to reproduce Röntgen's experiments, it is worth quoting this first
article in some detail. It reveals that Röntgen's findings consist

> in the discovery of a new conductor of light. Professor Rontgen, the
> well-known Professor of the Wurzburg University, has succeeded in
> photographing metal weights shut up in a wooden box, without show-
> ing anything of the casing on his negative. He is also said to have pho-
> tographed the bones of the hand, all the soft parts being invisible. He
> photographs by means of light of an exhausted Crooke's pipe, through
> which an inductive current is passed. The discovery appears to be so
> far that the rays in question penetrate wood and flesh, but not bone
> or metal. It is surmised that photographs of the kind mentioned may
> have a valuable practical application in the discovery and location both
> of fractures and of bullets. If this discovery is sustained it will cer-
> tainly take a first place among the many marvels of this scientific age.[16]

This short article gives the bare bones of Röntgen's rays: they are emitted by
a Crooke's vacuum tube through which an electric current passes; they are
akin to light in producing an image on a photographic plate, but differ from
it in penetrating certain solid substances; they can show metal objects in a
wooden box and the bones through the flesh; and their practical application
seems to be in detecting broken bones and metallic objects such as bullets or
needles lodged in the body.

Over the next few months, newspapers and journals reported further developments as other researchers sought to confirm and extend Röntgen's find-

---

14 'Cyclopia', *Evening Telegraph*, 23 May.   15 James Murray, 'The early formative years in
Irish radiology' in J.C. Carr (ed.), *A century of medical radiation in Ireland: an anthology* (n.p.,
1995), p. 6.   16 'Electric photography in surgery', *Dublin Evening Mail*, 10 January.

ings. The papers also editorialized on their possible significance. The volume of X-ray stories in Dublin's *Evening Telegraph*, which seems to be the Irish paper most interested in X-rays, may give a sense of public interest in the early part of the year. Its coverage began on 11 February, and in the seventeen working days to the end of that month, it had published 12 items on X-rays. In the same period, it published one moving picture story.[17] The X-rays were discussed in editorials[18] and in substantial feature articles in the Saturday editions of the dailies.[19] The content of these stories already locates the discovery firmly in the institutional frameworks in which it is still embedded: in medical diagnosis, in security applications and in industrial-scientific contexts. The medical uses extended from the surprisingly large number of metal items that were secreted in people's bodies to the investigation of mummies.[20] Of security uses, the defusing of anarchists' bombs, or 'infernal engines' as they were called, is of particular note[21]; and industrial-scientific applications include the detection of fake precious stones and of additions to Bordeaux wine.[22]

Several reports claimed that the interest in X-rays was not limited to the scientific, medical and photographic communities. 'The much talked about X Rays', began a report in the *Dublin Evening Mail*,

> have penetrated into the centres of the medical and scientific circles of Dublin, and are illuminating the minds of servants and students alike – to say nothing of the ordinary observant thinker – with irrepressible amazement and curiosity at the remarkable developments of Roentgen's great invention.[23]

One clear indication that the rays had caught the imagination at least of what were called the 'fashionable classes' is the fact that a man wearing a skeleton suit and styling himself 'Rontgen X Rays' won first prize in the fancy dress cycle parade (cycling was a middle-class obsession at the time) at the Carlisle grounds in Bray in August.[24] It is also signalled by the way in which reports

---

17 'The cinematograph: a startling invention', *Dublin Evening Telegraph*, 26 February. Focusing on the content of the films, this article began by showing how far the cinematograph was ahead of the kinetoscope, by pointing out that Edison's peepshow viewer was first exhibited in Dublin in April 1895.   18 See, for example, the editorial item 'The Rontgen rays', *Freeman's Journal*, 27 April.   19 See, for example, 'Shadowgraphs: the process described by Professor Barrett: its aid in a Dublin surgical case', *Evening Telegraph*, 28 March; and 'Dublin hospitals and the X rays: what Edison has been doing in America', *Evening Telegraph*, 11 April.   20 'Rontgen rays upon a mummy' and 'Mummies and the new photography', both *Evening Telegraph*, 17 February.   21 'The Anarchists and the new rays', *Evening Telegraph*, 4 March; and 'Bombs and the X rays', *Evening Telegraph*, 17 April.   22 'Photography and jewels', *Evening Telegraph*, 22 April; and 'The new tell-tale photography', *Evening Telegraph*, 6 March.   23 'The Roentgen rays: interesting demonstration', *Dublin Evening Mail*, 25 April.   24 'Bray fancy dress cycle parade', *Evening Telegraph*, 29 August.

of the discoveries were taken up as the year progressed by feature columns, editorials, humorous columns and cartoons. At times, it is difficult to distinguish whether a humorous article is discussing real scientific research or exaggerating for comic effect. One article described how an English photographer supposedly set about photographing his thoughts:

> First, he has drawn a large triangle on a sheet of paper. Secondly, he has gazed on that triangle until neither he nor geometry could stand much more of it. Then he has gone into a dark room and stared through a vacuum at a photographic plate until he has felt sick, keeping the image of the triangle in his head the whole time. Finally he has developed the plate, and found thereon a light impression, the size of a pin's head. This is his thought. It is not a bit like a triangle, but it is merely the photographic reproduction of the retinal reflection and projection of the thought image of the image of a thought of a triangle.[25]

Despite the clear comic intent of this article, it seems that there was serious speculation on how X-rays might be used to photograph thought.[26]

In this context of the apparent ubiquitousness of X-rays, it is difficult to explain the reversal in relative interest by the papers and perhaps by the public in the Röntgen rays and in cinematography at Cyclopia. The success of the animatographe was such that the exhibitor at the fete, Charles Augustus James, was able to advertize it as the 'wonderful triumph of Scientific Research, [...] which has been patronized by the Nobility and Gentry of Ireland at Cyclopia', when he presented it at his World's Fair Waxworks, Henry Street, Dublin, in the week following the fete.[27] While noting that it is a 'marvellous invention', a review of the World's Fair shows focuses on the details of some of the ten sensational films presented rather than on the technical details of the apparatus as is frequently the case with the X-rays.[28] This seems to be the crux of the difference between the two technologies. While both were able to produce spectacular visual artefacts, the images produced by the cinematograph were far more multifaceted in their appeal to an audience.

Unlike moving pictures, X-rays had a very brief period as a fairground or variety theatre novelty. In England, for example, William Friese-Greene, an inventor who had experimented with a motion picture camera in the early 1890s, brought his X-ray apparatus briefly onto the stage of the Old Oxford

25 'Professor Rontgen: Professor O'Mulligan emerges from retirement to cast some X-rays on a complicated subject', *Dublin Evening Herald*, 14 March.   26 See, for example, 'Wizard Edison's latest', *Evening Telegraph*, 21 December 1897; and Richard Crangle, 'Saturday night at the X-rays: the moving picture and "the new photography" in Britain, 1896' in John Fullerton (ed.), *Celebrating 1895: the centenary of cinema* (London, 1998), p. 140, n. 12.   27 See advertizements in *Evening Telegraph* during week of 26 May.   28 'The animatograph: on exhibition in the city', *Evening Telegraph*, 27 May.

Music Hall in 1896.[29] Among other showmen around the world who exhibit-ed X-rays were Mark Blow in Australia, Yokota Einosuke in Japan, William Paley in the United States and Jasper Redfern in Britain.[30] While X-rays could produce spectacular visual results, they failed to find a long-term place as an entertainment attraction.

In his account of the arrival of moving pictures and X-rays in Britain, Richard Crangle stresses that in terms of marketing, cinematography benefit-ed from its assumption into the programme of the variety theatre rather than remaining at the fairground.[31] It could, therefore, take advantage of variety's 'traditions of itinerance rather than ephemerality', whereby acts moved on to new audiences once their novelty value had been exhausted in a particular place.[32] Unlike early moving picture equipment, X-ray equipment was rela-tively delicate and required skilled operation to produce good results. The dif-ferences in the portability of the equipment meant that the potential subjects of the X-ray were limited by the fact that they had to be determined in advance, brought close to the apparatus and, if the end product were a pho-tographic image, held steady for the length of the relatively long exposure. The cinematographic subject, by contrast, was potentially limitless because the equipment could be brought to a location and await a subject, take subjects of varying sizes, and capture both still and dynamic subjects.

By the summer, the X-rays may have passed their peak as a novelty, and the detrimental effects of sustained exposure also began to be noted. In July the *Evening Telegraph* reported the findings of a German medical paper 'that Rontgen's rays burn the skin like the rays of the sun'.[33] The dangers were made more explicit in November when the scientific journal *Nature* made known the damage done to the exhibitor of X-rays at the Earl's Court Exhibition in London.[34]

For various reasons, then, the exhibition of X-rays was better suited to the more controlled environment of the hospital or lecture theatre than to the variety theatre or fairground. Initially, it was those with links to universities in Ireland who experimented with X-rays because 'the requisite apparatus was available in almost every physics department in the country'.[35] The first public exhibition of X-rays in Ireland occurred as part of a lecture given by the physi-cian Cecil Shaw, at the invitation of the Ulster Amateur Photographic Society, in the Museum, College Square North, Belfast, on 24 February 1896. 'The attendance in ... the hall of the museum was almost too large to be comfort-

29 Ray Allister, *Friese-Greene: close-up of an inventor* (London, 1948), pp 78–9.   30 Stephen Herbert and Luke McKernan (eds), *Who's who of Victorian cinema: a worldwide survey* (London, 1996), p. 124.   31 Crangle, 'Saturday night at the X-rays', pp 138–44.   32 Ibid., 142.   33 'The latest about "X" rays', *Evening Telegraph*, 11 July.   34 'The bad side of the X rays', *Evening Telegraph*, 5 November.   35 Murray, 'Early formative years in Irish radiology', pp 6–7.

able', reveals a detailed press account, 'but, notwithstanding the inconvenience of the crowding, the interest evinced was very great'.[36] Shaw offered an illustrated explanation of Röntgen's discovery and showed the results of some of his own experiments with the rays, but a live experiment seems to have been unsuccessful. He also acknowledged and sought to dispel some of the popular speculations on the effects of X-rays that constituted a substantial part of their attraction:

> A man might contemplate with comparative equanimity the idea of photographing the money in his purse, or the keys in his pocket, or the nails in his boots, but the line must be drawn at photographing his skeleton. That this last feat could be accomplished by the aid of Professor Rontgen's discovery was a widespread belief. It had been gravely declared that satin was the only dress material impervious to the new light, and it was even whispered that certain ladies' outfitters in the West End were doing a brisk trade in satin garments warranted Rontgen ray proof. (Laughter.)[37]

In April, the same month as the Cinématographe, 'The World's Most Scientific Invention',[38] premiered at Dublin's Star Theatre of Varieties, Röntgen's discovery was causing a sensation in the national press and among the medical profession. While the editorial in the *Freeman's Journal* of Monday, 27 April reported on the progress of Röntgen's experiments, an article on the same page reported on developments in Dublin:

> We understand that Professor Barrett has been continuing very successfully his investigations into the question of direct vision by means of the Rontgen rays. The Professor has now, we believe, succeeded in producing a fluorescent screen by which he has been able to see quite through the body of an adult – the ribs and vertebrae being well seen. He has also succeeded in seeing through a copy of a London directory of 3,200 pages with thick covers. These results seem to be equal to any of those reported from the other side of the Atlantic.[39]

Interest in Barrett's experiments was such that he gave a public lecture on them for '[a]ny of the medical profession or others particularly wishing to attend' at the Royal College of Science on 30 April.[40]

---

36 'The new photography: the Rontgen rays: interesting lecture in Belfast', *Irish News*, 25 February. 37 Ibid. 38 The phrase is used in the advertizement for the cinematograph shows in the *Irish Times*, 20 and 21 April. It is one of a series of hyperbolic expressions used to describe the phenomenon in the newspaper advertizements. 39 'The Rontgen rays' (editorial item) and 'The X rays in Dublin', *Freeman's Journal*, 27 April. 40 'The Rontgen rays', *Freeman's Journal*,

It was not until April 1897 before a successful attempt was made to combine the two phenomena in what would later be called cineradiography. This was accomplished by Dr John Macintyre, whose *X-Ray Cinematography of Frog's Legs* was discussed in the *British Journal of Photography*.[41] The high doses of radiation needed to produce a moving image made cineradiography too dangerous for the subject until electronic image-enhancement techniques were developed in the 1950s. G.A. Smith's 1897 film *The X-Ray Fiend* deals with the popular anxieties around the rays at their inception. In it, a mad professor turns his apparatus on an embracing couple to reveal their embracing skeletons.[42] Mad professors also haunt the pages of the newspapers in 1896.

> The news of a sensational development of the employment of Professor Rontgen's X rays comes from Rome. A distinguished Italian scientist, Professor Salvioni, of Perugia, has invented an instrument by means of which rays of invisible 'light' are made to impart to the eye the capacity of seeing through all objects which the Rontgen rays can penetrate, and of beholding the contents of opaque receptacles. [...] The head reels before the possibilities which this discovery opens up. Hamlet's appeal, 'O that this too, too solid flesh would melt',will have to be revised in the light of the new rays.[43]

The talismanic invocation of literature (possiblly the first case of X-ray spectacles) recalls Eglinton's more extensive remarks on its inadequacy in the face of technological developments. His generic classification of technology according to a classical literary hierarchy (steam engines are epics, cinematographs, lyrics) may suggest why generically superior X-rays continued to cause anxieties among cinephiles. An article in the cinema journal *Irish Limelight* in 1917 speculates on the implications of the recent discovery of what it calls 'beyond X-rays', which could give an image of the internal organs as well as the bones:

> You walk into an X-ray store (for there will be X-ray stores in every town soon), in broad daylight and fully dressed, and get a complete picture of a life that has hitherto been mercifully hidden from you [...] If this discovery (which is also positively indecent as well as dangerous) be proved all the mystery and happiness of life will be gone [...] Some people won't be satisfied unless they get a photo of their stomach after each meal, just to see how their dinner is being digested.

30 April.   41 *British Journal of Photography*, 44: 1929, 23 April 1897, p. 260. Partly reprinted in John Barnes, *The rise of the cinema in Great Britain: Jubilee Year 1897* (London, 1983), p. 199.   42 Denis Gifford, *The British film catalogue 1895–1985: a reference guide* (Newton Abbot and London, 1986).   43 'New photography – new sensation', *Evening Telegraph*, 11 February.

> There will be rows of photos – livers and spleens and stomachs – along every mantle-piece, and people will compare notes about them. The organs of private people will become public property. They may even be shown on the kinema if they happen to be distinguished people. The 'Spleen of a Cabinet Minister at work' would make a fine sensational draw as a moving picture.[44]

Among the remarkable features of these anxious speculations on the loss of somatic propriety (including the etymological links of the latter term to ownership: being in possession of oneself) is the fact of their comparative lateness. More than twenty years after Röntgen's discovery, and its increasing absorption into mainstream medical and surgical practice,[45] developments in radiography continued to fire the public imagination. The discourse on the body here may have an even more contemporary resonance in the incorporation of tanning studios into many of the video/DVD outlets that exist in every town in Ireland. In these, patrons can irradiate their bodies to conform to an image of health promoted by some distinguished people of the moving-picture media.

44 'Between ourselves', *Irish Limelight*, 1:3 (March 1917), p. 20.   45 Although radiologists did not organize into a professional body until 1932, many hospitals had X-ray equipment by the late 1910s. See Murray, 'Early formative years in Irish radiology', pp 6–29.

Theorizing Irish animation:
heritage, enterprise and critical practice

MAEVE CONNOLLY

Irish animation currently benefits from a relatively high public profile, both internationally and at home, partly as a consequence of the Oscar nomination of two Irish-made productions: *Give Up Yer Aul' Sins* (Cathal Gaffney, Alan Shannon/Brown Bag Films, 2000) and *Fifty Percent Grey* (Ruairí Robinson, 2001). Various newspapers articles, at least one international festival, and a high profile season of screenings on Irish television have been devoted to Irish animation, and specifically to the films funded by Bórd Scannán na hÉireann/the Irish Film Board.[1] Media attention has tended to focus primarily on the distinctive structure of the animation and digital media sector, or on the role played by agencies such as the Film Board and the Digital Hub, but some commentators have sought to situate animation in relation to the wider context of Irish film culture. For example, animator Andrew Kavanagh has suggested that Irish animation is particularly well-placed to reach global audiences because it is characterized by distinct, recognizable aesthetic qualities. He emphasizes that by comparison with much international animation, Irish work 'is a lot more *literate*' and he notes that Irish animation producers 'don't write as animators', but instead 'write as filmmakers'.[2]

Kavanagh's position is intriguing because it directs attention towards an exploration of the modes of production which might be particular to the Irish cultural context. This emphasis on 'literate-ness' also seems to echo a familiar trope in Irish cinema studies – the construction of the Irish filmmaker as an auteur with strong associations to literature and theatre.[3] In this respect

---

1 The Bradford Animation Festival presented a special selection of Irish animation in November 2003 and an extensive season of recent Irish animation, entitled 'Animating Ireland', was broadcast on RTÉ One in December 2002. Despite the prominence of this season, however, RTÉ has been criticized for its failure to *commission* new Irish animation for television. See Jan Battles, 'Cartoon Makers Cut Up by RTÉ Snub', *Sunday Times* (Irish edition), 24 October 2004. For more general coverage of the animation sector, see Karlin Lillington, 'Digital media gets animated about its future', *Irish Times* (Business and Finance supplement), 23 January 2004, and Jennifer O'Connell, 'Irish film-makers animated about Oscars', *Sunday Business Post*, 3 February 2004. 2 Andrew Kavanagh, cited by Lillington, 'Digital media', p. 55. 3 For evidence of the 'literary' status of certain Irish filmmakers, see Eugene O'Brien, 'Series Introduction' in Emer Rockett and Kevin Rockett, *Neil Jordan: exploring boundaries* (Dublin, 2003), p. i.

Kavanagh's comments also hint at a less obvious parallel between Irish animation and Irish cinema – the prevalence of adaptation as a mode of production. As this article sets out to demonstrate, adaptation from literature, folklore,
autobiography or popular fiction is widely prevalent in Irish animation.
Examples include Edith Pieperhoff's films *An Bonnán Buí* (adapted from an
Irish song; 1995) and *Orpheus* (based upon the Greek myth; 1996), Andrew
Kavanagh's From *An Evil Cradling* (adapted from Brian Keenan's autobiography; Moving Still Productions, 1998), Terraglyph's *Wilde Stories* (adapted
from the short stories of Oscar Wilde) and Steve Woods' *Window* (adapted
from the writings of Bobby Sands; 1997). It is also possible to find references
to Irish art and design in animation productions that are not funded by the
Irish Film Board, as in the case of *Sir Gawain and the Green Knight* (Moving
Still Productions). This film, commissioned by Channel Four and short-listed
for a BAFTA Award, is based upon the medieval poem and inspired by the
stained glass windows of Harry Clarke.

Adaptation has, of course, long been central to animated feature production but its prominence in Irish animated short films is perhaps less easy to
explain, and may be linked to a range of economic, cultural and political factors specific to the national context. As yet, Irish cinema studies has tended to
engage with Irish animation only as part of the broader field of digital media
production.[4] Paul O'Brien has offered one of the few accounts of Irish digital
media that is explicitly focused on cultural form and content. He emphasizes
that traditional conceptions of national culture are difficult to sustain in relation to digital media, because the internet (and its associated processes of production and distribution) 'challenges cultural nationalism in a radical way'.[5] But
he suggests that, despite this, Irish culture has come to occupy a privileged place
within digital media discourse because Ireland is 'seen as a repository of mythic
'pre-modern' values *and* as the locus of cutting-edge developments in technology'.[6] O'Brien theorizes a recovery of mythic form in various contemporary cultural practices, including 'bio-art, interactive art, digital film, computer animation and the developing VR/web/gaming interface' and cites, as specific

4 There is little in-depth discussion of animation in recent accounts of Irish cinema such as
Ruth Barton's *Irish national cinema* (London, 2004), Martin McLoone's *Irish film: the emergence of a contemporary cinema* (London, 2000), and Lance Pettitt's *Screening Ireland: film and
television representation* (Manchester, 2000). For a discussion of the Irish games industry, a
major site of animation production, see Aphra Kerr, 'Live life to power of PS2: locating the
games industry in the new media environment', *Irish Communications Review*, 9 (2003)
(http://www.icr.dit.ie/). My own interest in animation forms part of a broader exploration of
'marginal' practices in Irish cinema, but is also very directly shaped by the experience of teaching animation and film studies on the BA in Animation at Dún Laoghaire Institute of Art,
Design and Technology.   5 Paul O'Brien, 'Hyperlinks, changelings and the digital fireside', in
Ruth Barton and Harvey O'Brien (eds), *Keeping it real: Irish film and television* (London and
New York, 2004), p. 111.   6 Ibid.

examples, the referencing of James Joyce's *Ulysses* in hypertext theory and the framing of web cinema as a contemporary form of traditional storytelling.[7]

This complex relationship between mythic form and technological innovation is not, however, necessarily specific to digital media production. Instead it should perhaps be considered in relation to the processes (evident since the early 1980s) through which national culture is constructed within the global economy as a site of both 'heritage' and 'enterprise'. As John Corner and Sylvia Harvey have demonstrated with respect to British national culture, the recovery of the past in the form of commodity to be consumed is often intimately linked to political investment in entrepreneurialism.[8] Informed by the work of Corner and Harvey, and by related critiques in national cinema studies, this article approaches Irish animation as a site of practice structured around the interdependent discourses of heritage and entrepreneurial innovation.

THE UNWRITTEN HISTORY OF IRISH ANIMATION

While very little academic analysis of Irish animation has been published to date, a considerable number of *practitioners* have produced short, but valuable, studies of the field.[9] The Digital Hub has also published a short history of Irish animation on its website, focusing specifically on industrial production. Although it makes reference to aspects of indigenous independent practice, the text locates the roots of Irish animation in the state-supported industrial initiatives of the 1980s and early 1990s.[10] During this period, the Industrial Development Authority (IDA) offered American animation studios, such as Murakami Wolf and Sullivan Bluth, tax incentives and facilities to locate in Ireland. The arrival of these companies provided the impetus for various educational initiatives, at Ballyfermot Senior College and later at Dún Laoghaire Institute of Art, Design and Technology (then Dún Laoghaire College of Art). Many international studios had abandoned their Irish ventures by the mid

7 Ibid., 115. O'Brien's analysis is attuned to the cultural context of new media production and reception in Ireland, referencing events such as Darklight digital film festival and monthly screenings organized by the Dublin Art and Technology Association (DATA). Significantly, the programmes for these events encompass fiction, documentary, music videos, electronic arts installations and artists films, as well as various forms of animation. 8 See John Corner and Sylvia Harvey, 'Mediating tradition and modernity: the heritage/enterprise couplet', in J. Corner and S. Harvey (eds), *Enterprise and heritage: crosscurrents of national culture* (London, 1991), pp 45–75. 9 See Maeve Clancy, 'Animation in Ireland', in C. Lerm Hayes (ed.), *Thought lines: an anthology of research: Faculty of History of Art and Design, 6* (Dublin, 2002), pp 18–26; Paul Farren, 'Irish animation: a brief history', *Film Ireland* 87 (July/August 2002), pp 12–13; Steve Woods, 'Drawing the line', *Film Ireland* 43 (October/November 1994), pp 24–5; Cashell Horgan, 'The hard cel', *Film Base News* 10 (July/August 1991), pp 8–11. 10 This text, entitled 'Irish animation: a brief history' was published on the Digital Hub website in December 2003 and can now be accessed at http://www.thedigitalhub.com/digital_media/sectors_animation.asp?S=1

1990s, but their highly trained Irish personnel flourished, forming new companies such as Magma, Monster and Terraglyph.

The Digital Hub seems to present Irish animation as the product of commercial initiatives and state investment in enterprise and education. A somewhat different narrative of origins has, however, been advanced in the articles and film retrospectives produced by practitioners. In 2002, a retrospective of Irish animation was held at the Galway Film Fleadh and it opened with a three-minute work depicting a moving clock tower, dating from the 1910s. Entitled *Clock Gate Youghal*, this film was made by cinema owner James Horgan and defined in the Fleadh programme by Steve Woods as 'a pioneering piece in world animation'.[11] Woods acknowledges, however, that it represented a false dawn in terms of indigenous production, and in fact the only other early work included in the retrospective was a 1928 animated advertizement for soap. Woods is not the only Irish animator keen to reinstate a lost history of production. For example, in 'A Brief History of Animation' (published in *Film Ireland*), filmmaker and writer Paul Farren admits that there is little record of animation production during the 1930s.[12] But he states that the celebrated German animator Lotte Reiniger (the director of the first ever animated feature) produced a series of Irish language fairy tales for the National Film Institute of Ireland during the 1940s. In fact, Reiniger's films appear to have been simply purchased from the Canadian Film Board for dubbing and distribution in Irish.[13]

Irish animation did not re-emerge until 1956, with the production of a Bord Fáilte short entitled *Beau Geste*, which according to the Fleadh programme 'encourages us all to welcome foreigners'. The establishment of Telefís Éireann, at the beginning of the 1960s, also created new opportunities for animation in advertizing and educational programming and a brief account of this period has been provided by filmmaker Cashell Horgan.[14] He notes that a number of international filmmakers relocated to Ireland at this point, including Günter Wolf (director of the Lyons Minstrel TV ads) and the American Harry Hess. Hess had worked on UPA projects such as *Gerald McBoingBoing* and *Mister Magoo* and he began teaching graphic design and animation at the National College of Art and Design in the 1970s. Horgan notes that this period witnessed the rise of a new generation of independent animators including Aidan Hickey, Tim Booth, and Steve Woods, a development that pre-dated the intervention of the IDA.[15]

By the mid-1990s, this independent culture had given rise to short-lived but significant initiatives such as the Irish Animation Festival, and the Anamú

11 Steve Woods, 'Irish animation retrospective', Fourteenth Galway Film Fleadh (programme), 2002. 12 Farren, 'Irish animation: a brief history', p. 12. 13 I am indebted to Sunniva O'Flynn of the Irish Film Archive for providing details on the National Film Institute's commissioning and dubbing of Reiniger's work. 14 Horgan, 'The hard cel', p. 10 15 Ibid.

lobby group led by filmmakers Steve Woods and Cathal Gaffney. Anamú was instrumental in extending Film Board support for animation, in the form of the Frameworks initiative established in 1995, and subsequent schemes such as Short Shorts and Irish Flash.[16] During this period the Film Board also funded various one-off projects, including *An Bonnán Buí,* and Steve Wood's *Ireland 1848* (1997). This latter film differs from the vast majority of Irish animated shorts in that it does not use either digital media or traditional techniques such as cel or clay animation. Instead it is produced through the animation of photographic stills, which have been photocopied and interspersed with intertitles to suggest early film footage. As such it invites comparison with a number of avant-garde film narratives, which employ photography to explore the theme of memory.[17]

In the opening title, *Ireland 1848* is presented as the work of one 'Lucien P. Horgan Esq.' and his revolutionary 'portable artistic camera', a piece of equipment that is capable of producing moving images forty years before the invention of cinema. This imaginary invention is used to 'record' the suffering and destitution associated with the Great Famine, and the measures instituted in response to this suffering. Several scenes featuring groups of women and children dressed in rags seem to have been modelled upon other images of the Famine, such as those produced to accompany reports in the *Illustrated London News*. These images flicker continually, suggesting a static newsreel shot, but there is very little action in many of the group scenes. The static quality may be a function of budgetary constraints, or limitations intrinsic to the process of production, but it also suggests a certain refusal to animate images with such strong documentary associations. Other sequences, such as those depicting the ladling of soup into bowls, are more overtly animated and seem to reference early cinema rather than nineteenth-century portraiture.

These references to early cinema, illustration and photographic portraiture in *Ireland 1848* suggest a self-reflexive exploration of animation practice, and this project is echoed in recent animation studies. Paul Ward has noted that, although it is a relatively new field of academic inquiry, animation studies encompasses two quite distinct models.[18] One adheres closely to the film studies paradigms established in the 1970s, while the other is characterized by a more overtly interdisciplinary engagement with moving image culture. The latter approach, which seems to be in the ascendant, is highly attuned to the diffuse character of contemporary animation practice. Lev Manovich and Andrew Darley are among those who have drawn upon computer science and visual studies to theorize the emergent field of digital media production, sit-

16 Clancy, 'Animation in Ireland', p. 22.   17 It can be compared to Kieran Hickey's *Faithful Departed* (1966), a key early work in Irish independent cinema, and also Chris Marker's *La Jétee* (1962).   18 Paul Ward, 'Animation Studies, disciplinarity, and discursivity', *Reconstruction* 3:2 (Spring 2003), (http://www.reconstruction.ws/032/ward.htm).

uating animation in relation to gaming, the web, music video and virtual reality.[19] Even though these accounts of new media practice are not directly concerned with key issues in national cinema studies (concerning history, memory,
identity etc.) they offer a critical perspective from which to engage with developments in policy and education, which are of particular relevance to the
national context.

As noted already, academic analysis of Irish animation remains underde-
veloped and at this point it is perhaps useful to acknowledge some of the factors that may have shaped its occlusion within academic discourse. Firstly, and
perhaps most importantly, the history of production is clearly characterized by
discontinuity, to the extent that a critical mass of work simply did not come
into being until the mid 1990s, and was not well catalogued until relatively
recently.[20] A second factor, which complicates critical analysis of Irish animation and necessitates an interdisciplinary approach, is the gradual transformation of animation practice over the past two decades. Prior to the 1990s, the
Irish context of production seems to have been structured around two opposing (although necessarily interdependent) models. An indigenous artisanal tradition, characterized by a degree of experimentation, functioned as the alternative to the international industrial model. During the 1990s, however, artisanal
experimentation has given way to new forms of entrepreneurialism, leading to
the formation of a host of small companies engaged in various different forms
of production, from Frameworks-funded shorts to educational programming
and advertizing. This transformation of indigenous animation parallels other
developments within film and the arts, and can be considered within the context of a broader process of cultural and economic 'reinvention'.[21]

HISTORY, HERITAGE AND IRISH ANIMATION

As already noted, the complex relationship between heritage and enterprise in
British national culture during the 1980s has been theorized by Corner and
Harvey. Informed by some of the same concerns, Ruth Barton has developed
parallel critiques of heritage discourse in Irish cinema, focusing specifically on
a cycle of period dramas produced during the 1980s and 90s.[22] She situates these

19 See Lev Manovich, '"Reality" effects in computer animation', in J. Pilling (ed.), *A reader in
Animation Studies* (London, 1997), pp 5–14 and Andrew Darley, *Visual digital culture: surface
play and spectacle in new media genres* (London and New York, 2000).   20 Kevin Rockett has
provided the first comprehensive survey of animated films funded by the Film Board in *Ten
years after: the Irish Film Board 1993–2003* (Galway, 2003). Information on projects currently
in development is now also available on the Board's website (www.filmboard.ie).   21 For a discussion of the reinvention of Irish cinema during this period see Debbie Ging, 'Screening the
Green: cinema under the Celtic Tiger' in M. Cronin, L. Gibbons and P. Kirby (eds), *Reinventing
Ireland: culture and the Celtic Tiger* (London, 2002), pp 177–96.   22 See Ruth Barton, 'From

narratives in relation to Irish tourism imagery, which has tended to promote Ireland as a 'feel good' location and suggests that, through its cinematic and literary period dramas, Ireland has fashioned itself (and been fashioned) as a 'symbol of a living imagined history, a country hanging suspended in a pure and permanent past'.[23] Some of Barton's key points are specific to live action cinema and photographic media. For example, she suggests that *Michael Collins* (Neil Jordan, 1996) is characterized by a kind of 'history effect' because it echoes the lengthy running time and high production values of Hollywood epics, while its process of production involved the restaging of historical events with large numbers of extras. This restaging, which was itself the subject of considerable media attention, worked to incorporate the audience into the narrative.

Given her attention to the place of *live action* within period drama, Barton's critique does not seem readily applicable to animation at present.[24] Yet her analysis of the interplay between film and other media highlights the way in which heritage imagery circulates across multiple channels. One obvious site of circulation within the Irish context is the television ident or logo. Although lacking the cultural prestige of literary adaptations or historical drama, animated sequences have long been characterized by high production values and a pronounced investment in technological innovation. Since the 1960s, Radio Telefís Éireann (RTÉ) logos have drawn heavily upon the iconography of folk craft and Celtic myth. Many of the early idents were limited to static representations of the St Brigid's cross, but more complex animated sequences have developed since the early 1990s. These sequences often employed new technologies to represent a journey through a mystical rural landscape, complete with Neolithic burial monuments, swirling mist and (in the case of the 'millennium ident') spectral female figures.[25] Most recently, however, RTÉ has sought to articulate a more self-consciously 'modern' identity through a series of idents incorporating urban landmarks. One actually articulates the process of 'modernization' through the computer-generated transformation of Dublin's O'Connell Street Nelson's monument (blown up in 1966) into its millennial counterpart – the Spire.

It is also possible to identify a new emphasis on the construction, and transformation, of images of the past in another key site of Irish heritage discourse – the literary film. As Ruth Barton notes, adaptation from a literary (or theatrical) original has occupied a central role in Irish film production since

history to heritage: some recent developments in Irish cinema', *The Irish Review* 21 (Autumn/Winter 1997), pp 41–56, and Barton, *Irish national cinema*, pp 130–47. **23** Barton, 'From history to heritage', p. 54. **24** It is worth noting, however, that computer-generated imagery and visual effects – forming part of the field of animation practice – are widely used in historical epics, such as *Saving Private Ryan* (1998), *Gladiator* (2000), and *Pearl Harbour* (2001). **25** For a more in-depth discussion of Irish television idents, see Maeve Connolly, 'Between the seasons', in M. Connolly and O. Ryan (eds), *The glass eye: artists and television* (Dublin, 2000), pp 42–53.

the 1980s. In her most recent analysis of Irish period drama, she suggests that one set of source texts has gradually given way to another – signalling a wider shift in cultural discourse. It seems that, for the filmmakers of the 1980s, the 'Big House' novels of the late nineteenth and early twentieth centuries functioned as the principal literary source texts. These narratives often deal specifically with the experiences of the Protestant ascendancy; many explore the theme of traumatic memory familiar from Gothic literature. In contrast, many of the period dramas produced in the 1990s are adapted from a more recent series of novels, set in the 1950s and 1960s, and explicitly concerned with male subjectivity and national identity.[26] This second wave of film narratives, which includes *The Butcher Boy* (Neil Jordan, 1998) and *Korea* (Cathal Black, 1995), are often characterized by a self-conscious reworking of personal and cultural memory, and by the subversion of traditional nationalist iconography. Even though they return repeatedly to an earlier moment, Barton suggests that these narratives display 'an increasing confidence that the past can be overcome'.[27]

Irish animators also seem to have engaged quite directly with the discourses shaping the representation of the national past, and some have examined themes of literary heritage and political struggle through processes of adaptation. As already noted, adaptation from an original text is a widely prevalent process in Irish animation production. At least a third of the (forty) short films funded under the Frameworks scheme since 1995 are adaptations of one form or another. Developed in partnership with the Arts Council and RTÉ, Frameworks offers animators the opportunity to develop 'personal and creative projects'[28] and many adaptations are characterized by innovation and experimentation, rather than by fidelity to an original text. This is particularly true of From *An Evil Cradling* a work that employs a number of different stylistic registers, both figurative and abstract, to articulate Brian Keenan's traumatic experience as a hostage.

While From *An Evil Cradling* displays a profound sensitivity to the source text, some animated adaptations are distinctly irreverent. For example, *Ulys* by Tim Booth (1997) makes reference to the form and content of Joyce's novel but is far more directly concerned to lampoon the myth of Joyce's 'genius' through caricature than to transpose the novel into film. *Ulys* is just one of a number of Film Board funded animations that seems to propose a critique of Irish heritage culture. *Celtic Maidens* (Cartoon Saloon, 2003) is a three-minute work funded under the Short Shorts scheme, one of a number of pieces intended for theatrical screening prior to a Film Board feature. Taking the form of a fake advertizement, it pokes fun at the history of the Rose of Tralee contest and its place within the wider context of national and diasporic culture. The Rose of Tralee is clearly an easy target but *Celtic Maidens* sharply identifies it as a point of convergence for a set of enduring myths concerning

26 Barton, *Irish national cinema*, p. 134.   27 Ibid., 139.   28 Rockett, *Ten years after*, p. 134.

Irish emigration, feminine purity and rural identity. In one scene, for example, a 'maiden' trembles as she reads a highly sentimental account of emigrant hardship and triumph over adversity.

Much of *Celtic Maidens* is characterized by the linear aesthetic of cel animation and graphic caricature but the opening sequence employs photographic landscape imagery, evoking an array of cinematic and photographic texts, from *The Quiet Man* (John Ford, 1952) to the postcards of John Hinde and photomontage pastiches of Sean Hillen. This short film clearly articulates a certain scepticism with regard to the cultural, economic and political discourses shaping Irish media production. It is, however, produced by Cartoon Saloon, a company that is responsible for a feature project that is steeped in 'heritage' imagery. For several years, Cartoon Saloon has been developing a classically animated feature that seeks to capitalize on the fame of the Book of Kells. Originally called *Rebel*, now re-titled *Brendan and the Book of Kells*, the film tells the story of a young monk who must save the illuminated manuscript from marauding invaders. While the project has gone through a number of stylistic changes, the original showreel situates the production within the context of an indigenous artistic tradition that, by implication, can be traced back to the Book of Kells itself. It would seem that, although short animation may offer opportunities for satire, feature production is more constrained by the conventions of heritage discourse.

AUTHORSHIP, ENTREPRENEURIALISM AND CRITICISM

Ulys, Celtic Maidens, and *Brendan and the Book of Kells* all reference Irish traditions of representation (albeit in very different ways) but many recent Irish animations borrow from more international sources. *Ship of Fools* (Moving Still Productions, 1998) is an allegory of sectarian conflict and political intransigence in Northern Ireland, and was funded by the Film Board in collaboration with the Northern Ireland Arts Council and the Community Relations Council. The script was written by Art O'Bríain in collaboration with broadcaster (and narrator) John Kelly and, although the film is not identified explicitly as an adaptation, it borrows from the *Odyssey*. In visual terms the piece is characterized by constant motion and transformation but the plot is minimal, and centres on a ship's journey across a dark ocean, during which the vessel is repeatedly beset by a mythic creature. At various points, graphic references to the political landscape are interspersed with overtly fantastical images, ostensibly underlining the mythic character of political discourse in the North. In some respects this piece suggests a self-conscious reworking of images of the past, echoing that noted by Barton in live-action literary adaptations of the 1990s. But while narratives such as *The Butcher Boy* and *Korea* hint at the possibility of recovery, *Ship of Fools* seems to suggest an inability to escape from the past.

Ship of Fools is just one of a number of works to reference graphic and
literary traditions beyond the national canon and Andrew Kavanagh (of
Kavaleer Films) has repeatedly borrowed from Eastern European sources.
Intriguingly, although Kavanagh has claimed the quality of 'literateness' for
Irish animation, his own work is characterized by an absence of spoken dialogue or commentary and seems to be very clearly oriented towards an international audience. *The Depository* (2002), adapted from the graphic novel by
Andrzej Klimowski, is a fantastical narrative that can be read as a dream or
an allegory. It explores a conflict between a group of angelic figures whose
wings recall the opened leaves of a book, and who seem to function as emblems
of the imagination. The conclusion of the piece is ambiguous, but an ongoing
struggle against authority is evident.

Similar themes are explored in *The Milliner* (2003), also written and directed by Kavanagh. Although this piece is not identified as an adaptation, its plot
clearly echoes that of Jiri Trnka's 1965 film *The Hand*. In Trnka's allegorical
work, produced through stop-motion animation, a sculptor is forced to take
orders from a dictatorial power, represented by a gesticulating human hand.
Ultimately, the sculptor loses all control over his art.[29] *The Milliner* employs
computer-generated imagery and echoes the *Matrix* cycle of science fiction
films in its exploration of technologically mediated homogeneity and utopian
revolution. At the same time, however, it functions as highly stylized allegory set in an invented world where individuals are represented by jigsaw puzzle
pieces. These pieces fit together into a homogenous whole primarily because
they are created according to a standard design that includes a machine-made
bowler hat. Following an industrial accident, in which a number of faulty hats
are produced, one individual begins to create new designs, disrupting the jigsaw
pattern and sparking the collapse of the dominant social order.

The Milliner is set in a world that appears to be dominated by *corporate*
homogeneity, as symbolized by the bowler hat. In contrast, *The Hand* evolved
in response to the restrictions of a socialist system. Yet both films could perhaps be seen to explore the theme of state intervention in the arts, albeit from
different perspectives. As already noted, the Frameworks scheme provides an
opportunity to develop 'personal and creative projects', implying a particular
emphasis on individual experimentation and artistry. Yet the recipients of this
funding are, for the most part, production companies engaged in a range of
commercial projects, ranging from advertizing to educational programming.
Within this context, Frameworks supports a mode of production in which the
aesthetic preferences of animators and other authors can take precedence over
the considerations of clients. Inevitably, however, these projects remain constrained by the (perceived) priorities of the funding agency. The oblique ref-

29 For a discussion of Trnka's film, see Paul Wells, *Understanding animation* (London and New
York, 1998), pp 84–8.

erencing of Trnka's work in *The Milliner* could then be read as a commentary on the political and cultural factors that serve to structure the development of Irish animation.

CONCLUSION

An in-depth analysis of Irish animation practice is clearly long overdue and this article has simply sketched some possible starting points for further research. It would seem that many practitioners have attempted to counter the 'marginal' status of animation by seeking to recover a lost history of production. Others have embraced interdisciplinary approaches to imagine an alternative point of origin, countering a tendency by state agencies to locate the roots of Irish animation in the commercial initiatives of the 1980s. For all its marginal status, Irish animation offers clear parallels with live action cinema in the 1990s, not least because of the prevalence of adaptation as a mode of production. By contrast with many of their counterparts in live action production, however, Irish animators have often looked beyond the Irish canon or subverted aspects of Irish heritage discourse. This article has also identified several works, such as *The Ship of Fools* and *The Milliner*, which borrow from established international traditions of allegory and satire to explore the relationship between representation and ideology. Perhaps more that any other work mentioned, *The Milliner* suggests the emergence of a self-reflexive mode of practice, informed by a critical analysis of the position of Irish animation in relation to the intertwining discourses of heritage and enterprise.

Halas and Batchelor: animation, propaganda and *Animal Farm* (1954)

ELIZABETH COULTER-SMITH

The cartoon film adaptation of George Orwell's *Animal Farm* (1945) was produced by Halas and Batchelor Cartoon Films in 1954 and released in the
United States later the same year and in the UK in early 1955. While both
the British and the American governments had used the 'cartoon' during the
First and Second World Wars to influence public opinion, the film remains
an unusual example of an animated Cold War propaganda film. Made under
controversial circumstances, the film exploited the public's association of the
animated cartoon with childhood 'innocence' along with the cartoon's highly
flexible visual language to express explicitly political ideas and attitudes. This
article will examine John Halas and Joy Batchelor's partnership, identifying
the husband-wife team's concern to combine animation with persuasion and
how this lead to their involvement in the production of *Animal Farm*.

BEGINNINGS

John Halas was born Janos Halasz in Budapest, 1912 and died in London,
1995. His training as an animator came from two apprenticeships served with
major European figures in the fields of graphic design and animation. Halas'
first apprenticeship was with the Hungarian-born director and special-effects
expert George Pal who, from 1927 to 1930, taught Halas the art of cut-out
animation, camera loading, and action timing. Halas's second apprenticeship
was under Sandor Bortnyik at the Mühely Academy, nicknamed the
'Hungarian Bauhaus', where Halas learned typography and poster design. Halas
subsequently moved to Paris where he worked as an assistant sign writer and
graphic designer before starting to make animated films in Hungary in 1934.
Two years later, he moved to London where he met Joy Batchelor.

Joy Batchelor was born 1914, Watford, Hertfordshire; she died in London,
1991. Batchelor completed her formal education at the Watford Technical School
and School of Art and graduated with a number of awards in 1934. She was
accomplished in all areas of graphic design and illustration. After graduating,
Batchelor worked for one of the first British cartoon film studios in London,
British Cartoons, where she assisted on a series about a talking horse *Come on*

Steve (1936) produced by Roland Davies. In 1936 she was recruited by Halas to work at British Animated Films on a film entitled *The Music Man* (1937) and this proved to be the start of a longstanding professional and personal relationship.

Halas and Batchelor's work in the period 1938 to 1940 mainly consisted of commercial freelance jobs in poster, newspaper, and fashion design and included posters for British Gas and the General Post Office. In 1940 the couple married and in the same year were introduced to the J. Walter Thompson advertizing agency (JWT) by George Pal, Halas' mentor and earlier teacher in Budapest. Halas and Batchelor began to work as a commercial cartoon advertizing partnership for JWT. Initially they produced shorts for Lux, Kellogg's (*Train Trouble*, 1940) and Rinso. They also worked extensively with Alexander MacKendrick at JWT where he was a scriptwriter and storyboard artist. It was also in 1940 that they were commandeered by the British government to start production on animated shorts for the war effort.

The wartime animation studio of Halas and Batchelor consisted of a small group of enthusiastic young colleagues from JWT. The work was normally divided as follows: scriptwriting, Joy Batchelor; storyboards, characters, and layout, Joy Batchelor and John Halas; animation, Wally Crook, Vera Linnecar, and Kathleen Murphy; trace and paint, shooting, editing, administration and management, John Halas. Halas recalls:

> For the work load we would have needed 20 to 30 staff. We had only 7. It meant that it was work day and night. Scripts and storyboards at night and the physical execution of the film by day. We put the studio in motion in the middle of 1941, badly equipped with an old French stop-motion camera made by Eclair costing five pounds (eight dollars). Our staff was all our old colleagues who loyally waited for us until we were ready for them. It was some 15 kilometers from London. As the laboratories were in London, to bring in the rushes to be developed every day was very inconvenient'.[1]

A government information cartoon had two major aims: firstly, it had to communicate effectively the benefits of complying with government directives; secondly, it had to do so in an entertaining and memorable way. Halas and Batchelor employed clever narrative structures and intelligent caricature as well as a subtle use of tone, images and sound that distinguished their work from less sophisticated forms of wartime propaganda. In this way, the animated cartoon had the potential to become a powerful political weapon because it offered 'soft propaganda', or propaganda with a 'sugar coating'. As the producer Sydney Box observed in 1937:

1 John Halas, *The Story of Halas and Batchelor* (Unpublished, Halas and Batchelor Collection, Surrey Institute of Art, 1991), n.p.

The cartoon film offers the publicist far greater licence than any other type of propaganda picture because it is, by its very nature, divorced from reality. Over-emphasized advertizing, which would not be tolerated in a natural photography film, can be presented in an amusing manner by cartoon without giving offence to anyone.[2]

In blending animation with social persuasion, Halas and Batchelor therefore contributed to the establishment of this new genre of animated propaganda (though, it should be remembered, that the term 'propaganda' did not possess the negative connotations in the 1930s that it was later to assume).

DEVELOPING A DISTINCTIVE APPROACH TO ANIMATION

The Halas and Batchelor style was at least in part indebted to their admiration for Disney. Halas was happy to admit this when he recalled:

It was during 1934 when, with my colleague ... I took a round trip to attend the European premiere of Charlie Chaplin's *Modern Times* with the Disney cartoon *How to Play Polo*, with Goofy, in Vienna. We loved the films ... The experience of seeing the work of Chaplin and Disney was far reaching and inspired us for a long time.[3]

However, Halas and Batchelor's wartime 'social information' films stand in stark contrast to the more homogenized propaganda produced by the huge Disney machine during the war. Compared to the massive Disney apparatus, Halas and Batchelor were more like a cottage industry. However, this also invested their work with a much stronger individual sense than the output of Disney. It is also the case that after the war Disney ceased patriotic work to turn their factory-like operation towards lucrative childrens' entertainment such as *Cinderella* (1950), *Alice in Wonderland* (1951) and *Peter Pan* (1953) – all huge box-office hits. In contrast, Halas and Batchelor remained focused upon specialist propaganda and information film made for the Central Office of Information (COI), the successor to the Ministry of Information (MOI).

Initially this work was in support of the welfare reforms of the Attlee Labour government (1945–1951). These included animated films promoting public health (e.g. *Fly About the House*, 1950, *A Mortal Shock*, 1950, *Diphtheria Immunisation*, 1947) as well as a series of eight-minute shorts dealing with the Town and Country, and National Health and Insurance Acts. For the latter, Halas and Batchelor developed a cartoon character named 'Charley' who appeared in *Charley's Black Magic* (1948), *Charley's Junior School Days* (1949)

2 Sydney Box, *Film publicity: a handbook on the production and distribution of propaganda films* (London, 1937), p. 47.   3 John Halas, *The story of Halas and Batchelor*.

and *Charley's March of Time* (1948). Charley was intended to enjoy mass appeal and the 'Charley' films were shown in Britain to over 30 million people a week. As Paul Rotha observed:

> Though working in a wholly different medium, John Halas was among the first to show how the animated cartoon can be turned to documentary use. The Charley series which he and Joy Batchelor produced for the Central Office of Information in *1948–9* provided the best example.[1]

While there may have been cost factors involved, it seems that Halas and Batchelor's record as a specialist propaganda and public information unit was the main reason that Louis de Rochement approached them, rather than Disney, to produce the animated version of George Orwell's novel, *Animal Farm* (1945). Halas and Batchelor's propaganda filmmaking during World War Two was known to American officials in London administering the Marshall Plan funds designed to kick-start the European economy. Some of these funds were being used to make public information films that would stimulate the regeneration of Europe and Halas and Batchelor worked on one of these, *The Shoemaker and the Hatter* (1950). In this way, it can be seen that although *Animal Farm* – as a feature-length animated film – is unique within the context of Cold War film, it also links directly to Halas and Batchelor's work for the British government during the war and after.

Writing in 1972, Halas suggested that, historically, there have been four kinds of animation. The first of these, he argued, was the style of 'graphic realism' associated with Disney; the second was the abstract style associated with avant-garde filmmakers such as Len Lye and Oskar Fischinger; the third, he identified as a non-Disney form of stylized realism typical of Yugoslavia's Zagreb Studio or a film such as *Yellow Submarine* (1968). As for the fourth style, Halas clearly refers back to his own work and a film such as *Animal Farm*. 'It was developed in this country just after the war and it is likely that Joy Batchelor and I will be accused of establishing it', he argues. 'It is the creation of a new category of film animation appealing primarily to an adult audience and dealing with an adult subject, such as a social situation dramatized and simplified for a mass appeal'.[5]

Animal Farm is, in many ways, indebted to post-war Disney feature animation, employing the stylized graphic realism first developed in Disney's animated cel-based films, along with the Technicolor process (still a luxury in the 1950s) that was also typical of the Disney style. However, as in Halas and

4 P. Rotha, S. Road, and R. Griffith, *Documentary film* (London, 1952), pp 266–7.   5 John Halas, 'The emerging technique of computer animation', *British Kinematograph*, Sound and Television Society (London, 1972).

Batchelor's previous work, the film contains a serious political message that was aimed at adults as much as children. This leads to significant differences between the approach of the film and that of Disney. For example, *Animal Farm* avoids the careful emotional balancing evident in Disney cartoons, often permitting an unrelenting development of terrifying scenes. Thus, while there are painful scenes in *Bambi* (1942), such as the scene in which his mother is killed, the audience is spared the sight of this. In *Animal Farm*, on the other hand, there are several instances in which painful scenes are shown directly. These include the scene in which the fate of the animals is conjured up during the Old Major's speech; the slaughter of Snowball by Napoleon's dogs; the execution of the chickens and sheep for their crimes; and the scene near the end of the film when Boxer, the much loved and tireless worker, is sold for a crate of alcohol and taken to the knacker's yard. In order to communicate Orwell's dark vision, the film makes imaginative use of surreal yet visceral imagery that is not only highly potent but also potentially disturbing for a child.

The style of the film also departs from that of Disney feature films of the same period that aspire to 'realism' and three-dimensionality. In *Animal Farm*, by contrast, characters are drawn in a flat two-dimensional style and there is a lack of integration between characters and backgrounds. *Animal Farm*, in this respect, is more stylized than similar Disney productions and, while this may partly be the result of economic factors, it also befits the film's gloomy vision.

'ANIMAL FARM' AND IDEOLOGY

As Roger Fowler indicates, Orwell's novel was anti-Stalinist rather than simply anti-communist and his concern was to attack the 'Soviet Myth' that permeated the British intelligentsia and which, for Orwell, was harming the Socialist movement[6]. However, with the onset of the Cold War, such subtleties were lost. As Michael Shelden notes, Orwell's text 'caught the popular imagination just when the Cold War was beginning to make itself felt and, for many years 'anti-communists enjoyed it as a propaganda weapon in that war'.[7] It was certainly in this spirit that the novel was perceived by the CIA who were so impressed with it that they bought the rights to the book shortly after Orwell's death in 1950.[8] Cold War battles were fought by the British and American intelligence agencies primarily through the media, which included internationally serialized comic strips, novels, plays, newspaper serializations, drawings and posters as well as film. Thus, the contract with Halas and Batchelor not only involved the production of an animated film but also the illustrations for the republished

---

6 Roger Fowler, *The language of George Orwell* (Basingstoke, 1995) p. 163.   7 Michael Shelden, *Orwell: the authorised biography* (London, 1991), p. 404.   8 F.S. Saunders, *Who paid the piper? The CIA and the cultural Cold War* (London, 1999) p. 509.

version of the book and a syndicated comic strip version. What is also evident is that Orwell's original text is significantly altered throughout these adaptations suggesting how outside political influences were being exerted.

For instance if we look at the old Major's speech and the main differences between the film and the book, we see a number of changes taking place at the very outset of the film. In the film, the old Major dies at the end of his speech. In the book, however, old Major dies three days later. While this change may partly be explained by the need for dramatic effect, it also heightens the sense of fear, both in the audience and in the animals themselves. The cultivation of fear in propaganda is, of course, a powerful persuasive tool. The next obvious change occurs in the song that the animals sing at the end of Major's rousing speech. In the book, Orwell describes the melody as 'something between "Clementine" and "La Cucaracha"'[9] and has detailed lyrics to go with it. In the film you hear the animals singing along to what appears to be a modified version of a Russian anthem, which is quite a contrast to 'La Cucaracha'. Orwell's lyrics start out

> Beasts of England, beasts of Ireland,
> Beasts of every land and clime,
> Hearken to my joyful tidings
> Of the golden future time'.[10]

All of these are omitted from the film version.

Major's speech also shows signs of manipulation and the use of the word 'evil' is a prime instance of this. It appears in the first paragraph of the first scene in the film, yet in the book both its frequency and context are quite different. In Orwell's book the use of the word 'evil' is used twice in Major's speech, and is used in a very different way. To quote its first use in Orwell's book: 'Is it not crystal clear, then, comrades, that all the evils of this life of ours spring from the tyranny of human beings?'[11] Contrast this with the film: 'Overthrow this evil tyrant!' Thus, while it is quite clear that Orwell is suggesting that evil is not within any one thing or person, the film version encourages us to believe that 'evil' is, indeed, embodied in a particular person or animal – someone to identify and something to fear.

CONCLUSION

Halas and Batchelor's animated film adaptation of George Orwell's *Animal Farm* played a crucial role in the Cold War propaganda campaign and can be

---

9 George Orwell, *Animal Farm: a fairy story* (London, 1945), pp 12–13. 10 Ibid., 13. 11 Ibid., 10.

considered as a masterwork in the genre of the animated propaganda film. According to the analysis offered here the principal contribution of Halas and Batchelor to the medium of animation lies in their abilities to use cartoon animation as a means of persuasion. This began with their work in advertizing during the 1930s when they became influenced by the sophisticated techniques employed by American advertizers. This was a valuable preparation for their important contribution on the 'home front' during World War Two. Although their contribution to the Cold War seems less unquestionably praiseworthy, there is no doubt that at the time they believed that they were working in the interests of democracy and freedom. Having played such a key role in the British government's war effort, it probably seemed quite natural for Halas and Batchelor to accept another 'wartime' brief. Certainly there was no doubting the horrors perpetrated by Stalin and although these may have dissipated after his death in 1953 the regime remained aggressively imperialist as was evident in 1956 when Russia invaded Halas' original homeland, Hungary.

Cathal Black's *Korea*

EMILIE PINE

In a reflection of the critical hostility to which Irish rural drama was subject to in the 1990s, and an impatience for a modern urban cinema, film reviewer Vincent Browne argued in 1995 that:

> In recent years, what almost amounts to a '50s sub-genre of movies has emerged in this country. These films are prime examples of woeful tackiness and awful begorrahism, each one distinguishable from the last only by the new depths to which they are prepared to descend. These films appear to be either unbelievably dour or to be made with as many stereotypical blandishments as it is possible to stuff into one movie in order to make it appeal to the broadest audience.[1]

While Cathal Black's *Korea* certainly revisits much of the ground covered by the 'sub-genre' of 1950s Ireland, it does so with a difference.

Korea is an adaptation of John McGahern's 1970 short story of the same title. Originally, Black intended to make *Korea* as a short film but following Joe O'Byrne's script treatment, he decided to turn it into a full-length feature film. McGahern's story is expanded to include a romantic plot and the drama is extended from the original's focus on the father and son fishing together. Yet the film remains true to the sense of claustrophobia in the story. Indeed, it was this atmosphere that first drew Black to McGahern's work because, as he says, 'I thought that there was a dark heart to the country that wasn't being expressed but McGahern seemed to bring this out'.[2] In *Korea*, Black, a film-maker much concerned with the dark heart of Ireland, stays true to this tone of repressed emotion and violence.

The plot of the film centres on Eamon (Andrew Scott) and John Doyle (Donal Donnelly), a father and son who fish the nearby lake for eels for a living. It is set in the early 1950s as Eamon Doyle has just finished school and is awaiting his final examination results. Temporally, the film heralds a changing and modernizing country as electricity promises to transform rural Ireland. Yet, John Doyle is opposed to these changes, in large part because they are

---

1 Cathal Black, interview with Vincent Browne, *Film West* 24 (Spring 1996), p. 19.   2 Ibid. Black made this statement about 'Wheels', another John McGahern story, which he adapted for the screen in 1976.

championed by his civil war adversary, Ben Moran (Vass Anderson). Doyle is trapped in the past – by his memories of the civil war, especially the execution of a youth in Mountjoy Gaol. Indeed, death pervades the film as the title refers to the death of Luke Moran, Ben's son, in the Korean war, though the village gossip focuses on the report that the Morans received $10,000 in compensation for their son's death. When Eamon disobeys his father and starts seeing Una Moran (Fiona Molony), his father responds by trying to force him to emigrate to America, where he would most likely be drafted into the army to fight in Korea. Behind Doyle's motivation to separate Eamon and Una also lies the promise of financial security for Doyle from his son's migration as his livelihood as a fisherman is coming to an end.

Eamon's opening voice-over tells the audience that 'We were the last to fish the fresh water for a living', and his elegiac tone pervades the film. The shots of the lake are predominantly blue-green in composition, lending the lake images a melancholic air, while long shots of the lake predominate with the figures of the two men in the boat barely discernible in the background. One of the long shots early in the film dissolves to a shot of a clock face and the sound of the radio. The image of the clock signals that time is passing and that the Doyles are in danger of being left behind. Modernity and, specifically, the industrial power of electricity attract Eamon, but Doyle is opposed to it, partly because of the link between its installation and Ben Moran, a promoter of local enterprise, including tourism.

The first time the installation process is depicted, Eamon and his father are walking back from the lake. They walk past the base of an electricity pole where, just visible at the top of the frame, are a man's legs. Eamon is fascinated by the setting up of the electric cables and walks slowly past, staring up towards the man at work. Doyle impatiently calls Eamon to 'come on', paradoxically calling him forward into the past.[3] Even Doyle's demeanour makes it clear that he resents the intrusion of the electricity poles. That the electricity worker is visually so far above the two men implies that the developments of modernity are beyond them, and in this early scene the contrast between the traditional way of life on the lake and the faster pace of modernity is plainly set out.

The introduction of electricity to the area coincides with the tightening of regulations concerning the Doyles' fishing rights. Doyle and his son are the last men permitted to fish the lake and even then they are strictly controlled, only being allowed to use one thousand hooks in the lake at any one time. Coincidentally, it is Moran who oversees these controls. John Doyle has been told that these limits are because eel fishing 'impoverish[es] the fishing for the

3 Somewhat similar to the plot of Black's *Korea* is *The Promise of Barty O'Brien* in which a son must strive to convince his father, who fought in 1916, to introduce electricity into their home. See Kevin Rockett in Kevin Rockett, Luke Gibbons and John Hill, *Cinema and Ireland* (London, 1988), pp 82–4.

tourists'. Later in the film even this limited right is taken away when Doyle receives a letter telling him that his license has been terminated as the State wants to develop the lake for tourism.[4] Incensed and distraught, Doyle races to Moran's house to confront him. Though Moran tells him he tried to save his livelihood and that he can get him alternative work, Doyle does not listen to him. Instead, Doyle's mind is in the past. He confesses that Eamon's mother wanted to emigrate to America but Doyle wouldn't hear of it, saying 'I told her I'll never leave it, I told her that'. Doyle obviously cannot face the self-recrimination over his past actions and so continues to blame Moran.

Doyle's opposition to emigration to America is rooted in his patriotism and his deep connection to place, a connection forged by fighting for Irish independence. He sends Eamon to school, to get 'the education', to ensure that he will have the opportunity to stay in Ireland. Doyle's determination to believe in the future of Ireland becomes clear when father and son take their eel catch to the train station to be exported. In the back of the truck, Doyle comments to another passenger, 'Oh it's a great country right enough' to which the man nods agreement. The camera pulls back, and while the truck drives out of shot, a long shot of the wide, open countryside is sustained. This shot visually contradicts the image of America as the only open space available to Eamon, and confirms Doyle's judgment that it is 'a great country'. The film cuts to the noisy, bustling train station where the man taking delivery of the eels is pronouncing America to be 'the land of opportunity ... a big expanding country'. He contrasts it with Ireland, 'this pokey place. All there's room for here is fillin' holes and pints of porter'. To this diatribe Doyle replies:

> I wanted him to get the education. It'll stand to him for the rest of his life. There's no use scrapin' for the education then letting the yanks get the benefit. As long as there's the fishing there's something. Not many can say that. There's far too much talk about America, America.

Despite the fact that emigration figures were rising in this period – and one newspaper shown in the film carries this headline – Doyle is determined that his son remain in Ireland. Ben Moran, in contrast, allowed his son, Luke, to emigrate to America, where he was drafted to fight for the American army in Korea. At Luke Moran's funeral Doyle tells a neighbour, 'We didn't fight for our country to send our sons to Korea to die', demonstrating not only his bitterness towards the Morans but also his desire for Eamon to live in and for Ireland.

---

4 The reality of fresh-water fishing meant that eel fishing had to be re-introduced in several areas as eel populations increased to the extent that they endangered salmon stocks, in particular their young. Lough Neagh remains one of the only places in Ireland, however, where eels are commercially fished.

Yet, despite his support for educational progress, Doyle is fearful of it, too. It is not just their last summer on the lake because of stricter regulations, but also because Eamon's education gives him access to a world beyond fishing or manual labour. In an early scene Doyle uses Eamon's education as a weapon against Moran. When Moran comes to check that they are only using the regulation one thousand hooks, Doyle's riposte is that Eamon is educated and therefore 'well able to count to a thousand'. Yet later in the film Doyle also sees Eamon's education as an invasive weapon against his memories. When Eamon questions his father about his role in the War of Independence and the civil war – 'You did terrible things then didn't you, to make this a free country' – Doyle tells him that his 'schooling's over now'. Further, when Doyle tells Eamon about his memories of the civil war, in particular the execution of the young soldier, he rejects Eamon's view on the matter. Eamon asks his father if he thought that the young soldier 'stood to attention because he thought he might still get off if he obeyed the rules?' Doyle replies, 'Sounds a bit high falutin' to me. Comes from going to school too long'. Though Doyle champions Eamon's education, when it intrudes on his own version of the past, he shies away from it. Indeed, his reaction can be read as a desire not to think about the parallels between the young soldier's execution and his own situation, because abiding by the regulations on the fishing industry has not saved his livelihood.

John Doyle lives in the past, yet also thinks that it should be left alone. Both his waking hours and his sleep are disturbed by images of the past. He cannot move on, partly because he refuses to open up to his memories, and although he finally tells Eamon stories about the war, he will not allow them to be questioned. For Doyle, the past is framed and unchanging – just like the picture of him as a soldier hanging on his living-room wall.

FREEDOM?

Memories of the civil war in particular most disturb John Doyle. While in Mountjoy Gaol he witnessed the execution of two men, one a youth, and he has recurring nightmares about the event. The past refuses to be glossed over and breaks in on the present, rupturing it. However, Doyle's memories and the past do not always match. When Doyle narrates the story of the young boy being executed in Mountjoy, the film cuts to shots of the execution. Yet, the boy does not fall in the way that Doyle narrates and, indeed, the scene is not shot from Doyle's perspective but from the yard itself. Doyle is watching from his cell as the two men die, his hands gripping the bars across the window. This slight discrepancy points up the fallibility of memory and is further evidence of the necessity for figures such as Doyle to make peace with the past and to live for the future, rather than be constrained by memory.

As Eamon sees it, his father is not merely trapped by the past but does not *want* to move on, refusing to forgive Ben Moran for being a Free Stater. Even the link of fatherhood at the death of Luke Moran is not enough to bridge the divide between them. Doyle's 'civil war gun had hung on the wall for years, a reminder, he said, of a country he had fought for but was stolen from him'. This is made even more poignant in that the Doyles live in a border town in Cavan. Moreover, Doyle and Moran occupy different ends of the social hierarchy. Moran, the Free Stater, has benefited from his support for the Anglo-Irish Treaty and is now a prominent member of the community. His role now is to bring the 'electric revolution', whereas Doyle's revolution is still that of thirty years previously. While in the pub one night, the barman remarks to him that 'the electric will change everything', to which Doyle replies, 'There's lots of things the electricity *can't* change'. Doyle cannot see the social change that electricity can bring, refusing Eamon's request that they have it installed in their cottage, and derisively telling Eamon of the official Electricity Supply Board (ESB) launch, 'They lit the streetlamp, as if that will change anything'. Doyle's emphasis on 'change', or the lack of it, is a quiet but insistent indictment of the failure of the fight for independence.

Where Doyle represents the past, Eamon beckons the future: as the radio commentator puts it, he is one of 'the first generation to be born in freedom ...'. In the same year as Eamon's birth, 1934, the Minister for Defence Frank Aiken created a volunteer force made up of ex-IRA men, and which was designed to weaken the active IRA. Thus for his father, Eamon's birth signalled the beginning of a new life and an end to an old one.[5] Measures such as these were signs of the changes to come with the outlawing of the IRA two years later. Just as with the fishing license, John Doyle's past and identity were expunged and prohibited by the very authority he fought to put in power. When Doyle receives the letter informing him that he is no longer permitted to fish the lake, he tells the postman that 'There was a time when all I wanted was to see a harp on an envelope, instead of a crown'. The heavy irony here is compounded when we see that the letter is signed in Irish.

Doyle's distrust of authority and, by implication the government, emerges also when he talks to Eamon about his future. Eamon tells him that if his results are not good he will have to take what job he can get. In response, Doyle mutters, 'what you're *let* get'. His feeling of oppression is clear in this instance. Revisiting an earlier comment of his it is easy to trace this feeling of disrimination throughout the film. When Eamon asks his father of the 'terrible things' he did 'to make this a free country' one presumes that Doyle's

5 The Pension Act was passed to benefit those who had fought in the War of Independence in the same year. See J. Bowyer Bell, 'Introduction' in Uinseann MacEoin, *The IRA in the twilight years, 1923–1948* (Dublin, 1997), pp 4–8.

refusal to answer him is a reaction to Eamon's curiosity about the 'terrible things'. However, it is also possible that his refusal to speak is a reaction to Eamon's comment that it is a 'free country'. Doyle's feelings about freedom are made clear when Eamon remarks that he saw Una Moran walking, to which Doyle sarcastically replies, 'It's a free country, I suppose'. Doyle's sarcasm implies that for Una Moran it may be a 'free country' but that the phrase means little to him.

Doyle is haunted by the past; it will not leave him alone. He dreams of his honeymoon, on Howth head, but this dream is shattered by the memory of his internment during the civil war and the youth's execution. Doyle's dream recurs, on one occasion while he is waiting for Eamon to return with the boat. He falls asleep on the jetty and the film cuts to a sequence of images of the eels and the youth being shot and falling to the ground. The film then cuts to a shot of Doyle waking up on the jetty, in the same position as the boy lay on the ground in his dream. This visual match has a double implication. Firstly, Doyle thinks that it should have been him and not the young boy who was executed, a sentiment which is made explicit in McGahern's short story. Secondly, though Doyle was not shot that day, the link between him and the boy means that he cannot fully live his life; one part of him is dead.

While Doyle cannot move on, his paralysis also threatens to paralyse Eamon. He risks everything to separate Eamon and Una, by planning to send Eamon to America. This is in direct contrast to everything that he has previously said about wanting Eamon to get an education and stay in Ireland, to justify his part of the war. Distraught at the idea of being sent away, Eamon catches a fever from standing in the rain waiting for Una, and while sick he hallucinates images of Luke Moran in Korea. These hallucinations continue the theme of the destructive nature of war and show that, like his father, Eamon is plagued by images of war, though he has not even emigrated, let alone been drafted. Linking Korea and the Irish civil war is done not only through the death of two young men, but by the fact that both were captured in ambushes. These connections, though on separate continents and thirty years apart, create the sense that there is only one war, ever-present and continuing. The implication is that if Eamon does emigrate, the cycle will be repeated, and he will become either embittered like his father, or a sacrificial figure like Luke Moran and the young soldier.

EELS

One other image connects Eamon's fears of Korea and the images of execution that haunt his father: the eels. From the opening shot of the film – of the eels twisting in a box – they are established as the dominant image of the film. Their significance is threefold. Firstly, and most obviously, the eels rep-

resent a passing way of life. The Doyles have fished the lake for decades but
the changing attitude of the state towards the countryside means that the lake
will be used in future to create a different kind of revenue: tourism. While
the future beckons for Eamon, the future represents the death of his father's
way of life and, by extension, his own death. After Doyle has received the
letter officially informing him of the loss of his license, he goes out eel fishing
alone. In the boat, he looks out fondly on the lake, towards a growth of rushes,
seeing a sepia-toned image of other men in their boats, a community of fish-
ermen. When he looks back at the lake, the image of the past is gone and the
lake returns to its slate-blue colour. The film then cuts to a shot of one eel
twisting on a line. The link between the eel and Doyle implies that the future
holds the same for both of them because they are equally trapped. This link is
strengthened when, as Doyle sleeps on the jetty waiting for Una and Eamon
to return from the graveyard, the film cuts between shots of the eels in their
box and Doyle's dream of the young soldier.

The eels are also associated with moments of trauma. When Eamon asks
his father if he did 'terrible things' in the war, the film cuts to a shot of the
eels. Similarly, when early in the film Doyle is drunk and thumps the table,
saying of the executed boy, 'he died for this!', the film again cuts to the eels.
The eels are thus associated with the trauma of Doyle's past and Ireland's violent past. Finally, the eels represent the disturbance of war generally. The
connection between the eels and Korea is made early in the film, when there
is a cut to the eels after the radio announcement of Luke Moran's death.
Likewise, when Eamon is distraught at the thought of being sent to America
and he is faced with the possibility of being drafted to fight in Korea, he goes
to the jetty at the lake. The film cuts from an image of Eamon standing on
the jetty in the pouring rain, looking up at the inscrutable night sky, to a shot
of the eels twisting in their underwater box.

The eels, then, represent the traumatic effects of war and, by connecting
the Irish War of Independence, the civil war and the war in Korea, suggest
the recurring or cyclical nature of violence. On the surface, Ireland has moved
on from violence and is apparently more engaged in the 'electric revolution'
than in violent uprising. The transformation of the landscape thus seems complete: from the anarchic space as it was viewed under colonialism, to its role
as a space of resistance during the guerrilla war, to the marketing of it as a
space of leisure for tourists. Yet the presence of the eels – twisting in their
underwater box – suggests that there is still a dark underside to the attractive
facade of the Irish landscape that continually erupts, like Doyle's nightmares,
into the film. The banning of eel fishing, in this reading, appears to be not
only an economic initiative but simultaneously is an attempt to erase the dark
underside, indeed the memory of the past that the landscape holds.

RESOLUTION

The constant eruption of the eels at moments of trauma for the characters reveals that the past needs to be resolved. This is a very real need for Eamon because his father, refusing to forgive the role that Moran played in his past, seems willing to send his son to America to begin the cycle of violence again. What *Korea* achieves is to show how that cycle can be broken, the pattern changed. When Eamon and Doyle go out on the lake for the last time, Eamon brings his father's gun with him. In the boat he tells him that he wants to marry Una Moran and that he is not going to America. He takes the gun from his pocket and points it at his father. Eamon does not intend, however, to shoot him: he gives the gun to him and tells him that using it is the only way he will make his son emigrate. Eamon gives his father an ultimatum: to use the gun against his son or to throw it into the lake. Doyle's first reaction is that the gun should be on the wall at home hanging next to the picture of him in military uniform. By taking the gun from the wall, Eamon illustrates that he will un-frame the past and change the pattern of their lives.

By arguing that the gun should be thrown into the lake, Eamon forces Doyle to confront both the past and the future and shows him that he must move on; the gun belongs with the eels in the past. Furthermore, Eamon recognizes the need to put the gun where it belongs: together with the darker elements of the Irish past and landscape, and not where it had been, intruding into the home. Eamon stands up in the boat, towering over his father but also over the lake, and by extension, the landscape and nature. By standing in the boat, Eamon visually illustrates that he is imposing his will over the landscape and on his and his father's fate and, by so doing, changing the pattern.

There is, however, a qualification to Eamon's success in ridding his family of the gun. Though Doyle throws the gun into the lake it is not destroyed but merely hidden, lying under the surface. The film's visual emphasis on the disturbing presence of the eels under the water strongly suggests that, though these troubling images can be covered up, they do not disappear entirely. The presence of the gun under the water is a reminder that violence has not left Ireland entirely, and this implication is the film's only indirect reference to events in Northern Ireland.

The presence of the gun below the water's surface is also suggestive of Black's reconfiguring of Irish identity. Rather than land – the traditional symbol of Irish identity and security – *Korea* focuses on water, a more unstable and dynamic, shifting site of identity. The eels, moving and twisting underwater, further undermine the sense of a secure foundation for the self. Thus, the threatening power of the past and the instability of self, and thus, necessarily, also the future, are acknowledged.

Eamon is not capable of this independence without help. While he challenges his father in the boat, Una Moran is standing on the jetty, watching them and providing an anchor for Eamon on the shore. Una represents, at this moment, more than just Eamon's present and future. In this moment of crisis and resolution, Una stands in the role of Eamon's mother. Earlier in the film Eamon tells Una that if his mother were alive, he would be able to stand up against his father. When Eamon is sick, Una violates Doyle's rules and visits him. As she is looking after him, the film cuts to a photograph of Eamon's mother on his bedside table, and then cuts back to Una. The link between Una and Eamon's mother strengthens Una as an ally and also reveals that war is not the only issue from the past that needs resolving.

Doyle is distraught at losing his license to fish as he told his wife that he would never leave the lake and thereby hastened her death. Before they go out on the lake for the last time, Doyle refers to this, saying to Eamon that 'I did all I could for her, spent all the time I could with her'. The link between Eamon's mother and Una not only enables Eamon to confront his father, but also in turn enables Doyle to come to terms with his neglect of his wife. When they bring the boat to the shore, Doyle allows Una to help him out of the boat. Standing over Doyle, Una not only represents a link to Eamon's mother but also she occupies the same space as her father had done early in the film. With Moran, Doyle had chosen to reject any attempts at conciliation but by taking Una's hand he shows his willingness to forgive the past. Before he leaves, Doyle asks Una if she heard the kingfisher singing, the same question that Eamon had asked her on their first date. Doyle is thus following the path his son has chosen.

Throughout the film Doyle consistently argues for the future of Ireland as positive, dismissing the need to emigrate and insisting that he fought so that Eamon could remain in Ireland. His misery and resentment of Moran blinds him to this but, by the end of the film, Doyle realizes that the past should not define him. Indeed, the film taken as a whole approves of modernizing Ireland and facing the future pragmatically. Perhaps this reflects its moment of production, the mid-1990s when IRA ceasefires made it possible for films like *Korea* and Neil Jordan's *Michael Collins* (1996), to be made. The civil war could only be addressed once Ireland had started to acknowledge and move on from its violent past. *Korea*, made in 1995, looks back at the 1950s, which in turn is obsessed with the 1920s. The film is thus the ultimate backward look, yet for once it looks back in order to move on.

Escape from fantasy Ireland:
Martin Duffy's *The Boy from Mercury*

PÁDRAIC WHYTE

Written and directed by Martin Duffy, *The Boy from Mercury* was released in Ireland in 1996. The film allows for an exploration of the construction of both an Irish childhood and an Irish (national) past on screen. Duffy uses the idea of childhood fantasy in the film both as a form of escapism and also as a comment on the heterogeneous nature of Irish culture in the 1960s and in the 1990s. In merging constructions of children and history, the idea of childhood acts as a liminal space for the simultaneous production of a concept of self and of nation. Investigating the film in such a manner positions the analysis of childhood within the context of the family, modernization, and of the church, as well as in terms of the moving statue phenomenon of the 1980s.

The film focuses on the childhood experiences of Harry Cronin (James Hickey), an eight-year-old boy growing up in Dublin in the 1960s. Harry's father died five years earlier and, inspired by *Flash Gordon* films, Harry has retreated into a fantasy world, believing that he is from the planet Mercury. Each night he communicates with what he concludes is a Mercurian spaceship and claims that he has been sent to Earth with special powers. For Harry, childhood experiences consist primarily of interactions with his worried mother (Rita Tushingham), his angst-ridden older brother Paul (Hugh O'Conor), an eccentric Uncle (Tom Courtenay), and a school bully, Maguire (Kevin James).

Descriptions of the film as 'a winning slice of nostalgia'[1] and as an 'obvious but generally effective meditation on childhood escapism set in early 1960s Dublin',[2] tend to overlook and simplify the complex processes involved in the construction of the past in the film. Investigating the representation of the past in the text through an analysis of childhood, however, allows a greater understanding of the past-present relationship at work in projects that attempt to represent history from a contemporary perspective. Such a method of analysis finds its foundation in the writings of Michel Foucault and his concept of 'history of the present'; his problematization of modes of representation; and the examination of the role and function of memory in the creation of representations of the past. Combining these ideas with the work of Peter Hollindale

---

1 *Hot Press Magazine*, December 1996.   2 'Harvey's Movie Reviews' website, http://home-page.eircom.net/~obrienh/bm.htm, accessed 12 July 2004.

and his theories of 'childness' in children's texts allows for an in-depth examination of the intertwining of childhood and history in *The Boy from Mercury*.

The deconstruction of a metanarrative of history from a present-day perspective can be read by utilizing Foucault's idea of 'history of the present', a
term used in *Discipline and Punish: The Birth of the Prison* (1975) but which
as a concept can be traced back to his essay 'Nietzsche, Genealogy, History'
(1971).[3] In an article in *Magazine Littéraire*, Foucault discusses the problematization of representation stating that, 'I start with a problem in the terms
in which it is currently posed and attempt to establish its genealogy; genealogy means that I conduct the analysis starting from the present situation',[4] an
approach also expressed in 'Nietzsche, Genealogy, History' where genealogy
is used to deconstruct and explore historical narratives. For Foucault, traditional history is characterized by its constants and its aim to dissolve 'the sin-
gular event into an ideal continuity – as a teleological movement or a natural
process'.[5] However, drawing upon Nietzsche's idea of 'Wirkliche Historie',
Foucault believes that by dismantling these modes of historical tradition, an
'effective' history can be created introducing 'discontinuity into our very being'
as it 'deprives the self of the reassuring stability of life and nature' constantly disrupting 'its pretended continuity'.[6] In this sense, history is not simply
an eruption of an event followed by an ideal continuity, but is a series of conflicting discourses of power, a play of dominations. As is discussed below,
Martin Duffy uses his own genealogy and memories of childhood and of
Dublin to complicate ideas of a coherent continuous history and to comment
upon Irish culture of the past and of the present. As a consequence, the basic
premise of 'childness' can be used as a mechanism to explore this construction of the past in the present.

In his work, *Signs of Childness in Children's Books*,[7] Peter Hollindale problematizes the very notion of childhood in relation to children's texts, including film and television. He argues that there are two constructions of childhood involved in films produced for children; on the one hand, the adult
constructs an idea of childhood through writing and directing, while the child
viewer creatively constructs childhood while watching the film. Therefore,
childhood in the text is created through a negotiation or exchange between
author and child, the text functioning as a site of this interaction. In attempting to formulate a workable vocabulary for his analysis, Hollindale rejects the

3 Michel Foucault, *Discipline and punish: the birth of the prison*, trans. Alan Sheridan (New York,
1977, orig. 1975); 'Nietzsche, genealogy, history' (1971) in Paul Rabinow (ed.) *The Foucault
reader* (London, 1981), pp 76–100.   4 Michel Foucault, 'Le Souci de la vérité', *Magazine
Littéraire*, 207 (1984), p. 18; also cited in Robert Castel, 'Problematization' as a mode of reading history', in Jan Goldstein (ed.), *Foucault and the writing of history* (Oxford, 1994), p. 238.
5 Foucault, 'Nietzsche, genealogy, history', p. 88.   6 Ibid.   7 Peter Hollindale, *Signs of childness in children's books* (Gloucestershire, 1997).

use of words such as 'childish' and 'childlike' because of the predominantly negative cultural connotations inherent in such terms, and settles on the idea of 'childness', which he takes from Shakespeare's use of the word in *The Winter's Tale*. Childness, Hollindale proposes, is 'the quality of being a child – dynamic, imaginative, experimental, interactive and unstable' and that it 'is a shared ground, though differently experienced and understood between the child and adult'.[8] In this sense, he refers to childness as that distinguishing property of a film for children that sets it apart from other films.

The composition of childness varies for the child and adult spectator. For the child, it consists of an interaction of childhood self-identity with images of childhood in society such as standards of behaviour, social expectations and taboos. For the adult spectator, childness is a combination of adult memories of childhood, expectations regarding social norms and the behaviour of children, as well as ideas of childhood innocence and the potential fulfilment of future hopes and dreams. While arguably extremely broad in its approach, Hollindale's work offers a useful foundation for understanding the complexities of concepts of childhood inherent in both writing and reading children's texts within a specific cultural framework.

The composition of childness in the film is therefore a complex process and is not merely constructed through the presence of children on screen but also through Duffy's own personal memories. The influence of memory in creating the narrative is revealed in an interview conducted by Hugh Linehan, as Duffy reveals the autobiographical nature of the film by stating that 'A lot of it *is* me. When I was a kid I thought I was from another planet, which is the starting point for everything in the film. It brought back a lot of things from my childhood that I realized were quite sweet and precious'.[9] Linehan echoes this fondness for the past by stating that the film is 'an affectionate depiction of suburban Dublin life in the early 1960s, based very closely on Duffy's own childhood memories'.[10] This idea presents three distinct elements for consideration in an analysis of the rendering of the past, as memories of Dublin, memories of childhood and concepts of childhood in Irish culture become blended in composing the narrative. Combining these approaches with the theories of Foucault and Hollindale leads to possible *literal* and *metaphorical* readings of childhood in *The Boy from Mercury*.

In the construction of a literal form of childhood on screen Duffy attaches a childhood identity to Harry's character and brings to the fore a series of representations that are traditionally associated with childhood and with dominant images of children in culture. These include economic dependence, escapism and retreating into the realms of fantasy, Harry's closeness to animals, being bullied at school, attempting to live up to his mother's expectations, arguing with his older brother, and playing with his friend Sean. This

8 Ibid., 46–7. 9 *Irish Times*, 6 December 1996. 10 Ibid.

is paralleled by many images in the film reminiscent of *Cinema Paradiso* (Giuseppe Tornatore, 1989) and *My Life as A Dog* (*Mitt Liv som Hund*: Lasse Hallström, 1985), echoing ideas of childhood wonder and innocence. Such a listing merely offers a general overview of some of the main areas which contribute to creating concepts of childhood in the text. In Hollindale's terms, the child viewer then brings his/her own reality of experience of childhood to the film and creatively interacts with the version of childhood presented on screen in the production of childness. However, this reading of childness is complicated when childhood is explored in metaphorical terms. It is possible to see the child Harry as an allegory for the Irish nation as the character is used to comment upon Irish culture in the 1960s as well as in the 1990s.

In his analysis of Neil Jordan's *The Butcher Boy* (1997), released one year after *The Boy from Mercury*, Martin McLoone notes that the bomb that goes off in Francie Brady's head can also be read in metaphoric terms as 'the cultural explosion of Eamon de Valera's imagining, [that] went off in Ireland in the early 1960s with the beginning of a process of modernization which continues at a more advanced level today'.[11] McLoone continues to read the film in terms of the clash between tradition and modernity and the impact of American popular culture on Irish society. Similarly, as discussed below, it is possible to read the childhood character and experiences of Harry Cronin as a metaphor for Ireland, and the conflict between tradition and modernity in the 1960s.

As Harry is brought to the cemetery to visit the grave of his father (the film echoes many of the themes found in Irish cinema during the 1990s, particularly in terms of representations of a family with an absent father),[12] an event that appears to have been transformed into a ritual, his mother encourages him to talk to his dead father and tell him what a good boy he has been. Meanwhile, his older brother Paul has no interest in this ritual. The events take place during a period when Ireland was experiencing the transition from the isolationist economic policies pursued by Irish governments since the early 1930s toward a process of modernization and internationalization from the late 1950s onwards. As a child, Harry functions as a metaphor for the nation in the early 1960s, with his dead father possibly representing both ex-Taoiseach Eamon de Valera and the protectionist traditions with which he is associated. On the other side of Harry, separated by the cross (traditional religion) is his brother Paul who, obsessed with pop culture, possibly symbolizes progress and modernity. Harry's mother, uncertain of the correct course to take, yet wanting the best for her child, is constantly torn between pushing Harry

11 Martin McLoone, *Irish film: the emergence of a contemporary cinema* (London, 2000), p. 217.
12 These include films such as *Thirty-Five a Side* (Damian O'Donnell, 1995), *Last of the High Kings* (David Keating, 1996), *I Went Down* (Paddy Breathnach, 1997) and *This Is My Father* (Paul Quinn, 1998). For a further discussion of this topic, see Martin McLoone, *Irish film*, pp 168–83.

toward the rigid rituals of the past and urging him to progress like his older brother. It is significant that they repeat 'Glory be to the Father', stating 'as it was in the beginning is now and ever shall be'. Harry, like Ireland, is caught in a type of paralysis, constantly told to keep his links with the past, a past that is now dead, while simultaneously encouraged to become like his Americanized brother Paul.

This influence of global culture is evident in Paul's obsession with rock n' roll, and also in Harry's passion for *Flash Gordon* films and comic books. Similar to Francie Brady in *The Butcher Boy*, these elements of popular culture offer an escape route from the problems posited by everyday reality. The *Flash Gordon* films inspire Harry to create a fantasy life, where he believes he is in fact a Mercurian on a mission to investigate the social habits of Earthlings. The escapism offered by popular culture fills a void in Harry's life and he becomes increasingly immersed in the fantasy world that he has created.

Harry descends into the realm of fantasy through his retelling of *Flash Gordon* stories and the belief that he possesses superpowers. The lines between fact and fiction become blurred for him as he imagines that his Mercurian powers have wounded his friend Sean. Although Harry is perturbed that his belief in fantasy may have caused harm, he continues to embellish his tales of Mercury. He draws upon these fictions in times of crisis, particularly when threatened by the school bully. As Harry looks up in expectation of the arrival of a spaceship, the bully becomes distracted. Consequently, Harry seizes the opportunity to thump him and run. In the end, the imagined Mercurian space ship does not actually land and rescue him, but it is his belief in the fantasy that has saved him.

The imaginings that he has conjured up through his interaction with American culture, however, can only ward off the bully on a temporary basis. It is only when he accepts the aid of his big brother that he can permanently fend off the bully Maguire and move on with the reality of his life at school. Immersing oneself in a realm of fantasy can be useful to a degree but it will only delay the inevitable. Like the fantasy elements of films such as *Pete's Meteor* (Joe O'Byrne, 1998), the child character is relying on outside assistance, but support arrives from within in the form of his family and friends. Unlike Francie Brady, Harry's descent into a world of fantasy is halted. As the film concludes, Harry accepts his mother as his biological mother, addressing her as 'Mam', and signalling a return to his Dublin reality. If the metaphor of the child as the Irish nation is continued then perhaps this can be read as a comment upon Ireland's economic situation in the 1960s; Harry (as Ireland), is in need of assistance, is rescued by Paul (modernity and progress) and consequently accepts the reality of his Dublin home and family life. It is possible to interpret this version of events in terms of Ireland's changing economic policies. However, while Taoiseach Sean Lemass' economic policies moved away from the stifling protectionism of the de Valera era, there was a subse-

quent danger of the Irish economy becoming dependent on international mar-
kets (similar to the way in which Harry has become completely dependent
upon a fantasy provided by American culture). The film can be read as a comment on the need to strike a balance between these extremes by addressing
problems within Ireland as well as developing economic links abroad.

In common with *The Butcher Boy*, *The Boy from Mercury* can equally be
read as a text about the 1990s, particularly in terms of problematizing a cohe-
sive narrative of continuity between past and present as well as the role of
memory in this process. As Hollindale notes, in writing a text for children,
childness is created through the adult's memory of childhood. The semi autobiographical nature of Duffy's text allows for a depiction of both a personal
history and a cultural or national history. Thus a history of both self and nation
is created from a contemporary perspective, as it exposes the presence of the
present in a construction of the past through memory. In the search for origins or continuity of self and culture, the adult writer draws upon personal
memories of childhood that are located within the shared public memories of
Ireland of the 1960s as represented by the screening of *Flash Gordon* films,
new housing developments, and various elements of popular culture. Duffy
uses memory to create a story of his own past and a story of Ireland through
the lens of the 1990s. Therefore, the narrative of *The Boy from Mercury* is not
simply a nostalgic take on 1960s Ireland, but, as is debated below, may explore
issues of Ireland in the present. Consequently, the coherent linear narrative
of history is dismantled as the text conflates ideas of past and present. Drawing
upon a similar perspective in his discussion of *The Butcher Boy*, McLoone
notes that 'the film is not ultimately about the historical moment *per se*, but
about how it is remembered and interpreted in the present ... it is a profoundly contemporary film and is most interesting for the ways in which it
intervenes in the contemporary cultural debate in Ireland'.[13]

Duffy optimizes the use of fantasy in his exploration of the effect of modernization, particularly in relation to new housing developments. As Harry is
invited to visit his friend Sean, he adopts the guise of an anthropologist as he
researches the living habits of Earthlings and reports his findings to his home
planet. The use of soft focus photography creates a dreamlike quality, literally blurring the lines between fantasy and reality. Sean's home-life appears as
a fictional form of the potential of modernization and urbanization. This
sequence not only idealizes property developments of the future, but aligns a
particular family lifestyle with such developments. While Harry is in awe of
what he sees, the representation is ultimately conservative and is rooted in the
portrayal of family life in American cinema of the 1960s, reflected in Harry's
comments that 'it was just like something out of the pictures'. The representation of Sean's family in this sequence is in stark contrast to Harry's home-

13 Martin McLoone, *Irish film*, p. 217.

life. While Harry is over-awed by his trip to Walkinstown, his mother feels
threatened by his positive reaction to the experience. Harry is placed between
this juxtaposition of his mother's association with tradition and Sean's idealized family and the embracing of modernization. Once again it directs attention toward the influence of global culture in ambiguous terms. If the urbanization of Walkinstown is viewed as the possible future of Ireland through
progress and development, Harry's visit to Sean's house firmly positions the
Americanization of culture within that future.

The film also offers a complex representation of the Catholic church and
religion as an oppressive force in Harry's life. As noted above, Harry is forced
to pay homage to his father at the graveside, a ritual that appears to have
become a laborious family tradition. In school, Harry's teacher is a Christian
brother (Ian McElhinney) who is strict and violent toward his pupils. The
brother refers to the figure of Jesus on the cross in order to unearth the truth
regarding a threatening note left in the school bully's desk, and asks the children in the class to 'swear upon the name of holy Jesus on the cross' that they
did not write the note. In this sequence, the Catholic church becomes aligned
with images of oppression and force as well as with the feelings of fear and
guilt experienced by Harry. Similar critical representations of the Catholic
church were dominant in many films and television programmes produced in
Ireland from the early 1990s, from the screening of Cathal Black's *Our Boys*
in 1991 to *Song For a Raggy Boy* in 2003. However, Duffy's most interesting
critique of the church lies in his blurring of fantasy and reality and the trib-
ute he pays to films that deal with the moving statue phenomenon that
engulfed Ireland in the 1980s, most notably Margo Harkin's *Hush-a-Bye Baby*
(1989), a film on which Duffy worked as editor.

At the risk of over-simplifying the complex position of moving statues in
Irish culture, it may be useful to place it within the context of events in 1980s
Ireland. In 1985, many moving statues of the Virgin Mary were reported around
the country, attracting huge crowds of both believers and cynics. Elizabeth Butler
Cullingford notes how conservative commentators at the time believed that 'Our
Lady was grieved and angered by the terrible events of the previous year [1984],
including ... fifteen year old Ann Lovett dying as she gave birth to her illegit-
imate child in a grotto dedicated to the Virgin Mary'.[14] Butler Cullingford states
that 'Ireland's sexual morality, according to the conservative reading of the mir-
acles, needed to be restored to its former purity'.[15] Rather than questioning the
repressive role that the church may have played in the circumstances leading
to Ann Lovett's death, some religious leaders saw the phenomenon of the
moving statues as criticizing the young girl's behaviour rather than their own.

14 Elizabeth Butler Cullingford, 'Virgins and mothers: Sinead O'Connor, Neil Jordan, and *The
Butcher Boy*', in Dudley Andrew and Luke Gibbons (eds), 'The theatre of Irish cinema', *Yale
Journal of Criticism*, 15: 1 (Spring 2002), p. 189.   15 Ibid.

In *Hush-a-Bye Baby*, the statue of the Virgin Mary appears in the fevered dreams of a fifteen year old pregnant girl, Goretti (Emer McCourt). Later, as Goretti walks by a statue of the Virgin, she issues a warning to Our Lady, 'Don't you fucking move, I'm warning you!', signalling that religion does not function as a source of solace in this time of crisis, but acts as an oppressive force whose omnipresence perpetuates a feeling of guilt. It is constantly regarded with apprehension as opposed to awe.[16] It is possible to read Duffy's representation of religious iconography as a means of criticizing the church, as the concept of moving statues is aligned with the rest of Harry's fantasy world. As the fantasies become more intense and he begins to hallucinate, Harry imagines people coming through the door of his bedroom. Included in the hallucinations are images of monsters coming out of graves, a glowing Sacred Heart picture, and Jesus moving on the cross.

The theme of a young boy in mid-twentieth century Ireland having visions of religious icons is common to many films made in Ireland in the 1990s, particularly *The Butcher Boy* and *All Things Bright and Beautiful* (Barry Devlin, 1994). However, *The Boy From Mercury* is the only film that uses the male figure of Jesus as opposed to the female Our Lady. Such an approach reinforces the dominance of the patriarchal order in creating an oppressive society as opposed to the possible representation of the female figure as a source of maternal comfort and warmth as in the other two films. This is coupled with the Brother's warning that telling lies while swearing on the body of Jesus on the cross will lead to the blackening of the soul. In the context of the film, the figures that dominate Irish culture are represented as domineering forces whose primary function is to instil guilt and anxiety into children. By associating the image with the rest of the fantastic elements in the film, Duffy creates the idea that belief in moving statues is just as absurd as the belief that one is from another planet.

Subsequently, Duffy's film surpasses simplistic notions of a nostalgic childhood and exposes the complex processes involved in the construction of a narrative of the Irish past through the literal and metaphorical use of childhood. The disruption of a coherent linear narrative of history corresponds to Foucault's problematization of creating historical narratives in the present. The contemporary position of the writer/director greatly influences the composition of the narrative, as certain elements of history are foregrounded to comment upon both the past and the present. Hollindale's theories of childness offer a useful methodology in exploring possible readings of this history and culture in the text as the varying forms and uses of childhood are analysed. Ideas of childhood and Ireland are conflated as the past of self and the past of the nation converge in this liminal ideological space of film.

16 Neil Jordan expands upon this idea in *The Butcher Boy* in his ambiguous representation of the Virgin Mary, played by Sinead O'Connor.

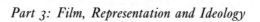

Part 3: Film, Representation and Ideology

From feminism to post-feminism:
Pat Murphy's love story *Nora*

DIÓG O'CONNELL

The Joyces moved to Switzerland, where he taught English and started a theatre to produce English plays. They were very hard up. One day when he was in the theatre rehearsing, a letter came announcing that a huge sum of money had arrived from an anonymous donor. Nora, all excitement, put on her hat, went to the theatre and, before all the company, announced their good fortune. Joyce always remembered that, in the midst of congratulations, the wife of an actor in the company turned to Nora and said with an edge in her voice: 'And so, Mrs Joyce, you open your husband's letters'.[1]

What makes Pat Murphy's film *Nora* (2000) most intriguing from a scholarly perspective is how it diverges from Murphy's earlier distinctively feminist work and reveals a trajectory reflecting key changes and developments within feminist film debates. Murphy's approach to the intellectual exploration of the relationship between feminism and republicanism in *Maeve* (1981) was modernist and avant-garde while *Anne Devlin* (1984) could be seen as part of the feminist project that sought to reclaim female historical figures from oblivion coinciding with the development of women's studies in 1980s Ireland. Much has been written about these two films probably because of the undisguised political and aesthetic feminist approach that lends itself to the socio-political discourse that has prevailed in Irish cinema studies since the 1980s. Murphy's earlier work emerged within a context of a developing interest and activity in feminist film studies in the 1970s and 1980s as well as being part of the radical first wave of Irish film.

   Nora is different however, principally because it is difficult to label or categorize either as part of Murphy's *oeuvre* or within the boundaries of feminist film. Brenda Maddox's biography *Nora: the Real Life of Molly Bloom* (1988) is part of the feminist project reclaiming neglected female historical figures. Murphy takes this publication as her inspiration, but while following the feminist trajectory established in the 1980s she deviates from it by moving it in a new direction. Its uniqueness is highlighted further when viewed within the context of the styl-

1 *Irish Times*, 20 April 2000.

istic tendencies of contemporary Irish film. Murphy herself denies that it is a feminist film due to the Joycean nature of the text stating that:

> [y]ou can never get to [Nora] separate from [Joyce]. You always have to use him as a way into her and that's one of the reasons *Nora* is not a feminist film in the way that *Anne Devlin* and *Maeve* are feminist films...[This film] is not trying to recuperate her and say that she was something else.[2]

In this paper I wish to explore where this film sits within the feminist film project and Murphy's work in general and posit a notion that it signals a move by Murphy away from overt feminist narratives towards what may be called post-feminism,[3] evidenced principally through the creation of a structure that simultaneously embraces and subverts conventional narratives, and thus reflects some of the emerging trends within recent Irish cinema and feminist politics. Murphy's film, I argue, is a contemporary love story that both uses and subverts conventional mainstream devices to articulate a radical discourse of equality. Murphy refuses simple explanations of emotional states and consequently presents an exploration of romance and love that incorporates both positive and negative outcomes, defying an assured position for the viewer.

Nora opens in 1904 when Nora Barnacle (Susan Lynch) runs away to Dublin from her native Galway. From the outset she is portrayed as an active, dominant character, an approach to narrative that recalls the emergence of progressive female characters in the 1970s as a consequence of feminist agitation. In a set-up that wastes no time, Nora meets Joyce (Ewan McGregor) on a Dublin street. Evoking a small, localized milieu, Joyce knows that she is a stranger in town and guesses from her accent that she hails from Galway. Nora from the start is confident and assertive. When Joyce introduces himself and arranges a date but fails to ask her name, she calls after him, 'Hey James Joyce, don't you want to know my name? ... My name is Nora Barnacle'. From the opening shot, when she is framed seated on a bench in Galway train station, to her declaration on a public street of who she is, Pat Murphy is privileging Nora in the narrative.

---

2 Pat Murphy quoted in Gerardine Meaney, *Nora* (Cork, 2004), p. 70. Meaney's book was not published at the time this paper was originally delivered at the University of Ulster at Coleraine in April 2004. While the original argument put forward at the UU conference does not change, it is further developed in light of Meaney's book.   3 Post-feminism is seen here, not as Susan Faludi sees it as backlash, but as a continuation of feminism. According to Ann Braithwaite, post-feminism captures the state of feminism today, 'complete with all [its] difficult debates and animosities, [its] conflicts and contradictions, [its] pleasures and desires. [It is] not *about*, not *against*, feminism; not an appropriation or distortion, but a shift in central categories and questions; not a depoliticization or trivialization, but an active rethinking; not wholly new phenomena, but a way of articulating changes in and the evolution of feminism'. See Ann Braithwaite, 'Politics of/and backlash', *Journal of International Women's Studies*, 5:5 (2004), p. 27.

Because film is primarily a storytelling medium and the prevailing narrative conventions determine how that story is told, biographical material presents a particular challenge to the writer and director. When the subject matter is the wife of one of the best-known writers of the twentieth century, the challenge becomes beset by obstacles and controversy. In many ways, Murphy's approach defies expectation. She does not present a biopic that remains truthful to the facts; this would be impossible in ninety minutes of screen time. Neither does she proclaim Nora as a figure ahead of her time, an off-shoot of the feminist project to reclaim previously forgotten female historical figures. Instead she chooses to focus the narrative on telling a story about the relationship between two people. The narrative's progression concentrates on the 'working-out' of the relationship, whereby the two characters journey through the stages of 'classic' narrative: equilibrium, disequilibrium and, finally, the achievement of a new equilibrium. Where this narrative deviates from the conventional love story, however, and follows on from Murphy's earlier work is by telling a love story that expresses a discourse of equality, that speaks of gender relations in a positive, progressive and complex way. In constructing the narrative, the director rejects the structure that pits one character against the other; neither character dominates while the other regresses. Furthermore, the common scenario whereby one character 'rescues' the other is discarded, thus setting this film aside from other recent Irish romance films (*About Adam*, Gerald Stembridge 2001; *When Brendan met Trudy*, Kieron J. Walsh, 2001) in which the narrative dynamic is structured around one party 'fixing' the other, through a dynamic of dominance and submission. As Murphy states in an interview with Gerardine Meaney:

> I felt that, in terms of cinema, there had never been a really great love
> story that came out of Ireland. A lot of the movies I was seeing then
> had a narrative vision of erotic love as something forbidden and trans
> gressional. No movie narrative seemed to be able to hold the notion
> that people could just be together, have this great passionate love affair
> and be together. There was always a level of punishment.[4]

Filmmaker Jim Sheridan echoes this position but situates it within the stunted national psyche that is a consequence of postcolonialism.[5]

A film that had the potential to proffer a radical discourse, *A Love Divided* (Syd Macartney, 1999), falls into the conventional trap of pitting one character against the other. Rather than meeting the challenge of telling a story (that was both factual and historical) whereby a married couple took on the might of the main churches in Ireland in the 1950s, this film explores the conse-

4 Pat Murphy quoted in Gerardine Meaney, *Nora*, p. 14.   5 Interview with Jim Sheridan, *Rattlebag*, RTÉ Radio 1, 24 October 2002.

quences of Protestant Sheila Cloney's actions for her and her children when she flees her home, having left her Catholic husband following her rejection of Catholic doctrine and its dictates. It could be argued that while this film started out as a political film, it became a conventional love story against the backdrop of a significant historical detail, the familiar episode in Fethard-on-Sea in 1957. However, the opportunity to present a story about a united couple engaging in a head-on battle with the Catholic church was missed, by privileging the actions of one over the other. Consequently what it reveals is the value in Murphy's approach whereby she uses the conventions to support and subvert her story rather than slavishly allowing the codes dictate the story direction and design.

The narrative of *Nora*, however, simultaneously plays with the potential of feminist and mainstream classical narrative while subverting both. While this film distinguishes itself from previous feminist texts that were overtly political at the level of form and aesthetic approach (*Maeve* and *Anne Devlin*), it is not a classical text in the manner of mainstream film. Moving beyond traditional feminism, Murphy appears to be working towards a post-feminist discourse but also, in keeping with the Joycean theme, she articulates this in a modernist way. In doing so, she tells a story in narrative form that conveys a progressive message and this is clearly the significant achievement of this film.

PERSONAL VERSUS POLITICAL

Central to the story told in this film is the sexual relationship between Joyce and Nora. On their first date Nora is shown as pro-active in their sexual encounters. It could be argued that this is because Nora was all too aware of the consequences of pregnancy outside of wedlock in Ireland at the time and was therefore more in control of avoiding such a situation if she guided their sexual encounters. Nevertheless, the 'first date' scene sets the tone for the rest of the film whereby mutual sexual pleasure is a key part of their relationship. Meeting in a city centre park the passage from daylight to night suggests that their courtship takes place outdoors and over a long time. Evoking the cityscape, they descend steep steps that lead to a secluded, dark alley. Here they start kissing. Nora reaches for Joyce's trousers and puts her hand inside. After bringing him to orgasm, she concludes the scene with the request, 'Do you have a hanky, Mr Joyce?' Sexual guilt or fear is not associated with Nora at any point in the film although there are some references to Joyce's sexual guilt, particularly when he is visited by his mother's apparition. His subsequent behaviour with their friend Roberto Prezioso also suggests a problematic response to his own sexuality and relationship with Nora. His emotional disposition is hindered by jealousy and a desire for control yet within the narrative these issues are presented as his not hers. Nora, while obviously affected by his emotional state, does not take on his problems as hers to fix.

From the outset, the narrative of *Nora* is distinctive in its portrayal of women of this era. As the subsequent plot details reveal, Nora leaves her employment to run off with her lover, unwed, to continental Europe. Challenging preconceptions of early twentieth-century Ireland, Murphy's text presents a refreshing modernist tale, one that attempts to give voice to female sexuality, a discourse that has been absent by and large in Irish visual culture. While Gerardine Meaney points out that 'Murphy's work mirrors a current interest in the history of spaces of sexual dissidence and difference within Irish culture and society', Pat Murphy suggests that Nora Barnacle could not have been that unique, firmly believing that there were women who were able to form decisions and create their own lives despite societal norms and traditions, 'the way women do all the time'.[6] Thus it could be argued that Murphy is telling a story that is far more representative than the critics have acknowledged and, rather than conveying the 'woman ahead of her time' message, Murphy is unravelling a hidden history that has contemporary resonances concerning female sexuality, echoing the aspirational intention of telling Anne Devlin's story which is similarly concerned with the common role women played in Irish historical rebellion.

The letters that Nora and Joyce exchange detail in a most intimate way their sexual relationship. While the letters that Nora wrote to Joyce are not available in the archives, Murphy does not doubt that they exist. The way Joyce writes, as if in dialogue, suggests that this discourse was two-way. Using the device of letters to illustrate the closeness of their relationship, Murphy says that in

> the movie it's a time when they are physically separate, yet you are aware of an incredible closeness between them. I feel they used the letters to hold on to each other when they were physically apart. So the most sexualized parts of the movie in terms of their relationship is actually not when they're together, it's when they are apart from each other. That really interested me.[7]

Avoiding the counterposing of opposites in this love story, the exchange of letters details both the positive and negative aspect of their relationship. Not only is the representation of female sexuality progressive and honest, the portrayal of a heterosexual relationship with all its complexities sets this film apart from its Irish cinematic counterparts, and continues the feminist path towards post-feminism.

6 Gerardine Meaney, *Nora*, p. 8.   7 Pat Murphy quoted in Gerardine Meaney, *Nora*, p. 70.

PUBLIC VERSUS PRIVATE

While I am arguing that this film is a post-feminist text, a love story based on
equality, this is not to say that it is a romance story without conflict. Clearly
Joyce's jealousy, as it manifests itself for the first time when Nora attends the
concert with his friend Cosgrave (Daragh Kelly), is an obstacle to their relationship and thus one source, possibly the main source, of conflict. Even though
Joyce arranged the escort himself, seeing Nora with Cosgrave sends him into
an irrational state of jealousy. By choosing to tell the story along these lines,
Murphy identifies Joyce's jealousy as one of the obstacles that have to be overcome as they develop in their relationship. However, the narrative, by main-
taining Nora's character in a dominant position, clearly positions Joyce's jealousy as his flaw, his obstacle to overcome. Nora doesn't take it on board or
identify with it, neither does she leave him as a consequence of this action.

Giving expression to the most intimate parts of their relationship through
the narrative devices of voice-over and personal letters is a trait of Murphy's
style, experienced before in *Anne Devlin*. However, rather than confining such
intimacies to the private sphere, Joyce's compulsive jealousy often catapults
their privacy into the public realm. When Joyce returns to Dublin to open
Ireland's first cinema, the Volta, his jealousy seems to grow and intensify. He
writes a letter to Nora accusing her of being unfaithful. As she is reading it
to herself, Joyce's brother Stan (Peter MacDonald) asks, 'is there something
wrong, Nora?' She hands him the letter and, as he reads quietly to himself,
she says, 'read it out, read it out where he asks if Giorgio is really his son,
read it out where he asks who else fucked me before he did'. She continues,
'people in Dublin are laughing at him for taking on a girl many men have
enjoyed, nice isn't it? That's your brother, the great writer!' This sequence is
particularly pertinent given that internal focalization is a narrative device that
reveals the interiority of the character. Murphy combines it with a device that
makes what is most private, manifestly public, by externally focalizing it
through Nora's dialogue.[8] Later Joyce refuses to come back to her until she
threatens to have Lucia baptized. When she receives the letter that announces
his return, she says to Stan, 'I knew I'd best him at this writing game'.

Despite living apart and having the destructive powers of jealousy impact-
ing relentlessly on their relationship, Murphy portrays them as managing to
conduct a sexual relationship, Joyce masturbating in the projection room of
his new cinema in Dublin while reading her letters and she doing the same,
at the other side of Europe. Unlike classical narrative that portrays such negative emotional states (i.e. jealousy) in polarized terms such as persecutor/
victim, *Nora* manages simultaneously to represent the destructive force of jeal-

8 The terms 'internal' and 'external focalization' are derived from Edward Branigan, *Narrative
comprehension and film* (London, 1998).

ousy alongside the ability still to engage in the act of love. What complicates the narrative structure of this film is the disavowal by Murphy of the simplistic polarization of emotional feeling that ideologically-driven texts often perpetuate. In the 1970s, feminist film theory identified the approach in Hollywood classical narrative cinema which relies on the confrontation of opposites (often along the lines of good versus bad) to express conflict, ensuring that the patriarchal, bourgeois ideological version of social order and the status quo is restored and reinforced by the end of the film. While feminist film sought to challenge this, sometimes the cinematic results had the effect of simply reversing the terms of the opposition. What makes the text of *Nora* particularly interesting is that Murphy rejects the structure of opposites to create dramatic tension and articulates a narrative that explores conflict by portraying two opposite states simultaneously rather than pitting the two states against each other.

Jealousy and adultery are closely entwined facets that threaten to unravel the relationship and undermine the argument that this film provides a progressive expression of equality. However, as Meaney states '[t]here are large and fascinating differences of interpretation of the significance of adultery in the Joycean imaginary between [David] Lloyd and Murphy, which arises from their equally different interpretations of female sexuality. Murphy is very clear that Nora cannot be defined antithetically, as the opposite of repression or convention'. Quoting Murphy as saying that '[s]ometimes people like Nora are represented in cinema and in literature as this earthy kind of sex goddess and that is just not all she is. It diminishes and limits her to propose that what liberates her from being a repressed, oppressed Irish woman is no more than the opposite of that image'. Examining the Prezioso affair in the film, Meaney argues that Nora's ultimate fidelity is to herself. In Murphy's reading of this episode, 'it is precisely because Nora refuses adultery that she maintains her sexuality and identity independent of her lover'.[9] Similar to the way she deals with female expression and identity in *Anne Devlin*, Murphy appropriates the feminist tool of silence and identifies Nora's power with the way she chooses to respond to the Prezioso affair.

POVERTY AND WEALTH – A STATE OF MIND

The narrative portrays Nora and Joyce at their happiest when they have nothing and are devoid of material possessions. This is not an uncommon device of mainstream narrative; a deep, loving relationship is often portrayed as anathema to material wealth, a traditional moral that is widespread in fairy-tales and myth-making. The ideological myth of linking poverty and happiness that

9 Gerardine Meaney, *Nora*, p. 61.

emerged in Ireland from the de Valera era has only recently been debunked, notably by Frank McCourt in his autobiographical novel *Angela's Ashes* (1996). In *Nora*, however, poverty is not employed as a device that lifts Nora and Joyce to a higher emotional plane. Negating the trend in cinema towards 'heritage' where the aesthetics of the picturesque dominate, Pat Murphy argues that the costumes are used as a kind of narrative, and that in the film flamboyance is a gesture against poverty.[10] When Nora and Joyce are evicted from their apartment and Giorgio gets hold of Joyce's writings, scribbling on them with a crayon, rather than portraying this as a double catastrophe, Nora laughs it off. They meet in a hotel; Nora has already ordered and has champagne chilling on the side. Joyce greets her and, looking at the spread on the table, suggests in an off-hand way that there's one month's salary before them. Nora shows him the defaced writings; he tells her that he has just handed in his notice at the language school. 'Is it my turn for bad news?', she replies, informing him of their eviction. True to their form she declares that 'we are staying here tonight'. Viewing them through a modernist prism, Murphy says '[y]ou go to the most expensive hotel, you buy new clothes and then you even stay in the hotel. I think it's very "them". I think it's quite a modern take on them so it's not about trying to slavishly recreate the period'.[11] Murphy plays with the trope of poverty, not idealizing it but rather subverting its potential to dominate.

At the end of the film when Nora and Joyce are re-united as a couple and decide to return to Europe together, Joyce says, broke again, 'I don't actually know how we are going to get back to Trieste, Stanislaus was supposed to send us some money'. Rather than being an obstacle to their future it is incidental to their story. What is important is that they are united and the audience can only assume that the rest will fall into place. As Harvey O'Brien states, '[t]he relationship issues between them and especially for Nora have been resolved satisfactorily as far as the narrative is concerned when the movie ends, and the rest of the adventure is for the viewer to pick up on by reading some books'.[12]

EXPRESSING EQUALITY

The scene illustrating Joyce questioning Nora about being pregnant sheds further light on the dynamic that Murphy portrays as she articulates an equality discourse. 'The landlady thinks you are pregnant', Joyce says from the bedroom door as Nora lies in bed at the other side of the room. Nora doesn't know for sure but suggests that the food is making her sick. 'Maybe you should write to your mother', Joyce says. 'What for?', she asks. 'For help', to

10 Pat Murphy interviewed by Ruth Barton, 'Portrait of a lady', *Film Ireland*, 75 (April/May 2000), pp 12–15. 11 Ibid. 12 Harvey O'Brien, Review of *Nora*, http://indigo.ie/~obrienh/nora.htm.

which she responds, 'I don't need her help'. Concluding the scene Nora says, 'It'll be alright won't it, might not be, might just be the food, I can't keep it down', thus confirming her state while also looking for reassurance. In disavowing a discourse of blame, Murphy presents this dilemma in a complex, human way. Joyce's initial reaction is denial and then he shifts the responsibility to Nora expressed through his absences and drinking. Rather than demonizing Joyce's behaviour, Murphy, by rejecting the device of pitting one character against the other, suggests that he, like Nora, is just not dealing with their predicament. In Brenda Maddox's biography, *Nora: The Real Life of Molly Bloom*, the author shows how Joyce reacted to the news of Nora's pregnancy by writing to his brother Stanislaus, asking him to sit down with Cosgrave and study some books on midwifery as he and Nora were 'adorably ignorant' about the facts of childbirth. Pointing out to his Aunt Josephine that he had not left Nora as his cynical friends had predicted, he asked her to 'write Nora a letter of instruction'.[13] In his own idiosyncratic way, through letters, he engages with the dilemma facing them, and with recourse to his friends.

One of the main challenges to interpreting this text is assessing the relationship between Nora and Joyce. An ideological reading might interpret it as one of abuse, whereby Joyce is so consumed by jealousy that he is cruel and uncaring to his partner and highly destructive of their relationship, as has been suggested by some responses directed at the film and its director.[14] Reminiscent of *Breaking the Waves* (Lars Von Trier, 1996) in which the main protagonist sets up his partner with others because he can no longer satisfy her, it is difficult to account for the behaviour of Joyce. Just as Von Trier's text may be read as misogynistic, Joyce's jealousy and expectations around male/female relations have the potential to negate the equality sought by Murphy's film. Furthermore, the absence of narratives that attempt such an 'equality discourse' means there is little by way of comparison either in the feminist film canon or mainstream cinema.

This text, it can be argued, is post-ideological (or post-feminist) by attempting to articulate a human, emotional discourse that rejects external rational explanations: rather character motivation, whether rational or irrational, comes from within the individual. While Joyce does not embrace Nora in the scene mentioned above, nor does he reject her. His response, it can be argued, is a human one to something that was not planned. His subsequent relationship with his son, Giorgio, as portrayed in the film, along with the way they are shown to

13 Brenda Maddox, *Nora: the real life of Molly Bloom* (London, 1988), p. 57.   14 Pat Murphy has observed that 'one of the things that has been said to me, particularly in the United States, is why did you make a film about a woman who is being abused by this man and who stayed with him when she should have left. I kept trying to say this isn't what abuse is … sometimes that's one of the situations where representation lags far behind and isn't flexible enough to adequately mirror what women's lives were truly like'. Quoted in Gerardine Meaney, *Nora*, p. 8.

co-parent in a modern yet not particularly responsible way, reinforces this. In
fact, both Nora and Joyce are depicted as equally neglectful.[15]

However, Nora does face her pregnancy alone. When Joyce eventually arrives
home one night after Nora sends a neighbour to find him, they lie in bed together and once again he suggests that she write to her mother for help. He accuses her of not being interested in his writing; her response is to recite, verbatim,
something he has written. Murphy does not present Nora as a victim or as a
sufferer. Nor does she present her as persecuted by Joyce, by circumstance or
by her time. Nora constantly re-asserts herself as an equal in the relationship,
regardless of outside pressures or norms. By constructing the film in this way,
Murphy articulates a discourse that is both contradictory and unifying. Through
the moments of resistance Nora displays in the text, she asserts the position of
'equal dignity' central to the philosophy of modern, liberal humanism.

Joyce's jealousy takes increasing control of him as the narrative progresses. When he goes back to Ireland to open the Volta cinema in 1909, taking
Giorgio with him and leaving Lucia with Nora in Trieste, he does not return
for more than two months. While Nora does not follow him to Ireland, she
attempts to persuade him to come home, first by issuing him with a wedding
invitation and secondly by threatening to have Lucia baptized. When he
returns, relations between them do not improve. Joyce tries to force Nora into
an affair so that he can write about it but she resists, finally leaving him when
he accuses Roberto Prezioso in public of having sex with Nora. Joyce tried to
manipulate Nora into an affair but Nora refused to be controlled. Yet Joyce
still uses it as a way of forcing a break-up. 'Did you fuck my wife?' he shouts
at Prezioso on the pier like somebody demented. It is after this incident that
Nora returns to Galway. 'This is over now', she says as she displays the inner
strength to walk away, returning to Ireland in 1912 an unmarried mother of
two. Her strength of character and state of mind are also exhibited and
expressed in the costumes she and the children wear.

Despite having made the break, she visits Joyce's publisher in Dublin to
discover why his book, *Dubliners*, has not yet been published. 'Mr Roberts,
my husband wants to know why you haven't published his book.' 'It's very
complicated, Madame, I will write again to your husband in due course'. 'You
tell me now', she says directly. 'Well, they are not things one would wish to
discuss with a lady'. 'Oh, you don't have to be afraid, myself and my husband
have no secrets' she says, reinforcing the relationship of equality that they
share despite the break-up. 'Well are you aware that one of the stories concerns a pervert?' 'Yes, of course'. 'There are also hidden meanings in these

---

15 When asked about the portrayal of their parenting skills, Murphy explains that 'the dynamic is always between Nora and Joyce and the children are peripheral to that...The facts of Nora's
life make a polarity between sexual expression and motherhood in the film inevitable'. Quoted in
Gerardine Meaney, *Nora*, p. 25.

stories that you madam may not be aware of. For example, the most recent one, "The Dead", frankly there is something dirty going on in that story if you ask me'. This blatant challenge to their personal and intimate relationship is revealed through a close-up shot of Nora. For a brief moment, what has been intensely private is revealed in public, sending Nora to a place she has heretofore resisted, separate from Joyce, and suggesting a point of no return.

However in classical narrative style, the film ends by supplanting the disequilibrium with resolution. Joyce visits Nora in Galway and finds her playing with the children on the beach. As Maeve Connolly points out, 'when they are together in her old bedroom, Nora's body language and appearance remains somewhat restrained. Instead of reacting to Joyce's provocations with her customary verbal outbursts she walks away from him, and stands outside on the street...But in sharp contrast to earlier scenes, her posture is upright and her subsequent return to the bedroom, and to the relationship, can be read as a deliberate choice'.[16] Nora has shown that she has the strength to walk away but also to return to the relationship. She does so as an equal, aware of what lies ahead. The final scene visually evokes the romantic tale whereby the two lovers, reunited walk off, hand in hand, into the sunset. Far from being a tacked-on ending to satisfy the demands for closure, Murphy plays with the classical and feminist devices that make this film difficult to classify.

CONCLUSION

If *Nora* was a feminist film told within a traditional ideological discourse the story one would expect would be a commentary on the social, cultural or political period; it would tell the story of Nora as 'a woman ahead of her time'; or Nora as 'victim of male dominance and abuse' or else it would be an attempt to reclaim an important female historical figure. Pat Murphy deviates from this feminist project in the film *Nora* by telling a love story that is framed within the structure of a post-feminist tale and the location, setting and backdrop of the film remain just that. Murphy does not attempt to be historically or chronologically true and even admits that she is sometimes factually inaccurate. It could be argued, therefore, that her concern for truth in this film is for emotional truth by telling a story about two characters who believe that love is the expression of equality and the narrative is the articulation of their journey in that direction. Murphy's rejection of a structure that determines the actions of the characters as a consequence of wider society or norms is what shifts this film away from traditional feminism in the direction of a post-

16 Maeve Connolly, 'An archaeology of Irish cinema: Ireland's subaltern, migrant and feminist film cultures (1973–1987)' (PhD thesis, unpublished, Dublin City University, 2003).

feminist discourse. Nor does the film have recourse to destiny or fate. The relationship between Nora and Joyce is constructed within the boundaries of the agents in the film – who they are and how they are defined. In Murphy's film, the relationship is delineated by the actions of the two characters – Joyce's actions push Nora away. She willingly leaves him as a consequence of his behaviour. When they are reunited, she decides to return to Europe with him. The relationship is an expression of who the two individuals are, not what society or fate determined them to be. As Meaney states, '[t]heir relationship is not outside of society nor does it have the tragic destiny usually associated in literature and film with lovers who are at one with storms and the sea. While the couple are socially marginalized, the film also celebrates the way in which they find their way in and around society'.[17]

The film reveals elements that link this film to various stages of feminist film as it developed and changed since the 1970s. The narrative reclaims a forgotten female figure and gives expression to a 'woman's story' but by appropriating and subverting classical structures, it presents a contemporary story framed in a post-feminist way. Far from being a heritage film which trivializes the past romantically, this film offers a text that plays with familiar cinematic devices yet uses them ultimately to subversive ends. Although not the function or narrative impetus of the film, *Nora* reclaims Nora Barnacle from historical oblivion, echoing Murphy's earlier film *Anne Devlin* which recreated the figure of Anne Devlin as a politically-motivated rebel. By presenting Nora as much more than the wild, primitive girl from the west, it succeeds in debunking many of the myths behind the image that is Nora Barnacle, wife of James Joyce. But it also offers a contemporary Irish love story that articulates a modern discourse, one of equality. When read in this way, *Nora* can be seen as echoing some of Murphy's earlier preoccupations, while evolving and developing her *oeuvre* by reflecting contemporary feminist issues.

17 Gerardine Meaney, *Nora*, p. 66.

The Snapper:
a contemporary crisis pregnancy?

DERVILA LAYDEN

It is striking how Irish cinema has picked up these traumatic episodes, discharging the excess that cannot be expressed in the language of the courtroom or of journalism ... In a country where both church and state paternalistically police women's bodies, it is significant that in virtually all of these films ..., paternity is thrown in doubt. The father hovers in the background, or is adrift from the action, or cannot be identified at all.[1]

Narratives of single female maternity are cast by Luke Gibbons (in the above quote) as operating on a political level, challenging a patriarchal-centred Irish state as women's previously repressed voices return, not just as voices but as a series of film narratives linked by both excess and closure with the child's birth. This latter tendency questions the possibility for these single women of having 'life after giving birth'.[2] Indeed, some of the films, notably *Hush-a-Bye Baby* (Margo Harkin, 1989) and *Reefer and the Model* (Joe Comerford, 1987), both of which end with women in labour whose outcome is uncertain, also cast doubt on the possibility of life for the child as well.

While Gibbons views these narratives in psychoanalytic terms as the return of the repressed, Fidelma Farley[3] re-examines their mother figures (particularly those of *Hush-a-Bye Baby*) as revising national and religious female icons. Both critics agree on the traumatic nature of transgression for the single women, but Gibbons reads this as rebellion against the father and the state, while Farley analyses it as self-reproach for having failed in the imitation of an impossible icon, namely the national mother/virgin mother. These readings are not mutually exclusive but they do mark two sides of the Irish maternity narrative. Stephen Frears' 1993 film *The Snapper* appears to position itself between these two narrative and critical positions. As the first Irish film to show a contemporary single mother safely delivering her child and remaining within her family unit, *The Snapper* explores the Irish maternity narrative in a new way. However, it examines the trauma of single pregnancy in a society that is not church-dom-

1 Luke Gibbons, 'On the beach', *Artforum* (October 1992), p. 13. 2 Ibid. 3 Fidelma Farley, 'Interrogating myths of maternity in Irish cinema: Margo Harkin's *Hush-a-Bye Baby*', *Irish*

inated, thus freeing this contemporary mother figure from much of the religiously-rooted trauma investigated by Farley. In its interrogation of the role of the father, it also reveals a desire to explore both the sidelining of men in other maternity narratives and the crisis of paternal identity – a crisis partly due to the breakdown of faith in patriarchy and institutions, and which is characterized by the return of the repressed identified by Gibbons.

Despite this the film has received relatively little critical attention, something which may be due both to its status as a British television feature film and its location at the beginning of Ireland's second wave or commercial cinema, rather than being part of the self-consciously independent and political films of the first wave. Academic comment positions the film within the fields of working-class and paternal narratives, but the maternal narrative is surprisingly neglected. Lance Pettit contextualizes it in terms of the 1992 abortion referendum and points to 'the social abuse that [Sharon] receives as a single mother' while noting that the film is just as interested in Sharon's father's reaction to his daughter's pregnancy.[4] This paper reads *The Snapper* not just as a film of social comment but one that takes on the yoke of the maternal narrative as it attempts to explore a middle ground between the contemporary crises of single maternity and patriarchy. In figuring the single maternity narrative as an evolving one, I also re-appropriate Gibbons' psychoanalytical approach to the maternity narrative by using an area of psychoanalysis, trauma theory, to consider the portrayal of the nature of single maternity. As I am focusing on contemporary maternity narratives, more historically-based films with similar themes such as *December Bride* (Thaddeus O'Sullivan, 1990) and *The Playboys* (Gillies MacKinnon, 1992) will not be considered, although their use of the past as a means of interrogating issues relevant to the present is part of a wider social and cinematic debate.

In a society which elevates the 'traditional' nuclear family above all else, it is unsurprising that until recently both church and state would be hostile to single maternity, and as a result it has a rather shameful history in Ireland, with single mothers being hidden, punished and demonized[5]. The difficulties of reconciling traditional notions of sexuality and maternity with the modernization process came to the fore in the 1980s with two particularly controversial cases (one of infanticide; the other of a teenager dying in labour[6]) and the start of a series of divisive referendum campaigns that continued for almost twenty years.[7]These clashes were indeed the return of the repressed as char-

University Review, 29:2 (1999), pp 219–37.   4 Lance Pettitt, *Screening Ireland: film and television representation* (Manchester, 2000), p. 123.   5 The Magdalene laundries were institutions where 'fallen' girls went to have their babies but were often kept for many years afterwards as their families were unwilling to sign them out are the clearest examples of this.   6 The Joanne Hayes case and the Anne Lovett case both occurred in 1984 and are outlined in Luke Gibbons, 'On the Beach'.   7 Though outlawed by statute law since the nineteenth century, the first abortion

acterized by Gibbons and this cultural anxiety about single maternity manifests itself in Irish cinema, particularly in the film's ending coinciding with
the birth of the child. In a move echoing the increasing legal[8] and social focus
on the single pregnant woman, the span of *The Snapper*'s narrative is shrunk-
en to that of the pregnancy term, thus intensifying the experience of pregnancy. Although the central character of *The Snapper* is Sharon Curley (Tina
Kellegher), the film focuses on her only as expectant (and finally as actual)
mother, confining her representation to that of her pregnancy. This is in contrast to the inclusion of other material in the earlier films – the teenage sexual
development narrative in *Hush-a-Bye Baby*, the other characters and social
dimensions of *Reefer and the Model*, the post-childbirth re-incorporation of
the transgressive woman into the social order in *December Bride* and *The
Playboys* – representations which provide opportunities for deeper examina-
tions of the social dimensions to the pregnancies.

The fact that the stages of pregnancy come to a successful conclusion in
The Snapper, with the child's safe delivery and the arrival of the chaotic but
welcoming Curley family to the maternity hospital, suggests a progression
within filmic pregnancy narratives. But this happy ending should not distract
from the difficulty of Sharon's journey through pregnancy, because, although
the child's future within a family unit is more certain, it is hard-won.
Additionally, the film's generic origins in comedy should not distract us from
the traumas evident within it. Laughter is not just the register of fun, it is
also the register of hysteria. Trauma theory, a field of enquiry that links psychoanalytic theory with history,[9] points to the fact that laughter can be an indication of trauma:

referendum in 1983 enshrined in the Constitution a notion of the equal right to life of mother
and unborn infant, thus seeking to ensure that the legislature would not provide for abortion
under any circumstances. In 1992, following the so-called 'X' case where a schoolgirl became
pregnant after alleged abuse but her right to travel was questioned despite the fact that she was
suicidal, a further three referenda were held. The outcome permitted women to travel, allowed
abortion information to be distributed in Ireland but refused to invalidate the threat of suicide
as a threat to the mother's life. In March 2002, another referendum was held attempting to
remove the threat of suicide as grounds for abortion but this was again defeated following a con-
fusing and divisive campaign where both pro-choice and strongly pro-life campaigners ended
up advocating a no vote. In the latter case, this was due to doubts over whether the abortion
bill allowed or banned the morning-after pill.   8 At one stage during the 1992 referendum campaign, people joked (not entirely without foundation) that women leaving the country would
have to take a pregnancy test before being allowed to board the plane/ferry. This focus reduces
woman to merely an agent of reproduction, subordinating her to the (potential) foetus she carries.   9 Trauma theory originated from studies of war veterans and holocaust survivors. It is
characterized by the study of recurrent memories or traces of traumatic events and investigates
how trauma survivors present or elide these recurrences as they seek both to express their personal history and move beyond it. The field has also expanded to consider more private traumas, particularly in relation to feminist trauma theory. Laura S. Brown, 'Not outside the range:

Laughter occurs as shock because it occurs semiotically as language, and as language, laughter is traumatic because it always refers to its inability to occur as anything other than a compulsively repeated reference that is never allowed to come to rest in the fullness of a final meaning. The laughter of language can only refer, infinitely and compulsively, that is, traumatically, to its inability to reach the fullness of pure thought and being from which it is infinitely separated.[10]

But laughter is not only an indicator of trauma, it can also be a way of negotiating one's way through it[11] and the situation of the film within the comedy genre signals the potential for Sharon and her family to effect such negotiation. The study of recurrence and repetition – with the aim of moving towards recovery and the ability to leave behind the traumatic event – is a particular feature of trauma theory. In representing the single pregnant woman, *The Snapper* is working through a national trauma that has already been much dealt with in filmic narratives, and is also presenting the particularities of Sharon's very personal trauma. Her pregnancy is presented as a series of traumas – cued variously by laughter, tears and the invention of her own conception narrative as she progresses through it. Much of her trauma centres around the process of telling, highlighting the socially-created nature of her trauma and the strategies she uses to approach gradually her traumatic memory – a memory which, like pregnancy itself, grows until it reaches a crisis point, after which it is delivered and separate, outside of her body, capable of being named. She successfully deals with this memory well before her delivery date, and it is this that allows her to progress towards the birth.

The first trauma is telling her family about the pregnancy, and the film uses a heightened aural register to represent her distress, foregrounding her nervous breathing and fading out the sounds of the squabbling family as she approaches the kitchen. She then blurts out the bare facts of her condition and there are a few questions but no real discussion. Sharon's father, Dessie (Colm Meaney) says, 'I should give out, I suppose – or throw a wobbler or

one feminist perspective on psychic trauma' in C. Caruth (ed.), *Trauma: explorations in memory* (Baltimore, 1995), pp 100–12, takes issue with the practitioner's definition of trauma as 'outside the range of human experience'. She points out that definitions of normal experience are based on the experience of the (male) dominant class and definitions of trauma are based on public events where the victims are not seen as contributing to their own traumatic experience, and argues for a recognition of both private actual trauma and insidious trauma (fear of the potential, yet very real, dangers faced by marginalized groups). 10 Kevin Newmark, 'Traumatic poetry: Charles Baudelaire and the shock of laughter' in C. Caruth (ed.), *Trauma: explorations in memory* (Baltimore, 1995), p. 251. 11 See my chapter on the use of comedy to overcome past trauma in relation to Northern Ireland film, 'Imagining the future: post-Troubles comic fiction' in Kevin Rockett and John Hill (eds), *National cinema and beyond: Studies in Irish Film 1* (Dublin, 2004), pp 105–14.

something, but what's the point?' Somewhat uselessly, he points out that if she had come to them before she got pregnant, they could have done something about it. The dynamic of the scene shifts between anger and tears (even the dog seems to sense the trauma and starts barking incessantly) but there is little sympathy for her. While in contemporary Ireland the single mother is no longer hidden in a convent or other institution until the baby is born and most probably adopted, there seems to be no appropriate words or new ways of talking about or dealing with the situation. Dessie's ineffectiveness as a father figure or leader is illustrated by his response – he decides to go to the pub. In a somewhat late attempt to bond with his daughter, and one that does not work particularly well – once again highlighting his ineffectiveness, he invites Sharon to join him for a drink. Sharon's mother Kay (Ruth McCabe) is shocked at the pregnancy and feels that this news deserves a more considered response, but, she, too, does not know what the response should be, and is concerned above all else with what they will tell the neighbours. This allows both Dessie and Sharon to move the focus away from Sharon's pregnancy, using the strategy of avoiding personal blame by listing other people who have already broken the rules – effectively an approach which denies the traumatic nature of the event.

Despite this avoidance of blame there is a staged release of the news, consistent with it being somewhat shameful. Sharon and her parents decide not to tell the other children immediately, and when they are about to tell the rest of the family, Kay laughs – an indicator of her own trauma, of the shock that she cannot yet assimilate. Although the younger members of the family greet the news with delighted surprise ('that's massive',[12] her youngest sister exclaims) or indifference ('is that all?' her bored younger brother adds), while her older brother, a soldier, who returns from abroad later in the film, believes that family honour is at stake, and asks, 'do you want me to sort him out for ya?'. As Sharon by that stage has told everyone and is visibly pregnant, she has already moved past the initial trauma and is able to dismiss (and devalue) this offer of patriarchal protection and tells her brother to grow up.

Sharon's 'telling' trauma then moves beyond the family to her group of friends. The dynamics of this group (four people, with two sub-groups of two) are similar to those in *Hush-a-Bye Baby* but the close friendship is much more supportive in the earlier film and there is less attempt to cover up the trauma. In the 'telling' scene of that film, Goretti (Emer McCourt) sits on the beach staring out at the sea, apparently seeking inspiration as to how to deal with the pregnancy that she has so far concealed. Her friend Dinky (Cathy Casey) arrives full of concern ('Dear God, Goretti. What's wrong?'), offering comfort. When Goretti eventually confesses to her, she bursts into tears and is pulled into a protective hug by Dinky. The scene is bracketed on either side

12 Dublin slang for 'great' or 'wonderful'.

by sounds of the sea and images of nature and these seem to resonate with an acceptance of Goretti's condition as natural. The music within the scene is a haunting, two-chorded stringed theme that suggests the rhythmic in/out of breathing and of waves. Yet despite these associations with natural processes this musical theme is used throughout the film as a cue for the emotional and physical distress connected with her pregnancy, an explicit highlighting of the clash between social norms and natural law. Dinky, the only other person in the scene, echoes nature's acceptance by her refusal to pass judgement on her friend. Goretti's spontaneous confession is in marked contrast to the 'telling' scene with Sharon's friends in *The Snapper*, which is carefully stage-managed by her. In an earlier scene, having just told her parents of the pregnancy, she responds to her friend's question as to whether she has any news with a blithe 'No, not really'. When she tells them some days or weeks later, she waits for a gap in the conversation – which is presented less as conversation then as cackles of laughter – before casually saying 'I'm pregnant – did I tell yis?' This is greeted firstly by laughter, then by stunned silence and finally by a round of rather insincere congratulations, the last one of which has the rider 'yeh thick bitch yeh', followed by more laughter. It is clearly an ordeal for Sharon, who admits 'I know, it's terrible really', but instead of getting sympathy from her friends, she gets an interrogation as to the name of the father, something she is determined not to reveal. Eventually, she protests that she doesn't want to talk about it and they agree to get drunk instead. This scene takes place in a rather drab, harshly-lit pub. Although surrounded by people, both they and the environment are hard, conveying a sense of surface rather than of depth. Despite Sharon's unsympathetic friends, there are occasional reminders of a more human core underneath the surface, with Jackie (Fionnuala Murphy) telling Sharon that they won't want her hanging around with them when her pregnancy starts to show as it will scare off men, but still she sticks by her friend throughout the pregnancy, both in private and in public.

There is a distinctly gendered reaction to Sharon's pregnancy. The women appear more shocked and even suggest (as Yvonne (Karen Woodley) does) that she has been stupid while the men – as part of the film's recovery of the paternal – take it more in their stride. This is verbalized by Dessie's friend Lester (Brendan Gleeson) who says 'sure having a baby is the most natural thing in the world', although the value of this assurance is undercut by Lester's loyalty and anxiety to please. This gendered difference is not just in reacting to the pregnancy, but it also manifests itself when the father, George Burgess (Pat Laffan) becomes known. Even though Burgess is married, it is Sharon who is regarded as having breached the moral code, and it seems to be women who most diligently police this code, while men are seen to boast and tell jokes about it. Similar gender policing is evident in *Hush-a-Bye Baby* where the girls themselves make a distinction between the nice girls who do not have sex and the bad girls who do. While they giggle at sexually-active men (the uncryptically named Clitoris Allsorts character, for example), they use the word 'slut' to describe a woman who does the same. Women are expected to say 'no' (as we notice from early scene between Goretti and her boyfriend Ciaran (Michael Liebmann), but are constantly under pressure to say 'yes' and yet are regarded as stupid for getting 'caught'.

In *The Snapper*, women are no longer expected to say 'no' – they are expected to be sexually-active – but the underlying value system does not seem to have changed. Although both sexes objectify the other through the use of the term 'ride' as a sexual descriptor, it is Sharon who bears all the blame for her condition. It is also Sharon who points out her father's double standards when he objects to the term being applied to 'daughters' ('Don't be thick, Da, all girls are daughters.'), so she also carries the role of educator – a role thrust upon her because of her situation as a pregnant woman at the junction of two conflicting value systems. This was also a role that was thrust on Goretti. While Dessie only considers whether he should 'throw a wobbler' at the news of Sharon's pregnancy, Ciaran actually does, alienating Goretti so completely that by the time he has come to accept it, she no longer sees marriage to him as a solution.

The difference between the two films with regard to attitudes towards pre-marital sex is also linked to the presence or absence of the Catholic church. *Hush-a-Bye Baby* is suffused with church buildings, clerical authority and the cult of the Virgin Mary. Indeed, a priest calls to the house while Goretti and Ciaran are making love, a sort of *clericus interruptus*. Goretti's trauma is clearly induced by both the religious mores imposed by the Catholic church and by the social valorizing of the mother/virgin figure.[13] The lack of options available to her is emphasized in a radio discussion about abortion where a church campaigner celebrates the abortion ban and the increased protection this affords to the unborn child. The other discussant points out that the ban has only increased the fear and isolation of pregnant Irish women. Goretti is seen to be afraid even to be found listening to such a discussion,[14] let alone confessing her pregnancy. *Hush-a-Bye Baby* also engages with the issues of infanticide, induced miscarriage and desertion of the new-born baby – all possibilities for the single mother who cannot reveal her pregnancy to society, yet cannot choose to get an abortion. The film is set in 1984, when the first constitutional amendment on abortion was being enacted, apparently ruling out abortion as a legislative option. Interestingly, Goretti voices the very thought that led to the right to travel (for an abortion because of a suicide risk) being granted in the 'X' case when she tells her friend that that she wants to die. And

13 See Fidelma Farley, 'Interrogating myths of maternity in Irish cinema: Margo Harkin's *Hush-a-Bye Baby*', 1999, for a detailed discussion of the religious and Mariolatry references in this film.   14 The reasons for this are two-fold; both the nature of the discussion itself and the fact that it is in English (she is in the Gaeltacht).

although she does not attempt suicide, she tries to induce a miscarriage, but wonders if miscarrying would be an abortion, too, an indication of the lack of sexual education in Ireland for such women.

In contrast, there is no mention of religion at all in *The Snapper*, although there are frequent references (by George Burgess or others in joking imitation of him) to swearing on the bible, and there is a small crucifix in the Burgess's hallway. His weakness and vacillation are linked to a falseness and hypocrisy about religion, which is implicitly contrasted with the down-to-earth and up-front Curley family. Within the Curley home, the only presence of religion is a picture (it appears to be a calendar) of the Virgin Mary holding the baby Jesus that we see on the wall behind Kay in the 'telling' scene. The juxtaposition of the head and shoulders of both women has the effect of comparing Kay's situational shortcomings with the Virgin Mary's divinely-assisted maternal plenitude: Mary cradles the baby Jesus while Kay is divided from her daughter by a table and cannot offer the solace associated with motherhood or with the Virgin Mary. Although Kay wonders if they should tell the other children that what Sharon did was wrong, religion is not mentioned in this scene. For a country where public debates on morality have been so influenced by the church, this silencing of the church voice is very significant and, as audiences, we implicitly read the contrasting church view into the narrative. Yet, Sharon's parents do not pass on this moral judgement to the other children, who accept her pregnancy uncritically. Abortion is definitely ruled out from the start by Sharon herself, although it is not condemned in the strict terms that it is in *Hush-a-Bye Baby*. Yet *Hush-a-Bye Baby* allows a space for the dissenting voice through the mechanism of the radio interview, while *The Snapper* refuses to engage in debate on this topic or consider this as a possible option for Sharon. Again, a contemporary audience very recently exposed to the 1992 abortion referendum debates read the sub-text of those debates into the film, thus leaving space for the viewer's personal morality.

Both Goretti and Sharon must deal with the trauma of unexpected pregnancy, but while Goretti cannot admit her actual pregnancy, Sharon cannot admit the circumstances surrounding hers and this difference is reflected in their traumatized imaginings. Goretti's disturbed nightmare visions occur twice in *Hush-a-Bye Baby* – after hearing the abortion discussion on the radio and at the end of the film as she goes into labour. Her nightmares are flashes of her growing pregnancy, intercut with blood-pulsing close-ups and with the image of the Virgin Mary. Likewise, Sharon has two visions: one is a drunken imagining of the reaction to her pregnancy, the other is a flashback to the actual scene of the conception. The first is comic, substituting the reproachful gaze of the Virgin Mary in *Hush-a-Bye Baby* with the accusing faces and voices of gossiping neighbours, who are mostly women. Sharon enjoys imagining their shocked tones and laughs out loud, but she then stops as her laughter brings her back to the memory of the conception. Later in the film, the full memory returns as she hears Dessie's reaction to speculation that George Burgess was the father. She blocks her ears but his roars of Burgess's name from downstairs are the cue for the flashback to a drunken night when Sharon can hardly stand and Burgess's enquiry as to whether she is all right quickly turns into a car bonnet coupling during which Sharon is only barely conscious. She cries and keeps her ears blocked but the memory replays in her mind as we hear Burgess say 'that was A1 – good girl' and we see him pocketing her knickers as a souvenir before returning to the party, leaving her to stumble home. In some ways, Sharon's situation is potentially more traumatic (and certainly more morally problematic) than Goretti's. Although Goretti's youth and isolation exacerbate her trauma, she is in a relationship (albeit one where the pregnancy is not, at least initially, supportively received) where sex was consensual; Sharon's more contemporary trauma follows a possibly non-consensual (and less than) one-night stand. It is the absence of the church and the presence of family that allows Sharon to work through her trauma.

Family is presented as much more durable than friendship, which is seen to be superficial and unable to move beyond laughter in order to deal directly with the trauma itself. The laughter of her friends takes the place of the reproach of her parents (which would have been expected in earlier pregnancy narratives) but there is no real support network to help Sharon. Her friends never seem to evince real sympathy for Sharon and she seems to have no one with whom she can discuss the physical details of her pregnancy. Her remark that 'you should see the state o' me nipples' is followed by her friend's rapid change of subject with 'Frank Kinsella's a ride, isn't he?' Such is Sharon's sensitivity concerning the as-yet unnamed father that she assumes this is a suggestion that it is Frank Kinsella and she counters aggressively, 'it wasn't him, right' followed by a tirade as to who else is not the father. After the revelation that Yvonne's father, George, is the father, family loyalties prevail over friendship and Sharon is left with just Jackie as a friend. Yet, Sharon never acknowledges the full truth even to her.

Because Sharon can tell people about her pregnancy, her trauma is much more externalized than it is in the earlier films and the focus is on how she constructs (or avoids) the pregnancy narrative for herself. Having acknowledged her pregnancy, she initially refuses to talk about how or by whom she became pregnant. This strategy frustrates those around her but works until George Burgess leaves home, giving others the fuel for a different narrative. Having dealt with her initial trauma, a new trauma is created by this narrative which leaves her exposed to constant taunts and derision. Sharon refuses to acknowledge the truth of this narrative and creates her own – the Spanish sailor story. Trauma theory tells us that the ability to elide or distort the story is part of understanding it, part of the 'cure'. No-one really believes the story but this (temporary) construction of an alternative reality is an important part of her recovery process and allows her to refute the middle-aged crisis narrative of George Burgess (framed by him in carefully practised and clichéd words). Having done this, she can then push him out of the narrative altogether, telling him that he was 'off-target'.

The revelation of the father is a trauma for the rest of her family, too, almost all of whom defend her honour in some way, generally by physical means.[15] This lashing out at others seems to be their way of expressing their anger; although they blame Sharon for exposing them to ridicule, they won't easily admit it. Having dismissed George Burgess from the narrative, Sharon becomes the active agent in the film, realizing that she also needs to offer her family a way out of their trauma. Accepting responsibility for her actions and offering a pragmatic apology to Dessie for shaming the family is the turning point in the narrative, the cue for complete family reconciliation and the tacit acknowledgment by both Sharon and Dessie that George Burgess is the father. It is worth noting not only that it is Sharon's actions which bring about this reconciliation, but that she effectively manipulates and appeases Dessie, much like a parent does with a recalcitrant child (a point which will be returned to shortly). Having faced and eventually even spoken of her own trauma, Sharon is strong enough by the film's close to resolve that she will name the baby Georgina and her laughter at this idea contains both the shock of others and the trace of her own trauma.

It is a commonplace at this stage to refer to the absent or inadequate male in Irish family narratives and George Burgess is certainly that. However, Sharon's pregnancy offers Dessie (another inadequate male) a second chance at fatherhood. Indeed, after the turning point he becomes the more important parent as he takes on the maternal role, too, as Kay recedes into the background. His interest in the pregnancy amounts to virtual participation in it, his parenting of the other children becomes more responsible (he trains Darren's cycling team) and his appearance even changes as we see him wearing a suit and tie in the final scene. Somehow he has become simultaneously more masculinized and more feminized. The sequence that cuts between the baby feeding and Dessie's pint in the pub seems to establish a parental bond between them. However, this sequence can equally be read as Sharon becoming the parent – not just of her own child but also of her own father. Taken together with Sharon's education and manipulation of Dessie, it seems that he has somehow become the child. Thus, gender and chronology are distorted as Dessie is masculinized, feminized and infantilized all at the same time.

This distortion of chronology and Dessie's opportunity for rebirth returns us to the issue of life-cycle and hence to the consideration of *The Snapper*'s place in the cycle of pregnancy narratives. These narratives taken as a group

---

15 Craig breaks windows in the Burgess's house, Kay hits Mrs Burgess, Kimberley scratches her schoolfriend (and – the ultimate injury – scribbles on her sums), and Dessie provokes a brawl in the pub.

offer a view of Irish society and its development in relation to the issue of single maternity. The films all end with childbirth but in chronological order these births are respectively marginalized and without family, within the family but unknown to them, and within a supportive family.

The final scene of *Reefer and the Model* shows Teresa alone on the trawler, heading towards Reefer who is rowing to meet her. As her labour suddenly starts, she seems desperately alone as a combination of the sea and the very male environment of the trawler seem to be carrying her away from the world. As the pains worsen, she lashes a rope to the ship's wheel to keep it on course for the rendezvous with Reefer and to brace herself for the labour pains. Taken over entirely by the child inside her, she is unable to help Reefer board the ship and it smashes his small rowboat in pieces, leaving him thrashing around in the cold, grey Atlantic. As the film ends, the trawler is drifting on the sea leaving him further and further behind as a haunting Dolores Keane song suggests both a funeral keening and a mythical dimension to the film's refusal of the life offered by Ireland at the time. It is the soundtrack throughout this scene that provides much of the power, as Teresa's screams are heard over the chugging of the engine and a traditional chanted ballad of male voices with a slow bodhrán beat. This ballad stops only when her screams cease (and they are not replaced by the screams of a new born infant) and then the Dolores Keane song begins. As an instrument that new pupils are told to start playing with the use of their heartbeat as guide, the final beat of the bodhrán seems to indicate the end for both mother and child. The counterpointing of Teresa's screams with male voices, of the trawler against the sea, of Reefer in the sea against the funeral ship sailing towards the looming headland, all suggest a complex, almost impossible existence for both women and marginalized men in Ireland.

The final scene in *Hush-a-Bye Baby* takes place in Goretti's bedroom. The haunting stringed theme starts again as Goretti's voiceover recites the Memorarae (a prayer of intercession to the Virgin Mary). The scene recalls Goretti's earlier nightmare while in the Gaeltacht – a nightmare brought on by the radio discussion of single pregnancy and her awareness and fear of the physical changes within her. This fear (signalled by her horrified fascination with breaking eggs and their effect on the white – thus virginal – flour into which they are released) manifests itself in her nightmares and in the final labour as an almost alien possession of the body from inside. Unlike Teresa's instinctive reaction to the start of her labour, Goretti remains caught between nightmare and reality, unable to really believe that her body has been taken over by this pregnancy. While Teresa's labour is gritty and real, Goretti's is intercut with images of the Virgin Mary, of Goretti herself dressed as Mary, and of transparently-skinned fingers which show the blood pulsing through them as they clutch the pregnant belly. The physical terror is related to primeval maternal anxiety (exacerbated by her youth and the lack of anyone experienced to discuss it with) and overlaid with a mental terror caused by religious guilt and social expectations. Her screams

eventually wake her parents up to the reality – that she is in labour – and we
see their surprised faces before Goretti's face again fills the screen, in a final
admission of her pregnancy.

The fact that Sharon can admit her pregnancy seems to allay much of this
maternal anxiety. That this anxiety is not merely related to single maternity
can be seen by its manifestation in science-fiction (such as the *Alien* films,
1979–1997) and often in horror (*Rosemary's Baby* (1968) is an example). In
the two earlier Irish films, and particularly in *Hush a-Bye Baby*, this anxiety
is clearly linked through the use of imagery to nature, particularly water. The
opening underwater sequence of *Hush-a-Bye Baby* with its swirling movements is suggestive of drowning as well as the massing of bodily fluids in both
sex and pregnancy. The physical rhythm of the sequence takes all of these
processes outside our control as the female body appears to be possessed from
the inside by something unknown but insistently growing and finally discernible as a baby's hand. This imagery is linked to Goretti's pregnancy later
in the film, where she must conceal both the growing foetus and the fact that
her body is not menstruating. She burns the sanitary towels that her mother
buys her, avoids activities that will show her pregnancy and forces her swelling
abdomen into uncomfortably belted jeans. While in the Gaeltacht, she stares
at the sea as if it might provide some sort of answer. The sea's ebb and flow
– emphasized by the brownish-red tide mark behind her – drives home the
anxiety about her menstrual lack, the lack of the basic bodily process which
her social conditioning ensures carries such enormous weight. Indeed Goretti's
contemplation and discussions with Dinky seem to always take place near water
and these scenes are echoed by the sea scenes in *Reefer and the Model*. The
fact that the sea provided the means of escape[16] for so many pregnant women
is surely no coincidence.

The Snapper seems deliberately to shun the association between pregnan-
cy/childbirth and nature, preferring the less essentialist, more alienating but
ultimately safer environment of the urban hospital. In this environment Sharon
is reduced to a mere body but here, too, she tries to assert what control she can
over the narrative – when, with apparently little preamble, a nurse asks how
her bowel movements are, she retorts in a bored voice, 'Fine, how are yours?'
When her labour arrives, it is potentially the most traumatic of the three cinematic depictions as the child's heartbeat becomes distressed and a forceps has
to be used. Yet, her access to this clinical environment – an access not previously available to many young women concealing their pregnancies – saves her
and the child. This clinical environment has replaced nature in the earlier films

16 Many single pregnant women either chose or were forced to emigrate, usually to England.
Others (estimates suggest about 5,000 Irish women per year) go to England for abortions.
Although many such journeys are now by air, the 'boat to England' persists within the discourse.
17 Eithne Donnellan, '1 in 3 experience crisis pregnancy', *Irish Times*, 21 April 2004, p. 3.

and *The Snapper*'s only view of the sea is when Kay and Dessie stare out at it through the van window. They appear to be contemplating the likelihood of Sharon's Spanish sailor story and decide that the idea of this 'invasion' from outside is preferable to admitting the truth in their midst, itself an interesting insight into Irish society's way of dealing with trauma.

This refusal of discussion is also a wider problem in relation to pregnancy. Sharon is reduced to buying a book in order to understand her pregnancy, suggesting that the link between female instinct, or supportive community, and childbirth appears to be broken. Not only does she find the hospital and medical process alienating, but there is a complete lack of crisis pregnancy support services. She doesn't even get the friendly sympathy that was provided by Dinky in *Hush-a-Bye Baby*. Indeed, a recent survey by the Crisis Pregnancy Agency (conducted ten years after *The Snapper*) found that more than half of women who had experienced a crisis pregnancy said 'other services or supports could have made the experience easier'.[17] The same survey notes that twenty-eight per cent of women who had one or more pregnancies had experienced crisis pregnancy and that seventy-five per cent of the women who experienced crisis pregnancy chose to have the baby.[18] Sharon's pregnancy thus seems rather typical in this regard.[19] Not being married decreased as a concern over time, with only eight per cent of women whose crisis pregnancy occurred in the last ten years citing this as the main cause of the crisis. Within Sharon's age cohort generally (18–25 at age of crisis pregnancy), being too young or the pregnancy not being planned were more likely reasons for the pregnancy to be described as a crisis one. Again, Sharon's experience is very typical. Despite the fact that the pregnancy is clearly a crisis for her, this crisis is not related to being unmarried, and marriage is very quickly dismissed as an option early in the narrative. Crisis in the narrative is triggered by telling other people about the pregnancy and having to deal with their reaction to it. This reaction (and hence Sharon's trauma) comes in two stages – first the actual fact of the pregnancy, and second the identity of the father. As she tells George Burgess, 'I don't mind being pregnant but I do mind people knowing who made me pregnant'. Shortly afterwards is a scene that shows the general approval for Sharon's pregnancy when she performs a karaoke version of 'Papa, Don't Preach'. This approval dissipates remarkably quickly when the father's identity comes to light and the second (and more traumatic) stage of Sharon's crisis begins.

18 The *Irish Times* article (above) was an extract from ongoing research work into crisis pregnancy. The full report was published by the Crisis Pregnancy Agency in September 2004 and all subsequent information cited is taken from that report. See Kay Rundle et al., *Irish contraception and crisis pregnancy (ICCP) study: a survey of the general population* (Dublin, 2004). 19 It should be noted that the survey asked respondents if they had ever experienced a crisis pregnancy; many of those responding had experienced that pregnancy some time ago and before the establishment of the Crisis Pregnancy Agency in 2001.

In conclusion, I will return to my initial question as to the portrayal of the trauma of single maternity and its associated crises. *The Snapper* presents a crisis whose nature has changed as it becomes more externalized, but brings with it a new set of challenges to be negotiated. Women are no longer banished from the family for becoming pregnant outside marriage, but their trauma can be more public and our laughter at the narration of Sharon's pregnancy can be seen as a mark of our own unease at the collision of two value systems. In confronting these systems, the film offers a way out of the cycle of paternalistic repression and outburst identified by Luke Gibbons, with the role of the father (and, by extension, the church and state) no longer one of attempted control but rather becoming one of attempted understanding. Yet this attempt to recuperate the male, offering him an alternative to the traditional patriarchal role, is compromized both by Dessie's relegation to the place of a child and by George Burgess's exclusion from Sharon's narrative. By its omission of the church, the film also offers a way out of the veneration of the maternal icon, but this, too, is compromized by the sidelining of Kay within the narrative.

Although offering a potentially strong mother figure in Sharon, the film refuses to efface her difficulty in reaching this position. Society is not fully able to work through the trauma as is revealed by Dessie's compromized identity, the refusal to talk about the circumstances of the pregnancy (or the availability of other options), the differing attitudes of the community towards Sharon and George Burgess, and Sharon's lack of any real external support. The survival of the single mother and her child is a significant advance in the progress of Ireland's pregnancy narratives but the fact that this pregnancy breaks with earlier Irish films in actually producing a healthy child is not a denial of trauma; rather – like Sharon's naming decision – it is a reminder of it. However, the healthy baby is also a sign of optimism for the future. That this can only be a cautious optimism is borne out by both the Crisis Pregnancy Agency survey and the unresolved issues of paternity, maternity and sexual politics within the film itself.

'Ebony saint' or 'demon black'?
Racial stereotype in Jim Sheridan's
In America[1]

BETH NEWHALL

In her analysis of Irish director Jim Sheridan's Oscar-winning *My Left Foot* (1987), Ruth Barton notes that in a feature so driven by character, it proves essential that the film immediately 'establish the identifying traits of its central characters and, in order to achieve this, Sheridan draws on a range of existing archetypes with whom audiences might already feel some sense of familiarity'.[2] Stereotypes, like archetypes, function as cinematic devices that provide characters with an almost instant knowability and, in his most recent film, *In America* (2002), Sheridan once again relies on this type of device to facilitate his storytelling. In addition to rendering characters, and the conflicts that attend them, more easily recognizable, stereotypes serve to make the unknown or unfamiliar fathomable to those who have not experienced it first-hand. In this way, stereotypes assist in reducing exposition and drawing audiences into the world of the film. Nevertheless, invocation of stereotype is not without its potential danger. Stereotypes operate by 'reducing other landscapes, other peoples, and other values... to a normative paradigm' that can be read and understood by the uninitiated.[3] The genesis of this paradigm often occurs through the framing of the unknown, or 'Other', in terms familiar to the 'Self', or home culture.[4] Through this opposition, the figure of the Other comes to be viewed not as an individual of equal status, but as a being symbolically representative of a culture or people only understood or valued to the degree that renders it recognizable to the Self. In *Unthinking Eurocentrism: Multiculturalism and the Media*, Ella Shohat and Robert Stam argue that many stereotypes thus

---

1 This paper is distilled from 'Going to America but not getting very far: magic, race and gender in Jim Sheridan's *In America*', a dissertation submitted for the MPhil in Irish Theatre and Film at the School of Drama, Trinity College Dublin (2004). 2 Ruth Barton, *Jim Sheridan: framing the nation* (Dublin, 2002), p. 23. 3 V.Y. Mudimbe, *The idea of Africa* (Bloomington and Indianapolis/London, 1994), p. 6. 4 In discussing the stereotypical depictions of the Irish in nineteenth-century Britain, Elizabeth Butler Cullingford notes that the Irish stereotypes 'were theatrically effective because they differed from a norm called Englishness'. See 'Gender, sexuality, and Englishness in modern Irish drama and film', in Anthony Bradley and Maryann Gialanella Valiulis (ed.), *Gender and sexuality in modern Ireland* (Amherst, MA, 1997), p. 159.

operate on the assumption of 'undergirding binarisms: order/chaos, activi-
ty/passivity, stasis/movement'.[5] In this simplified breakdown, because of the
privileged position of the Self, in conjunction with lack of experience with the
culture of the Other beyond its stereotypical representation, the stereotype
becomes open to manipulation for various political, religious and moral ends,
so that the binarisms mentioned above easily translate into cultural value judg-
ments. 'Spatial tropes such as high/low devolve into symbolic hierarchies that
simultaneously embrace class (the "lower class"), esthetics ("high" culture),
the body (the "lower bodily stratum"), zoology ("lower" species), and the mind
(the "higher and lower" faculties)'.[6]

As the 'normative paradigm' of stereotype is repeated and reproduced, it
gains an authority disproportionate to its truth or reality, and the same could
be said of the hierarchical positioning encoded within the stereotype. In the
face of this authority, the ideological underpinnings that inform cultural products, and the political, religious, or philosophical agendas that these products
in turn serve, become increasingly invisible. Postcolonial theorist Edward Said
therefore cautions:

> There is nothing mysterious or natural about authority. It is formed,
> irradiated, disseminated; it is instrumental, it is persuasive; it has
> status, it establishes canons of taste and value; it is virtually indistin-
> guishable from certain ideas it dignifies as true, and from traditions,
> perceptions, and judgments it forms, transmits, reproduces. Above all,
> authority can, indeed must, be analyzed.[7]

The stereotypes employed in narrative cinema often rely on this implicit
authority, so that our enjoyment of cinema works on an exchange of sorts: the
film world 'presents itself to us as almost wonderfully benign. It offers us pleasure and makes no demands on us, except that it asks us not to think about
it'.[8] It is this aspect of narrative cinema, its apparent benignity within the 'triv-
ialized space of entertainment', that proves most dangerous, for it encourages
us not to question what we see, even when, as I argue in relation to *In America*,
what we see involves the deployment of retrograde ideas of race and gender.
In a sense, this paper takes as its project the analysis of authority Said discusses. While the much-lauded *In America* (2003) may seem innocuous, in his
depiction of the African man Mateo, director and screenwriter Jim Sheridan,
however unwittingly, invokes representational strategies common to imperialist ideology. By failing to question the film's use of stereotype, we participate
in the very process that naturalizes authority. Through the focus on *In*

---

5 Ella Shohat and Robert Stam, *Unthinking Eurocentrism: multiculturalism and the media* (London,
1994), p. 140.   6 Ibid.   7 Edward W. Said, *Orientalism* (London, 2003), pp 19–20.   8 Richard
Maltby, *Hollywood cinema* (Oxford, 2003; orig. 1995), p. 34.

America, I hope that this paper will offer a model of critique for the passive acceptance of the images relayed in classical narrative cinema, probing and elucidating the stereotypes through which regressive ideologies are propagated and perpetuated.

On a first viewing, one might find little to offend in Sheridan's story of a family that illegally immigrates to New York after the death of a young son in Ireland. Sisters Ariel (Emma Bolger) and Christy Sullivan (Sarah Bolger) take in their run-down Manhattan surroundings with wonder as their parents, Sarah and Johnny (played by Samantha Morton and Paddy Considine), settle in and struggle to make ends meet. Johnny doggedly attends auditions, trying to make a go of it as an actor, but has little luck. The death of his son Frankie has left Johnny so emotionally and spiritually bereft, he cannot muster sufficiently convincing emotion to win any roles. As Sarah tells him, 'That's why you can't get a job acting, Johnny, because you can't feel anything'. Additionally, after arriving in New York, Sarah becomes pregnant with a fourth child, and soon learns that the pregnancy could be life threatening, both for her and for the baby. The family's only good fortune comes from two unexpected sources: the friendship of a mystical Black neighbour, Mateo (Djimon Hounsou), and the three wishes that Christy believes Frankie has bequeathed to her. The crisis of the film revolves around the restoration of the family's happiness and stability, relying on Christy's wishes and Mateo's magic to save the family at crucial moments.

In her review of *In America*, Ruth Barton identifies Mateo as a sort of 'guide' for the Sullivan family as they journey toward emotional well-being.[9] This paper focuses on Mateo, whose magical intervention proves so crucial to the salvation of the Sullivan's baby, and the way in which the film constructs the mystical and spiritual elements of his character so as to make the miracle believable. In its treatment of Mateo, however benevolent he may seem, the film nonetheless embraces a representational strategy that draws upon tropes of imperialist and racist discourse. The film, in fact, relies on the ingrained assumptions that coincide with the stereotypes embodied by Mateo to render his character knowable and believable, even as that believability masks the stereotypes for what they are.[10]

Christy and Ariel are the first members of the Sullivan family to meet Mateo, and their encounters with him are characterized by his overt affirmation of his own magical propensities. For example, at dinner with the family on Halloween night, Mateo talks about how he can hear the voices of dead ancestors. When Ariel asks Mateo what they say, he considers for a moment, as if listening, then replies, 'Ah... they complain. "You don't pay attention to me. You don't feed me. I'm hungry"'. By having Mateo admit to a magical her-

9 Ruth Barton, Review of *In America*, *Film Ireland* (Jan./Feb. 2004), p. 42.   10 In my thesis, I also explore the gender stereotypes underpinning the character of Sarah.

itage, and draw on it for the benefit of the girls, the film uses Mateo's sanction
as a way of naturalizing a stereotype whereby an 'exotic' character possesses an
elevated spiritual awareness. In addition to his dialogue with the girls, the film
also reinforces the magical characterization of Mateo through other cinematic
means that begin long before Mateo first meets the two Sullivan sisters. We
hear Mateo before we see him, as the Sullivan family first enters the 'junkies'
building', the apartment house where they will make their new home in New
York. When they approach the building, Christy's voice-over intriguingly tells
us, 'We looked all over Manhattan for a place to live 'til finally we found the
house of the man who screams'. Climbing the stairs to their flat, the family
hears enraged screams coming from behind a door marked 'Keep Out'. Ariel
questions, 'Why does he scream?' to which Christy replies, 'Maybe he sees
ghosts'. Ariel, curiosity piqued, responds, 'Is this a haunted house?' Although she
does not get an answer, as the film soon reveals, in Sheridan's world, the answer
is yes, and the man lurking behind the door turns out to be the figure most in
communion with the film's ghosts. Even at this early stage, with the screams
and mention of a haunted house, the mood surrounding the unseen 'man who
screams' forbiddingly suggests a connection to the supernatural.

The first time we actually see Mateo, his appearance does nothing to allay
the frightening impression generated by the film thus far. After winning Ariel a
coveted *E.T.* doll at a carnival, Johnny playfully chases his daughters up the
stairs of their building, shouting 'Fee fie fo fum, I smell the blood of an Irish
woman'. For a brief moment, we see Mateo peer out from his uninviting doorway. As Johnny continues to play with the children, Mateo stands, brooding, listening pensively behind his door, which is painted with the face of a tiger. Later
that night, as Johnny and Sarah passionately make love, in interwoven shots, we
see Mateo raging with equal passion in his apartment below. A violent thunderstorm outside underscores the tumult within the building, throbbing drumbeats emphasize the primal nature of the scene, and Mateo contemplates a canvas,
much as a lion looks at his prey. As the shot angle switches, we see the image
on the canvas – a distorted, bleeding face painted in lurid reds and browns.
Suddenly, Mateo yells and lunges at the painting, slashing it with a knife. As
the scene continues to cut between Mateo and the Sullivans, a shot appears in
which a white canvas takes up the entire frame. Red droplets slowly hit the canvas
until an apparently bloody hand, and eventually the back of Mateo's head, come
into view as he leans across the canvas to impress his red handprint on it.

Throughout this sequence, from the frenetic arrangement of the shots to
the painting of the distorted face, the images we see and sounds we hear emphasize the primitive in Mateo's characterization. In addition to the storm and the
drumbeats, a haunting song with unintelligible (or, at least, non-English) lyrics,
generates a further feeling of otherworldliness in the scene.[11] Even the way the

11 The song is 'Tempest', sung by Lisa Gerrard and Pieter Bourne.

sequence progresses, with the disconnected shots meant to withhold information – we see Mateo tense and looking at something before we see what he sees,
the red drops splatter the white canvas before we see that it is, or the film suggests that it is, Mateo's own blood – and the intercutting with action set elsewhere, creates a sense of instability, disorganization, and violence. Mateo represents the exotic and unfamiliar, and unlike the wholesome Irish family, does
not conform to safely conventional values or codes of conduct. With such a
characterization so firmly established, long before Mateo utters any coherent
lines, his affinity with the supernatural comes as no surprise.

When Mateo finally does have dialogue in his first interactions with Christy
and Ariel, rather than the 'lonely raging madman' we have seen up until this
point, Mateo instead turns out to be more of a 'kindly uncle-figure'.[12] With the
girls, 'Mateo becomes the fairy godfather in this harsh but hopeful urban fairy
tale, the catalyst for bringing the family together and ultimately saving it'.[13] The
girls knock on Mateo's door on Halloween while trick-or-treating in the limited – and their parents hope, safe – confines of their apartment building. Shirtless
and muscular, Mateo flings his door open, shouting, 'What?' and stops abrupt-
ly when he sees the girls. Suddenly quiet, Mateo begins to talk with the children: 'This is Halloween? … Where are you from?' Christy replies, 'Ireland'.
Mateo asks, 'You came all the way to America to trick-or-treat?' Even with this
sudden gentleness, however, Mateo loses none of his primitive characterization,
or the spirituality that goes with it. Looking at Christy and Ariel as they stand
in the doorway, Mateo asks, 'There are only two of you?' Christy affirms, 'Two
girls', and Mateo ushers the girls into his apartment. Once the girls have passed,
we hear the soft sound of a gong and a rattle, primitive like the drums, but also
contributing to the mystical atmosphere, as Mateo peers out his door as though
looking for something. Because we know that Christy's answer is loaded, that
the 'two girls' used to have one brother, this brief moment taps into Mateo's
implicit spirituality to suggest that his connection to the supernatural somehow
alerts him to the presence of the lost child. Strengthening this suggestion, the
camera itself moves like the ephemeral presence Mateo seems to perceive,
switching from the shot-reverse-shot set-up of Mateo's conversation with the
girls to suddenly pull out the door and to the side, as though moving out of
Mateo's way as he leans out the door. The camera itself seems to have agency,
so that the audience momentarily assumes the point-of-view of the supernatural presence Mateo senses.

The film further generates a sense of Mateo's mystical benevolence
through cinematic imagery that constantly connects Mateo to Sarah and the

12 Review of *In America*, *The Guardian*, 31 October 2003, p. 17.   13 Wendy Weinstein, Review
of *In America*, *Rotten Tomatoes* 2004, 5 June 2004 <http://www.rottentomatoes.com/click/movie-
1125557/reviews.php?critic=columns&sortby=default&page=1&rid=1213202>.   Originally
reviewed for *Film Journal International* <http://www.filmjournal.com>.

new baby – right from the moment of the child's conception – making it nearly impossible to misinterpret Mateo's magical involvement in the survival of the infant. Over the thunderstorm in which Sarah and Johnny make love while Mateo rages below, Christy's voice-over tells us that this 'was the moment the baby was conceived', and in this sequence, the film establishes the pattern by which Mateo and the new baby will be linked, visually, throughout the film: through the movement of shots from Mateo to Sarah, and the significant focus on characters' hands. As discussed earlier, the shots in this sequence jump between Mateo and Johnny and Sarah, indicating his impending influence on the family and specifically, once Christy informs us of the conception, the new baby. Although the significance of Mateo planting his bleeding hand on a white canvas is less immediately clear, the sudden slowness of Mateo's previously manic movement confers automatic gravity on the moment, foreshadowing its thematic importance. In fact, because the drops of blood linger in the frame, imposed over some of the shots of Sarah and Johnny, it almost seems as though Mateo plants his hand on the conception, sealing his fate to that of the new baby. Critic Brett Buckalew remarks, 'in the film's most masterful passage, Sheridan gracefully cross-cuts between Johnny and Sarah's intense lovemaking, and Mateo's creation of a blood-crimson portrait (the thematic parallel becomes apparent later on)'.[14]

This connection between the hand imagery and the Sullivan's new baby comes to fruition when Sarah delivers prematurely and the newborn needs a blood transfusion, fulfilling a prediction by Mateo that the baby's 'blood is bad'. After the baby has been given new blood from Christy, and the family waits for the baby 'to show some sign of life', the film resumes the style of interwoven jump cuts used in the sequence in which Johnny and Sarah make love. Now, however, Sheridan contrasts images of the baby slowly opening its eyes and starting to cry, with Mateo on his hospice deathbed as he succumbs to an unnamed illness (the film strongly indicates that Mateo has AIDS) that has been steadily debilitating him. In the hospice, Mateo, who had been in a deep sleep bordering on coma, suddenly begins murmuring, with his eyes closed, in his native language. Although the words remain unintelligible to an English-speaking audience, the image is one with which we are familiar: the spiritual Mateo appears to mutter some sort of magical blessing or spell – a reading of the scene activated by the 'primal Black man' stereotype. As Mateo dies, the baby comes to life, and we see a close-up of the bawling infant reach out and find her parents' fingers, which they had inserted into the incubating unit. She grasps a grown-up finger in each of her tiny hands and calms. In the intercut shot, with an initial close-up on two hands, a nurse gently lowers Mateo's hand, which

14 Brett Buckalew, Review of *In America*, *Rotten Tomatoes* 2004, 5 June 2004 <http://www.rottentomatoes.com/click/movie-1125557/reviews.php?critic=columns&sortby=default&page=5&rid=123779>. Originally reviewed 29 October 2003.

she must have held during his passing, to the bed. Johnny and Sarah withdraw their hands from the incubator with much the same gentleness in the next shot. Carlo Cavagna considers that 'the juxtaposition of Mateo in the hospital at the same time as Sarah and Johnny's new born baby accounts for one of the most powerful moments in the film', and certainly, with the baby's life in the balance, much is at stake in the scene.[15] The simultaneity of Mateo's passing and the recovery of the baby, as presented in the cross-cutting sequence, indicates the causal relationship between Mateo's death and the baby's survival. The accompanying shots of the hands, however, render the miracle unambiguous, so that Mateo's death, especially given his mystical depiction, can only be read as a transferal of his life energy to that of the baby.

In these manifestations of Mateo's spirituality, Sheridan relies on stereotype to tap into an assumed cultural knowledge on the part of the audience – that African people partake of a primitive mysticism that leaves them emotionally and spiritually in tune with the supernatural world – to inform and encourage his audience's belief in the film's magic. Even before we see Mateo, his screams alert us to his special status, and once we see that he is Black, his subsequent mystical characterization becomes all the more explicable. As critic Bob Westal notes, 'In the movies, people from Africa are sometimes crazy, afflicted people are usually crazy, and artists are always crazy. So Mateo fits right in'.[16] The movie spends very little time explaining the cause of Mateo's rage, offering us just a scene between Johnny and Mateo, wherein Johnny angrily asks if Mateo is in love with Sarah. Mateo responds, 'No. I'm in love with you. And I'm in love with your beautiful woman. And I'm in love with your kids. And I'm even in love with your unborn child'. Mateo now roars, 'I'm even in love with your anger. I'm in love with anything that lives'. Realizing that Mateo's own life, therefore, must be running out, Johnny states, 'You're dying'. With almost no personal background, this scene offers the film's sole exposition for Mateo's initial scariness and his subsequent adoption of the Sullivan family, and it certainly gives us no explanation as to the source of his spiritual power. Because Mateo acts according to established stereotypes, the film expects us to accept his characterization with very little character development – such is the function of stereotype in film. I would argue, however, that the specific stereotypes Sheridan invokes, in the case of Mateo, in fact stem from racist preconceptions, so that 'Without the presence of the cardboard caricature played by Hounsou, *In America* would be merely

15 Carlo Cavagna, review of *In America*, *Rotten Tomatoes* 2004, 5 June 2004 <http://www.rottentomatoes.com/click/movie-1125557/reviews.php?critic=columns&sortby=default&page=5&rid=804297>. Originally reviewed October 2003 for *AboutFilm.Com* <http://www.aboutfilm.com>.
16 Bob Westal, Review of *In America*, *Rotten Tomatoes* 2004, 5 June 2004 <http://www.rottentomatoes.com/click/movie-1125557/reviews.php?critic=columns&sortby=default&page=1&rid=1224210>.

a reasonably competent yet ruthlessly manipulative tearjerker; with that presence, though, the film acquires an uncomfortably racist dimension'.[17]

In his depiction of Mateo, Sheridan relies on two stereotypes encoded in opposing images: the uncontrollable, beast-like savage, and the innocent, servile saint. When we first encounter Mateo, the film taunts us with only brief shots and auditory snatches of Mateo's screams, all of which build the portrait of the raging 'scary African artist'.[18] After meeting the Sullivan family, however, Mateo assumes the stereotype that will characterize him for the majority of the film, becoming entirely docile and much more like 'the Uncle Remus (naïve, congenial folk philosopher)' full of unsophisticated advice and hopeful prophesy.[19] When Mateo offers Christy a jar of coins as a Halloween treat and she protests because it's 'too much', he counsels her, 'When luck comes knocking on your door you can't turn it away'. In another scene, as Sarah and Johnny get ready for bed, he remarks that she seems happy, and Sarah replies, 'I am. It's something Mateo said ... He said everything's going to be all right... And the baby will bring its own luck'. When the baby girl is born in critical condition and needs a blood transfusion, Johnny tries to explain the situation to Sarah, who is still under the influence of anesthesia. Sarah nods as though she expected such news and reveals another of Mateo's prophesies: 'All the blood is bad. Mateo said all the blood is bad'. Even Johnny gets a bit of mystical folk wisdom from Mateo, as the two sit outside together on a winter's day. Mateo asks, 'What was Frankie like?' and Johnny replies, 'A warrior'. Mateo then says, in his native language, 'Masselo masela', which means 'A warrior who is not afraid to go to the other side'. Johnny queries, 'The other side a what?' Mateo, once again revealing his spirituality, gestures around them, 'This'. With his simple phrases and intuitive predictions, Mateo indeed comes to seem like an updated Uncle Remus for the family.

In giving his life for the sake of the family, however, Mateo's character takes on a disturbing level of martyrdom. Brett Buckalew argues that Hounsou's 'commanding' performance 'is wasted on a twisted hegemonic fantasy vision of the Black man who suffers so that the White man can succeed'.[20] In *Unthinking Eurocentrism*, Shohat and Stam identify a tradition in literature and media of limiting Black and minority characters to a subservient, even sacrificial position, in relation to their Caucasian counterparts. They argue that 'in order to be equal, the oppressed are asked to be better, whence all the stoic "ebony saints" ... of Hollywood, from Louise Beavers in *Imitation of Life* (1934 version), through Sidney Poitier in *The Defiant Ones* (1961), to Whoopi Goldberg in *Clara's Heart* (1988)'.[21] Mateo's sacrifice is not only noble, it is believable because it partakes of longstanding conventions whereby an ideal-

17 Buckalew, Review of *In America*.   18 Review of *In America*, *Guardian*.   19 Shohat and Stam, *Unthinking Eurocentrism*, p. 195.   20 Buckalew, Review of *In America*.   21 Shohat and Stam, *Unthinking Eurocentrism*, p. 203.

ized Black character willingly gives up his or her life for White characters – a telling comment on the inequality with which the media depicts the lives of minorities, as well as audiences' willingness to accept those depictions.

Mateo's assumption of the position of the 'ebony saint' dehumanizes him in other ways as well. Inherent in this depiction is the docility of the Black character, to the extent that he utterly lacks sexuality, predatory or otherwise. After Mateo meets the girls and the family invites him upstairs for dinner, in addition to donning a paint-spattered shirt, he arrives at their apartment with a colorful blanket wrapped around his shoulders, a combination that diminishes his muscularity and sexuality, yet, given the blanket's color and print, nonetheless reminds us of Mateo's exotic origins and his difference from the family. For the rest of the movie, Mateo, who spent several of his introductory scenes shirtless, always appears fully clothed. A stereotypical 'saintly Black', Mateo is 'desexualized, deprived of normal human attributes, along the lines of the "Black eunuch", cast in decorative or subservient poses'.[22] The denial of Mateo's sexuality becomes pronounced in his interactions with Sarah, especially in a scene in which Mateo plays with the children as Sarah watches. Earlier, in the action leading up to the scene in which Johnny and Sarah make love, Sarah ties a scarf around Johnny's eyes as he chases the girls around their apartment, chanting 'fee fie fo fum'. Sarah soon sends the children off to the ice cream parlor across the street where she works during the day, and where a co-worker does not mind keeping an eye on the girls, and has Johnny all to herself. As they make love, Sarah has Johnny keep the blindfold on, so that he wears a mask of sorts throughout their lighthearted foreplay. In a later scene, as Mateo plays with the girls he too wears a mask, holding an African mask up to his face, and reaches out for the children. Mateo's version of 'fee fie fo fum' does not end with he and Sarah in bed, however; in the next scene we simply see Mateo with Christy and Ariel, painting angels on their bedroom walls, content in his position of family playmate and caretaker, subverting his sexuality to fulfill a predetermined angelic role.

In conjunction with this 'ebony saint', Shohat and Stam note its stereotypical opposite: 'the saintly Black forms a Manichean pair with the demon Black'.[23] Although Mateo reveals himself to be more like a benevolent Uncle Remus, at the beginning of the film, his character much more closely resembles the violent foil of that gentle saint. We have already remarked upon Mateo's screaming, shirtless rage – a rage that seems so unpredictable and violent that, in conjunction with Mateo's prowling muscularity, it leads Buckalew to see Mateo's 'buffed-out masculinity as being inherently threatening'.[24] When the girls first knock on Mateo's door, given the film's set-up of Mateo, the audience certainly has been directed to expect the worst. Additionally, in his

22 Jan Pieterse quoted in Shohat and Stam, *Unthinking Eurocentrism*, p. 203.   23 Ibid.   24 Buckalew, review of *In America*.

early appearances in the film, Mateo seems beast-like, with his violent motion
and constant half-nudity. Shohat and Stam identify this as a 'key colonialist
trope' of 'animalization':

> This was rooted in a religious and philosophical tradition which drew
> sharp boundaries between the animal and the human, and where all
> animal-like characteristics of the self were to be suppressed. Colonizing
> discourse, for [Frantz] Fanon, always resorts to the bestiary.
> Colonialist/racist discourse renders the colonized as wild beasts in
> their unrestrained libidinousness, their lack of proper dress, their mud
> huts resembling nests and lairs.[25]

The film, in its initial depictions of Mateo – although he clearly does not live
in a mud hut, the few shots of the interior of Mateo's apartment reveal lots
of paintings and art supplies but little in the way of homey, conventional fur-
niture-operates within the colonialist terms Shohat and Stam describe.
Moreover, one could even interpret the love scene between Johnny and Sarah
as more symptomatic of Mateo's wildness than the passion of the husband and
wife. Or rather, because Johnny and Sarah's passion matches and coincides
with that of Mateo, the Sullivan's sexual interlude, the film's only sex scene,
reads as a foray of the married couple into the illicit and primal realm that
Mateo inhabits.

Mateo's transition from animal status to kindly friend of the family thus
embodies both poles of stereotypical representation, signifying 'On the one
hand … benevolence, harmless and servile guardianship and endless love', and
on the other, 'insanity, illicit sexuality, chaos'.[26] In the film's world, which
inherits its tropes from colonial and racist rhetoric, Black men, it seems, can
be either super-sexualized predators, or neutered subordinates – there is no,
more human, middle ground. Within these stereotypes, the Black figure symbolizes that which is highly evil and that which is impossibly good – both
repressive, unnatural identities in their own right. What registers as most problematic in the depiction of Mateo is not simply that *In America* features both
ends of the symbol spectrum (with no intermediate ground), but that Mateo's
transition from 'scary bogeyman' to 'Black angel' is accomplished only through
the intervention of the young, White protagonists.[27] On Halloween, Mateo

25 Shohat and Stam, *Unthinking Eurocentrism*, p. 137. E. Ann Kaplan in *Looking for the other:
feminism, film, and the imperial gaze* (London, 1997) identifies this same trend, noting that 'ani-
malizing minorities – showing their similarities to animals' and 'sexualizing minorities as lusty,
libidinous' are strategies 'common to many Hollywood images of others' (p. 80).   26 Toni
Morrison quoted in Shohat and Stam, *Unthinking Eurocentrism*, p. 203.   27 Dennis Schwartz,
review of *In America*, Rotten *Tomatoes* 2004, 5 June 2004 <http://www.rottentomatoes.com/
click/movie-1125557/reviews.php?critic=columns&sortby=default&page=5&rid=1231937>.
Reviewed 23 December for *Ozus' Movie Reviews* <http://www.sover.net/~ozus>.

storms to his door, flings it open to confront his unwanted guests, and something in the countenance of the young girls calms him immediately; his 'defens-
es quickly crumble when Christy and Ariel charmingly demand their
Halloween goodies'.[28] From this point on, Mateo assumes the role of gentle,
wise companion, and gone are any hints of violence or sexuality. In befriend-
ing him, the girls appear to tame the animalistic Mateo, enacting the colonial
rhetoric whereby a dominant culture that perceives itself as superior soothes the
amenable savage, who cannot attain the same status as the colonist, but only
grovel in subservient awe.[29] Matco ultimately appears as a willing participant
in his own repression on screen, if we in the audience even perceive that
repression. Imperial ideology infiltrates social consciousness through this very
process of naturalization, and in Sheridan's film, we witness the extent of its
effectiveness, for in accepting the magic of the film's world, we accede that a
(Black) 'man who screams' can be instantly tamed by two charming (White)
children. Thus, to those who would trumpet the enlightenment of contemporary filmmakers, feminist critic Gerardine Meaney cautions that 'blithe
assumptions that Irish cinema has become too modern and sophisticated to
reproduce the old myths risk reproducing them unchallenged'.[30] In developing critical subjectivity,[31] audiences can challenge the assumptions of these old
myths and the ideological authority that informs them. After all, 'Whoever
defines the code or the context has control... and all answers which accept
that context abdicate the possibility of redefining it'.[32] In following Sheridan's
film family to America, let us not abdicate that possibility.

28 Mark Caro, review of *In America*, *Rotten Tomatoes* 2004, 5 June 2004 <http://www.rotten-tomatoes.com/click/movie-1125557/reviews.phy?critic=columns&sortby=default&page=5&rid=804297>.   29 In discussing the phenomenon whereby the literature of hegemonic or colonialist powers depicts subordinated peoples as happily embracing their inferior status, Shohat and Stam identify a nineteenth-century example: 'The Black who comes into contact with Whites, claims a Belgian novel of 1868, "loses his barbarian character and only retains the childlike qual-ities of the inhabitants of the forest"' (p. 139 quoting Jan Pieterse).   30 Gerardine Meaney, 'Landscapes of desire: women and Ireland on film', *Women: A Cultural Review* 9:3 (1998), p. 251.   31 I borrow the term from Mary C. Gentile, *Film feminisms: theory and practice* (London, 1985), p. 77.   32 Claire Johnston quoted in Teresa de Lauretis, *Alice doesn't: feminism, semi-otics, cinema* (London and Basingstoke, 1984), pp 106–7.

Revisioning vision in the
Bloody Sunday films[1]

ELLEN E. SWEENEY

In January 2002, two of Britain's terrestrial channels – Channel Four and ITV – broadcast two docudramas within a week of each other to commemorate the thirtieth anniversary of Bloody Sunday when soldiers of the First Parachute Regiment killed thirteen civil rights marchers and mortally wounded another on 30 January 1972 in Derry, Northern Ireland. Both Channel Four's *Sunday* and ITV's *Bloody Sunday* depart from the majority of Troubles films which have relied on the stereotype of the atavistically violent Irishman which both John Hill[2] and Martin McLoone[3] argue has served to absolve the British state of responsibility for the violence. The films both represent the First Parachute Regiment's actions that day in Derry and the subsequent Widgery Inquiry which exculpated them from all wrongdoing as a turning point in contemporary Northern Irish history, effectively destroying the Northern Irish non-violent civil rights movement and reviving the Irish Republican Army.

At the root of my engagement with these two films is the question of the relationship of the image to historical memory. Both films foreground the relationship of the film image to the British public memory of Bloody Sunday. In their attempts to reconfigure the signifiers connected with Bloody Sunday and the Troubles in British memory, the films return to what Homi Bhabha has called the 'primal scene/seen' of Northern Irish Catholics in the British

1 This research would not have been possible without the support of Professor Paul Greenough and the Crossing Borders Program at the University of Iowa that funded my research trip to Ireland, Northern Ireland and London in the summer of 2003. In addition, I would like to thank my cousins in Ireland (North and South) for their hospitality and all-round helpfulness and kindness to me during the summer of 2003 when I was researching this paper. I would like to thank John Hill, University of Ulster at Coleraine, and Kevin Rockett, Trinity College Dublin, for meeting with me during the summer of 2003, and for giving me the opportunity to present this research at the Irish Film Postgraduate Conference in April 2004, in Portrush, Northern Ireland. I also owe a debt of gratitude to John Hill for his trenchant comments on an earlier draft of this paper. At the University of Iowa, I am grateful to Professors Cheryl Herr, Rosalind Galt, Corey Creekmur and Louis-Georges Schwartz and doctoral candidate Amit Baishya for their insightful criticisms of various drafts of this paper. In India, I thank Elliott McCarter and Professor Suzanne Ironbiter for their assistance.   2 John Hill, 'Images of violence,' in Kevin Rockett, Luke Gibbons and John Hill, *Cinema and Ireland* (London, 1987).   3 Martin McLoone, *Irish film: emergence of a contemporary cinema* (London, 2000).

imaginary. Like the signifier, the spectral film image, superficial and easily manipulable through editing, calls up the ghosts of the primal scene/seen and repositions them for a British television public. Problematizing the primal scene/seen through an engagement with the 'objectivity' of the filmic image, the films suggest that the 'objective' image cannot provide the truth about Bloody Sunday. In reading the relationship of the image to objective representation and to memory, I draw on Gilles Deleuze's theories regarding the relationship between the objective and subjective image in film. In Paul Greengrass' *Bloody Sunday*, individual biases and limited visual capabilities determine the ways in which both the marchers and members of the First Parachute Regiment comprehend and react to the events of Bloody Sunday. Instead of producing a totalizing visual account of the events, *Bloody Sunday* produces a fractured text in which human subjectivities are the veil through which the objective images are encountered. By contrast, Jimmy McGovern's *Sunday* posits that 'communal memory', a second-hand experience of the event, offers a more complete understanding of a historical event than that given by first-hand witness. In their engagement with the image, the films point to the problem of the image as supplement to interiorizing and inscriptional memory. In my thinking about the supplement, I draw from Jacques Derrida's writings that posit the supplement as an image that calls forth an absent present, to contain it and keep it at a distance. In calling up the ghosts of Bloody Sunday, do the films recuperate a repressed history, or do they indicate the impossibility of ever recovering the past?

The films are shaped by international, national and local influences. With regard to the international, both films belong to an international film genre that a recent issue of *Screen* has designated trauma cinema;[4] Greengrass's *Bloody Sunday* is also an international co-production. In relation to the national, both films draw upon British traditions of film and television docudrama and were produced in the context of British television film funding, production and terrestrial broadcast. The local appears in terms of the return of a repressed 'local' history through the metropolitan-based filmmakers' engagement with victims' families and Derry-based activists. While Greengrass' *Bloody Sunday* was explicitly produced with international distribution in mind and McGovern's *Sunday* was limited to strictly terrestrial broadcast, both films bear the marks of these three influences which themselves reflect British television's emergence as a primary player in the support and development of a British national cinema.

It is the films' different influences (both formal and funding) and their intervention into a national debate about military responsibility for Bloody Sunday that drew attacks from certain quarters of the London press. The films were criticized on the following grounds: the potentially explosive content of

4 'Special Debate: Trauma and Screen Studies', *Screen*, 42:2 (2001).

the films, it was argued, could negatively effect the peace process in Northern Ireland;[5] British public monies were being used to produce *Bloody Sunday* that was characterized as having an 'Irish nationalist' view of events, which might adversely affect the publicly-funded Saville Inquiry into Bloody Sunday;[6] while the contribution of 'foreign' funding in the case of *Bloody Sunday* (Irish director Jim Sheridan's production company Hell's Kitchen and Bord Scannán na hÉireann/Irish Film Board co-produced the film with Britain's ITV) was seen as calling into question the film's national identity and allegiances.[7] In their border policing of 'dangerous' influences in national cinema, the criticisms indicate a firm belief that a 'national cinema' should shore up myths of the nation, not critique them. The respective films' engagements with representations of the conflict draw a connection between the way in which the British establishment and army saw the civil rights marchers and how the Northern Irish Catholic community was represented in the news media.

Robin Wilson has argued that the majority of British reporting of the conflict has been reported from the squaddie's eye level, so 'fostering a partisan perspective in which the army was indeed no "real part of the trouble", but [merely] reacting stoically to the inflammatory Irish with a restraint no other force would show'.[8] In their return to Bloody Sunday, the films foreground the news media's representation of the conflict. Martin McLoone has pointed out that *Bloody Sunday*'s 'washed-out colours' suggest the 'grainy texture of black-and-white news footage' in an attempt to 'replicate the feel of the actual news footage of the events that is indelibly imprinted on the consciousness of an entire generation of people in Ireland and Britain'.[9] In referring back to the British media's presentation of the events of that day, *Bloody Sunday* provides a fictional supplement that problematizes the issue of perception by showing how a scene can be read in radically different ways according to individual and collective identifications such as nationality and religion. By contrast, *Sunday* represents the British media reportage of Bloody Sunday as uncritically relaying the state's account of the events to the wider world. By drawing on the textualization of the conflict in the British media, the films connect how the British army saw the marchers to the issue of the way in which the Northern Irish Catholic nationalist community and the conflict has been represented in the British imaginary. Homi Bhabha has argued that 'primal scenes illustrate [...] that looking/hearing/readings as sites of subjectification

5 Martin Fletcher, 'Open wound,' *The Times*, 19 January 2002, p. 29.   6 Unnamed author, 'Bloody Sunday films are part of the whole truth,' *Independent*, 13 January 2002, p. 26; Alexander Walker, 'Monstrous wounds of Ulster,' *Evening Standard*, 9 January 2002, p. 20.   7 Alexander Walker and Luke Leitch, *Evening Standard*, 4 January 2002, p. 2.   8 Robin Wilson, 'DD Papers: the media and intrastate conflict in Northern Ireland,' http://www.democraticdialogue.org/working/media.htm, accessed on 1/26/04.   9 Martin McLoone, '*Bloody Sunday*', *Cineaste*, 27:4 (2002), p. 42.

in colonial discourse are evidence of the importance of the visual and auditory imaginary for the *histories* of societies'.[10] Returning to the historical moment which transformed the way in which the Northern Irish community and the British establishment and army saw each other, the films foreground the ways in which the marchers and the paratroopers perceived each other that day, and how these perceptions were related to positions of power and submission.

In order to reposition the British viewer away from the squaddie, both films are squarely aligned with the civil rights marchers. In *Sunday*, the viewer is identified with the Young family, a Derry Catholic working-class family. In *Bloody Sunday*, the viewer is most clearly aligned with the Protestant civil rights leader, Ivan Cooper, played by popular television actor James Nesbitt. The two films are similar in presenting the actions and motivations of the 'Derry Young Hooligans' as the result of economic and political impotence, showing that neither *Sunday*'s John Young and *Bloody Sunday*'s Gerry Donaghy, both of whom were killed, were armed that day. The two films part ways in their representations of the British establishment and the British army. *Sunday* estranges the viewer from the First Parachute regiment by representing them as trained bloodthirsty killers sent by the government in London to teach the marchers a lesson. The film represents Lord Widgery as agreeing to give the Prime Minister the ruling he wants (exculpation of the army of any blame for the killings) before he has even gone to Northern Ireland to convene the inquiry. By contrast, *Bloody Sunday* represents the state as more fractured, with divisions within the Regiment and military command headquarters. Unlike the transparency of the motivations of the Young Derry Hooligans, the film deliberately obstructs understanding of the soldiers' actions that day by restricting the access of the viewer to their point of view.

In both films, the British soldiers are denied interiority, so the viewer is left to guess what drives them to kill innocent civilians. In the prelude to the massacre, both films establish how the soldiers have been taught to 'see' IRA men in the crowd: in *Sunday*, the voice of a commanding officer is heard psyching the soldiers up to attack by describing the marchers in derogatory terms; and in *Bloody Sunday*, the soldiers, waiting to enter the Bogside, tell each other about recent IRA killings of British soldiers and disparage the civil rights march as a front for the IRA. The orally recounted stories suggest the way in which the soldiers of One Para, motivated by fear and loathing, were prone to see every Derry marcher as a potential IRA gunman. Both films use a mediating character, the 'Good Brit', to substantiate the camera's vision of the events of Bloody Sunday.

In the two films, the 'Good Brit' is the lone member of the parachute regiment who 'sees' what really happened and whose vision gives credibility to

10 Homi Bhabha, 'The other question: stereotype, discrimination and the discourse of colonialism', *The location of culture* (New York, 1994), p. 76.

the local community's remembering of Bloody Sunday. When members of One Para begin shooting young men standing on the barricades, the 'Good Brit' comes to see as the camera sees following what Gilles Deleuze has characterized as the trajectory of the story. According to Deleuze, the story concerns the development of two kinds of images, objective and subjective, and their 'complex relation which can go as far as antagonism'.[11] The story's narrative resolution occurs when the subjective and objective images are resolved into 'an identity of Ego=Ego; identity of the character seen and who sees, but equally well of the camera/film-maker who sees the character and is what the character sees'.[12] In both Bloody Sunday films, this resolution occurs when the 'objective' soldier's vision is similar to that of the Derry marchers: unarmed marchers were gunned down by members of the First Parachute Regiment. I will analyze here a sequence from *Bloody Sunday* that complicates the narrative resolution of subjective and objective perspectives.

In a fourteen-shot sequence in *Bloody Sunday* in which the soldiers from the First Parachute Regiment begin to pick marchers off the barricades, the sequence is bookended by two long shots from the position of the firing soldiers. The sequence begins with a medium-long shot of a soldier standing behind a wall, with the unit commander's voice off-screen crying, 'He's got a weapon', followed by a cut to a long shot of a teenaged boy, with no weapon apparently visible, falling behind the barricades. The medium shot prevents the viewer from having any kind of perspective on the firing soldier's point of view, and the status of the long shot is ambiguous: is it objective or subjective, and if it is a point-of-view shot, whose is it? The temporal lag (of a second) between the aural description of what is seen and the subsequent image sets up the viewer to expect to see a gunman, only to have this expectation subverted. The ambiguous status of the long shot questions whether it is a 'subjective' point of view and thus possibly 'false' (and if it is, whose fantasy perception was it), or if it is 'objective', and thus true, contradicting what the commander says that he sees. In their representation of a hierarchically-based division in the Army between those who 'see' and those who shoot, these three shots suggest that, in this enactment of the 'primal scene/seen', the soldiers themselves are positioned in a regime that interpellates them into shooters.

Following these three shots, there is a cut to the other side of the barricade showing a boy lying wounded and a frantic Gerry Donaghy crouched near him. Whether it is the boy who has just been shot in the previous image is uncertain as his face is not in the frame. This shot is followed by a close-up of Ivan Cooper telling someone off-screen that the soldiers are shooting live bullets. There is intercutting between the terrified marchers hiding from being shot by the paras, and tight medium shots of the paras firing. As these shots

11 Gilles Deleuze, *Cinema 2: the time-image*, trans. Hugh Tomlinson and Robert Galeta (Minneapolis, 1989), p. 148. 12 Ibid.

of the soldiers are not followed by shots of what they are firing at, the spectator's access to the soldiers' point of view is restricted. Similarly, the images of the marchers do not show what they see. Significantly, the viewer's sense of the geographical positions of the soldiers, Ivan Cooper and the other marchers is severely distorted because of the assemblage of restrictive medium shots and the absence of an establishing shot. Although the scene cuts between the two groups, the editing and framing severely limits the spectator's grasp of the scene, and thus refuses a totalizing gaze.

At shot eleven, the sequence takes a turn when the radio operator (Para 027), the 'Good Brit', asserts that he cannot find a 'target' and asks at what the soldiers are shooting. There is then a cut to a medium shot of the soldier standing next to Para 027 who shoots, followed by the second long shot of the barricade showing another unarmed boy falling back, picked off by the bullet, as a Derry woman is heard to exclaim off-screen, 'They are just picking children off the barricade'. Unlike the previous long shot, which was of indeterminate identity, this image is marked as objective by a zoom in and out of the scene that identifies the shot as captured by a camera. In these shots, there are three 'spectators' – the objective camera image, that of Para 027 (the 'Good Brit') and that of the female marcher. However, Para 027 and the woman read the scene according to their own backgrounds – he as a trained soldier, she as a member of the community. Para 027 reads it negatively – there are no 'targets', while the woman (the maternal voice) asserts positively that she sees 'children.' In their reading of the scene, neither the soldier nor the woman accurately describes what the camera sees, but explains it according to how their own respective cultural backgrounds have trained them to read it. Further, the 'objective shot' appears to confirm what Para 027 sees after he has said it and is no longer looking at the barricade, but trying to convince the soldiers to stop shooting. Instead, it is the woman who appears to react to the same shot the camera sees. As the voice and the image coincide, it is as if the voice speaks the truth of the image, when the commander's reading of the first long shot was apparently incorrect. However, since the British soldier has already asserted there are no targets, the spectator has been encouraged to believe the Derry woman's reading.

Following Para 027's assertion that there are no 'targets', there is a splintering of vision within the group. Soon after Colonel Wilford orders the soldiers shooting to take only aimed shots (the implication being that his soldiers have been shooting randomly). When the soldiers chase the fleeing marchers, Para 027 and other soldiers shout out the call for a ceasefire that goes unheard or ignored by the soldiers who open fire on the marchers. While it is the 'Good Brit' whose vision of the events is most closely aligned with the objective camera and the view of the marchers, his testimony is heard at the end of the film narrating the unit's version of the events. The sequence suggests the way in which the 'individual' perspective is repressed by the state's vision. This vision will become the definitive narrative account of the events of Bloody

Sunday, and will influence readings of the Troubles. While *Bloody Sunday* shows us the denial of one soldier's first-hand experience of the event, *Sunday* suggests that communal memory of an event can be witnessed and denied.

In *Sunday*, a female marcher's testimony concerning Bernie McGuigan's murder before the Widgery Inquiry is shown in terms of close-up shots of the witness, images of what her testimony is describing, and shots of various people in the courtroom. The images from McGuigan's murder are striking for two reasons: except for the sound of his handkerchief fluttering in the wind and the sound of the rifle shot that killed him, they are unaccompanied by a sound-track; and they are clearly not all hers as she did not see the man to whose aid McGuigan had tried to go. The sequence begins with a close-up of her face, a cut to the image of the wounded man crying for help, followed by a pan around the courtroom. The state's lawyer at first cannot make eye contact with her, but in the sequence's sixth shot, he is framed in a tight close-up, looking at her, apparently unable to look away from her testimony. In shots seven through thirteen, there is an alteration between shots of the witness testifying and the recollected image: McGuigan holding out a white handkerchief trying to make his way to the wounded man; a close-up of the handkerchief; a long shot of McGuigan as he crumples to the ground, mortally wounded by a head shot. Except for the witness' voice, only the flutter of the handkerchief and the rifle shot are heard on the soundtrack. Significantly, in shot eleven, as the woman testifies, there is rack focus from herself then to Widgery in the background, looking pained and embarrassed by her damning testimony, as a rifle shot is heard, which serves as a sound bridge to the recollected image of McGuigan being shot in the head. In shot thirteen, there is a cut back to the same close up of the girl, this time a reversal of the order of the rack focus, with Widgery first in focus, then the witness, symbolizing his immersion in that moment of the testimony and his emergence from it.

The sequence represents powerlessness before the state in three separate moments: when McGuigan was killed, the woman's testimony at the Inquiry, and Widgery's later denial of her testimony through his ruling excusing the Paras from wrongdoing. This sequence is remarkable in the ambiguous nature of the recollected images: if they are not all the witness's (most of the shots of McGuigan are clearly not from her point of view), to whom do they belong? I would argue that the sound and image texts of McGuigan's murder are not exclusively recollected by the witness, but are to a great extent the affective responses of the people hearing her testimony, in particular those most antagonistic to it. This sequence represents the affective aspect of communal memory.

In thinking through the problem of communal memory and the image, I turn here to Gilles Deleuze's writings on the free indirect semi-subjective image, which draws from Pier Paolo Pasolini's writings on the subject. Pasolini drew his theory of the free indirect in film from Italian and Russian theories about free indirect discourse in literature, which is 'an assemblage of enunciation, carrying out two inseparable acts of subjectification simulataneously'.[13] There is no 'mixture' of two subjects, but a 'differentiation of two correlative subjects in a system which is itself heterogeneous'.[14] With reference to Pasolini's theory, Deleuze suggests an image in which the camera both gives the spectator a vision of a character and her world, but also imposes another 'vision in which the first is transformed and reflected'.[15] In the courtroom sequence, the woman gives her testimony and the courtroom witnesses listen to it. The woman's voice-over testimony, the non-diegetic sounds of the gunshot and the flicker of the handkerchief, and the imagined images of McGuigan's murder together form a semi-subjective image. As opposed to the cinematic tendency to oscillate between 'subjective' and 'objective', the free indirect semi-subjective image is 'an immobilization' between the two.[16] These shots are neither subjective, nor objective, but semi-subjective representing a communal experience that is another kind of vision. In contrast to the problematization of perception in *Bloody Sunday*, this sequence in *Sunday* presents testimony as eliciting and imposing a collective experience that transcends, however briefly, nationality and class identifications and divisions. These semi-subjective images see and experience more than the witness did that day in Derry. The question arises, however, how this collective memory papers over the fissures in the witness's own individual experience. In the film, this communal coming together in the image will be denied in the Widgery Inquiry's exculpation of the First Parachute Regiment.

Both films deal with the spectral relationship of the image to experience. As a medium, film has long been fascinated with and haunted by spectres. The Bloody Sunday films are possessed by spectres, with calling them back and attempting to bring them to heel. Neither film would have been produced if it had not been for the release of evidence that only became public in the 1990s, and which was the impetus for regional and international pressure to estalish a new Inquiry into Bloody Sunday.[17] Greengrass[18] and McGovern[19] had an idealistic motivation behind their involvement in their Bloody Sunday films: to produce British acknowledgement for their role in Irish suffering by

13 Gilles Deleuze, *Cinema 1: the movement-image*, trans. Hugh Tomlinson and Barbara Habberjam (Minneapolis, 1986), p. 73. 14 Ibid. 15 Ibid., 74. 16 Ibid., 76. 17 The following provided the impetus to form a new Inquiry: the 1997 publication of *Eyewitness Bloody Sunday*, a collection of the eyewitness accounts from that day which had been discounted by Lord Widgery in 1972; Channel Four's Bloody Sunday reports which undermined the official account; the release of army and police radio messages that had been intercepted by a local Derry man; analysis of recently available testimonies of implicated soldiers by University of Limerick law professor, Professor Dermot Walsh which showed that they changed their stories at least four times before the Widgery Tribunal; and an Irish newspaper's publication of Parachute Soldier 027's testimony that he had seen soldiers shooting unarmed marchers that day. Due to pressure from the Irish government, Prime Minister Tony Blair called for a second inquiry into Bloody Sunday, which commenced on 3 April 1998. 18 Paul Greengrass, 'Making history,' *The Guardian* (G2), 11 January 2002, pp 4–5. 19 Claudia Joseph, 'The Irish suffered, but it was a great tragedy for Britain, too', *Independent on Sunday*, 20 January 2002, p. 12.

attempting to provide what Alison Landsberg calls a 'prosthetic memory' for the British public of the event.[20] Landsberg argues that cinema can provide a 'prosthetic memory' of an historical event that can 'have the possibility in awakening in the viewing subject a feeling of empathy by developing an 'intimate relationship to memories of the events through which one did not live'.[21] According to Landsberg, unlike collective memory, which is tied to a certain ethnic community and serves to reinforce group identity, prosthetic memories do not belong to a certain group and are able to cross racial and ethnic lines as they borrow from the mass-media's technologies of remembrance.[22] In certain ways, the films take a local understanding of Bloody Sunday – and its ritual of commemoration – and translate it for a mainland British audience through the form of the docudrama and working-class drama.

I have referred to Landsberg's theory because the statements made by the Bloody Sunday films' creators and their critics suggest a similar understanding of cinema as working to interpellate people into a particular understanding of an event. However, the way in which a message is written does not determine how it is received.[23] Although those behind the Bloody Sunday films might wish for an interpellation such as that occurs to (and is denied by) Lord Widgery in *Sunday*, the film *Bloody Sunday* shows the way in which an image is radically unstable and open to a plurality of readings.

My second reason for referring to Landsberg concerns the problem of historical memory and the relationship of film or any other media to it. I return again to the ghost of the film, of history, of memory that preoccupies the two films, by turning here to Avital Ronell who has found in television the perfect metaphor for contemporary memory. Ronell writes that

> TV is ...the residue of an unassimilable history. Television is linked crucially to the enigma of survival. It inhabits the contiguous neighborhoods of broken experience and rerouted memory. Refusing in its discourse and values to record, but preferring instead to play out the myths of liveness, living color and being there, television will have produced a counterphobic perspective to an interrupted history...[24]

In their marks of trauma cinema – specifically McGovern's flashback structure and Greengrass' fade-outs – the two films foreground their identities as traumatic texts, referencing a broken history, but try to recuperate it. *Sunday* superficially marks this 'interrupted history' with its flashback structure and multi-person narrative focus, but all the characters, from Widgery to the 'Good

20 Alison Landsberg, 'Prosthetic memory: the ethics and politics of memory in an age of mass culture', in Paul Grainge (ed.) *Memory and popular film* (Manchester, 2003), pp 144–61. 21 Ibid., 148.
22 Ibid., 149. 23 Richard Dienst, 'Sending postcards in TV Land,' in David Wills and Peter Brunette (eds), *Deconstruction and the visual arts* (New York, 1994), p. 305. 24 Avital Ronell, 'Trauma TV: twelve steps beyond the pleasure principle,' *Finitude's score* (Berkeley, 1994), p. 308.

Brit' to the Derry Marchers, have a similar understanding of the event, although Widgery represses this knowledge in his ruling. Thus, the film presents us with the impossible: a seamless memory of an impossible history. *Bloody Sunday,* on the other hand, gives us both 'sides of the story', but this does not mean a total and complete understanding of the events. In its attempt to provide an 'accurate' reconstruction of the events of Bloody Sunday, the film necessarily shatters the possibility for anyone to have a complete understanding of the events. All perspectives will necessarily be fractured, incomplete. However, this representation drew ire from some for having the appearance of letting the British 'off the hook.' In his criticism of the film, Martin McLoone argued that:

> In the end, what all these esthetic devices do is to create a sense of irredeemable confusion. The message of the film, therefore, seems to be that the tragic events of *Bloody Sunday* were the result of confusion on all sides (even if especially so on the side of the army authorities) ... In other words, for all of its realistic strategies and its sympathetic treatment of the victims and their families, the film seems to let the British authorities and the army off the hook.[25]

I would suggest that the film does represent soldiers of the First Parachute Regiment shooting clearly unarmed people, such as in the sequence when the marchers are fleeing across the courtyard and one paratrooper opens fire on them, after a ceasefire has been called. Further, the film shows the doctoring of photographic evidence by the Army, and soldiers lying to the Army's in-house inquiry. I argue that the film represents the profound limitations of the state's reading of the Northern Irish conflict. The state's story about the Troubles has been one of a fantasy of a totalizing gaze it did not and does not possess. Media representations that mimic this control over the scene are likewise false. However, it does problematize the possibility of ever having a complete understanding of what happened that day in Derry.

My final critique of Landsberg's argument comes from Jacques Derrida's thinking about the 'supplement'. According to Derrida, the supplement 'occupies middle point between total presence and total absence', marking a determined lack.[26] The sign does not and has never referred to a signified, or to presence, but has only worked in relationship to a play of signifiers. The Bloody Sunday films are a confrontation with the national through the different writings through which national consciousness about Northern Ireland generally, and Bloody Sunday in particular, has been constructed. In the films' attempts to recall the trace of the event, they rely on the recreation of Bloody Sunday's iconic moments – Bernie McGuigan lying dead on the ground, the paratroopers firing

---

25 McLoone, '*Bloody Sunday*', p. 42.   26 Jacques Derrida, *Of grammatology*. trans. Gayatri Chakravorty Spivak (Baltimore,1976), p. 153.

at the crowd, Father Daly holding out a white handkerchief as he tries to guide a wounded man to safety – to give their reconstructions credibility. In their use of iconic signs, the films ultimately suggest the problem of all forms of memory.

In the reliance on language, experience has to be converted into verbal signs, and thus are disconnected from their original visual or emotional form. Thus all speaking subjects are ultimately constructed by their submission to the laws of language. Although the film image would appear to have a closer relationship to the experience of the event, and thus to be able to bypass the effacing strictures of language, what the film image reveals is the way in which it plays out the relationship between interiorizing memory, *Erinnerung*, and inscriptional memory, *Gedächtnis*,[27] which Jacques Derrida characterizes as one of 'rupture, heterogeneity, and disjunction'.[28] The 'rupture' and 'disjunction' between the sign and meaning, between *Gedächtnis* and *Erinnerung*, can never be closed or bridged. In the subject's recollection of the event, access to the event is forever lost to interiorizing memory, with only video clips that call to the 'lost memory' that can never be recovered.[29] Thus, acts of memory are similar to the surface, or superficiality, of the image, with the presence of the event forever lost to the subject.[30] Although in their imitation of the international film genre of 'trauma cinema', the respective films' creators may have been attempting to instill a 'prosthetic memory' of the event, thirty years after the fact, the ruptured relationship between memorialization and interiorized experience prevents this from ever being possible. Jacques Derrida has written about the troubling nature of the supplement:

> The supplement has not only the power of procuring an absent present through its image; procuring it for us through the proxy of the thing, it holds it at a distance and masters it. For this presence is at the same time desire and feared. The supplement transgresses ...[31]

Although representing the repressed histories of Bloody Sunday was important for the peace process in Northern Ireland, the extent to which the films could actually instill in the British television public an experience of the event is inhibited by the nature of the sign itself in relation to interiorizing memory. I would argue that the films, by trying to represent the unrepresentable, seek to contain the ghosts of Bloody Sunday and hold them at bay. In their engagement with a traumatic history, the Bloody Sunday films foreground the way in which all representations are haunted by their relationship to that which it represents. If trauma is defined as a recurring mental image to which there is no direct access, that is pure surface, then all representations mimic the relationship to the traumatic event as they are 'born from the abyss'.[32]

27 Ronell, 'Trauma TV', p. 312. 28 Jacques Derrida, *Memoires for Paul de Man* (New York, 1989), p. 56. 29 Ibid. 30 Ronell, 'Trauma TV', p. 327. 31 Derrida, *Of grammatology*, p. 155. 32 Ibid., 163.

Notes on contributors

DENIS CONDON, an IRCHSS Government of Ireland Scholar, was awarded a PhD at the National University of Ireland, Maynooth in 2005 for his thesis 'Cinematographing Ireland: The Irish Cinema, 1895–1921₃.

MAEVE CONNOLLY, an IRCHSS Government of Ireland Scholar, was awarded a PhD at Dublin City University for a study of Irish film and the avant-garde during 1975–87. She is currently a lecturer in film studies, specializing in animation, at Dún Laoghaire Institute of Art, Design and Technology.

ELIZABETH COULTER-SMITH is completing a PhD on the films of Halas and Batchelor and currently lectures in digital imaging and new media at the University of Central England.

JOHN HILL is Professor of Media at Royal Holloway, University of London, and Visiting Professor of Media Studies at the University of Ulster. His most recent project, a history of the cinema and Northern Ireland, is due to be published by the British Film Institute.

MIKA KO is completing a PhD at the University of Ulster at Coleraine on the representation of 'otherness' in contemporary Japanese cinema.

DANIJELA KULEZIC-WILSON is completing a PhD at the University of Ulster at Coleraine working on a thesis on screen musicality, examining the relationship of film and music.

DERVILA LAYDEN is working on a PhD at the Centre for Film Studies, University College Dublin focusing on the examination of stories told in both written and filmed literature in Ireland between 1991 and 2001.

MEAGHAN MORRIS is Professor of Cultural Studies and Co-ordinator, Kwan Fong Cultural Research and Development Program, Lingnan University, Tuen Mun, New Territories, Hong Kong. She is Chair of the Association for Cultural Studies (ACS), and is senior editor of *TRACES: A Multilingual Series of Cultural Theory and Translation*.

SARAH NEELY recently completed a PhD on the screen adaptation of Scottish and Irish literature at the University of Glasgow and lectures in media studies at the University of Paisley.

166   *Contributors*

BETH NEWHALL was awarded an MPhil in Irish Theatre and Film at Trinity College Dublin in 2004.

DIÓG O'CONNELL is completing a doctoral thesis on contemporary Irish cinema at Dublin City University and lectures in Film and Media Studies at the Dún Laoghaire Institute of Art, Design and Technology.

EMILIE PINE, an IRCHSS Government of Ireland Scholar, was awarded a PhD at Trinity College Dublin in 2004 for her thesis on Irish film and theatre in the 1930s.

KEVIN ROCKETT is a fellow of Trinity College Dublin, where he is a Lecturer in Film Studies. His most recent book is *Irish Film Censorship: A Cultural Journey from Silent Cinema to Internet Pornography* (2004). He has been awarded a 2005/06 IRCHSS Government of Ireland Research Fellowship to complete a history of Irish film exhibition and distribution.

ELLEN E. SWEENEY is undertaking comparative research in the Film Studies Program at the University of Iowa into the cinematic representations of trauma and their relationship to national history in Irish and Hindi (popular) cinema.

PÁDRAIC WHYTE, an IRCHSS Government of Ireland Scholar, is studying for a PhD at Trinity College Dublin. His research is examining film and literature for children in Ireland. He is currently vice-president of the Irish Society for the Study of Children's Literature.

Index

About Adam, 119
Aiken, Frank, 101
Alexander, Mike, 50
  Dreaming
Alice doesn't: feminism, semiotics, cinema,
  153n
Alice in Wonderland, 92
Alien films, 140
*All our yesterdays: ninety years of British
  cinema*, 47n
All Things Bright and Beautiful, 113
Allister, Ray, 75n
Almost Famous, 63
An Bonnán Buí, 80, 83
Anamú, 82–3
Anderson, Paul Thomas, 10, 57, 58, 61–5
  Magnolia
Anderson, Vass, 98
Angela's Ashes (Alan Parker, 1999), 50
Angela's Ashes (Frank McCourt, 1996), 124
Anglo-Irish Treaty (1921), 101
Animal Farm: a fairy story (Orwell, 1945),
  90, 93–5
Animal Farm (Halas and Batchelor, 1954),
  11, 90, 93–6
Anne Devlin, 12, 117, 118, 120, 121, 122,
  123, 128
The Arts Council (of Ireland), 86
Ashes of Time, 26
Attlee, Clement, 92
Auster, Paul, 62
Australian Football League, 18

BAFTA, 80
Ballyfermot Senior College, 81
Ballykissangel, 49
Bambi, 94
Barber, Samuel, 62
Barnacle, Nora, 12, 117–28
Barnes, John, 77n
Barr, Charles, 47
Barrett, Professor, 73n, 76

Barton, Ruth, 48, 53, 54, 80n, 84, 85, 86,
  87, 124n, 143, 145
Batchelor, Joy, 11, 90–6
Battles, Jan, 79n
Beau Geste, 82
Beavers, Louise, 150
Before the Rain, 60, 61
*Being in time: selves and narrators in
  philosophy and literature*, 57n
Bellbird, 23
*Between home and world: a reader in Hong
  Kong cinema*, 27n
Beverly Hills 92010, 23
Bhabha, Homi, 154, 156–7
Biró, Yvette, 61
The birth of Nanto ideology, 37n
Black, Cathal, 11, 86, 87, 97–105, 112
  Korea
  Our Boys
Blair, Tony, 161n
Bloody Sunday, 13, 154–64
Blow, Mark, 75
Blue Velvet, 55n
BoB & Partners, 24
Bolger, Emma, 145
Bolger, Sarah, 145
Book of Kells, 87
Booth, Tim, 82, 86, 87
  Ulys
Bord Fáilte, *see* Irish Tourist Board
Bord Scannán na hÉireann, *see* Irish Film
  Board
Bordwell, David, 26n, 58
Bortnyik, Sandor, 90
Bourne, Peter, 146n
Bowyer Bell, J., 101n
Box, Sydney, 91
The Boy from Mercury, 10, 11–12, 106–13
Boyle, Danny, 54
  Trainspotting
Bradford Animation Festival, 79n
Braithwaite, Ann, 118n

Branigan, Edward, 51, 122n
Braveheart, 48, 49, 54, 55
Breaking the Waves, 125
Breathnach, Paddy, 109n
    I Went Down
Brendan and the Book of Kells, 87
Brion, Jon, 62, 65
Brisbane Lions, 18
British Animated Films, 91
British Cartoons, 90
*British cinema and Thatcherism: fires were
    started*, 47n
The British cinema book, 49
British cinema, past and present, 49n, 52n
*The British film catalogue 1895–1985: a
    reference guide*, 77n
British historical cinema, 48n
British Tourist Authority, 49
Brown Bag Films, 79
Brown, Laura S., 131n
Brown, Royal S., 60, 63
Browne, Vincent, 97
Buckalew, Brett, 148, 150, 151
The Butcher Boy, 50, 51, 54, 55, 86, 87,
    109, 110, 111, 112n, 113
Butler Cullingford, Elizabeth, 112, 143n

Campbell, Joseph, 63–4
Canadian Film Board, 82
Caro, Mark, 153n
Carradine, David, 23
Cartoon Saloon, 86, 87
    Celtic Maidens
    Brendan and the Book of Kells
Casanova, 61
Casey, Cathy, 133
Cavagna, Carlo, 149
Celebrating 1895: the centenary of cinema,
    74n
Celtic Maidens, 86, 87
Central Office of Information, 92, 93
*A century of medical radiation in Ireland:
    an anthology*, 72n
*The challenge for higher education in
    Australia*, 20n
Chan Chi-fai, 29
Chan, Jackie, 23
Chan, Jordan Siu-chun, 24, 27
Chan, Stephen Ching-kiu, 26

Channel Four, 80, 154, 161n
Chaplin, Charlie, 92
    Modern Times
Charley's Black Magic, 92
Charley's Junior School Days, 92
Charley's March of Time, 93
Cheng, Ekin Yee-kin, 24, 27
Cheung, Pinky, 25
Cheung, Roy, 29
Chiau, Stephen, 26
Chin, Wellson Sing-wai, 26n
    Street Kids Violence
Ching Siu-tung, 26
Chion, Michel, 51n
Chow, Raymond, 24
Chow Yun Fat, 26
Chu, Yiu-wai, 27n
Chura-san, 39
CIA, 94
Cinderella, 92
Cinema and Ireland, 98n, 154n
Cinema 1: the movement–image, 161n
Cinema Paradiso, 109
Cinema 2: the time-image, 158n
Circle of Friends, 49
City on fire: Hong Kong cinema, 26n
Clancy, Maeve, 81n, 83n
Clara's Heart, 150
Clarke, Harry, 80
Clock Gate Youghal, 82
A Clockwork Orange, 27
Cloney, Sheila, 120
Come on Steve, 90–1
Comerford, Joe, 12, 129, 131, 139
    Reefer and the Model
Community Relations Council, 87
Companion to British and Irish cinema, 50n
Condon, Denis, 11
Connolly, Maeve, 11, 85n, 127
Considine, Paddy, 145
Constitution of Ireland (1937), 131n
Contemporary Irish cinema: from The Quiet
    Man *to* Dancing at Lughnasa, 53n
Cooper, Ivan, 157, 158, 159
Corner, John, 81, 84
Coronation Street, 23
Coulter-Smith, Elizabeth, 11
Courtenay, Tom, 106
Crangle, Richard, 74n, 75

Crisis Pregancy Agency, 141, 142
Crocodile Dundee, 23
Crook, Wally, 91
Crowe, Cameron, 63
  Almost Famous
Cyclopia charity fete, 70, 71, 72, 74

Daly, Father Edward, 164
Darklight digital film festival, 81n
Darley, Andrew, 83, 84n
Davies, Roland, 91
Dawkins, John S., 20
The Dawning, 53
de Bary, Brett, 19n
de Rochement, Louis, 93
de Valera, Eamon, 109, 110, 124
The Dead, 49
December Bride, 49, 130, 131
Deconstruction and the visual arts, 162n
The Defiant Ones, 150
Deleuze, Gilles, 13, 155, 158, 160, 161
The Depository, 88
Derrida, Jacques, 155, 163, 164
Devlin, Anne, see *Anne Devlin*
Devlin, Barry, 113
  All Things Bright and Beautiful
Dick, Leslie, 61n
Dienst, Richard, 162n
The Digital Hub, 79, 81, 82
Diphtheria Immunisation, 92
Discipline and punish: the birth of the prison, 107
Disney Corporation, 11, 92, 93, 94
  How to Play Polo
  Cinderella
  Alice in Wonderland
  Peter Pan
  Bambi
Dissolving views: key writings on British cinema, 47n
Documentary film, 93n
Donaghy, Gerry, 158
Donnellan, Eithne, 140
Donnelly, Donal, 97
Dreaming, 50
Dublin Art and Technology Association, 81n
Dubliners, 126
Duffy, Martin, 10, 11–12, 106–13
  The Boy from Mercury

Dún Laoghaire College of Art, *see* Dún Laoghaire Institute of Art, Design and Technology
Dún Laoghaire Institute of Art, Design and Technology, 80n, 81
Dyer, Richard, 50n

Earl's Court Exhibition (1896), 75
Eastenders, 23
Éclair, 91
Edison, Thomas Alva, 73n, 74n
Eglington, John, 69, 77
1848, see *Ireland 1848*
Electricity Supply Board, see ESB
Elizabeth, 48
Elton John 63
Enemies of promise: publishing, perishing and the eclipse of scholarship, 34n
English heritage, English cinema, 47n, 48n
The Englishman who went up a hill but came down a mountain, 49
Enterprise and heritage: crosscurrents of national culture, 81n
ESB, 101
Everwide (H.K.) Limited, 24n
Eyewitness Bloody Sunday, 161n

Faithful Departed, 83n
Faludi, Susan, 118n
Fanon, Frantz, 152
Farley, Fidelma, 129, 130, 135n
Farren, Paul, 81n, 82
Fellini, Federico, 61
  Casanova
Fifty Percent Grey, 79
Film as social practice, 34
Film feminism: theory and practice, 153n
Film publicity: a handbook on the production and distribution of propaganda films, 92n
Finitude's score, 162n
First Parachute Regiment, 154, 157–61, 163
Fischinger, Oskar, 93
Flash Gordon films, 11–12, 106, 110, 111
Fletcher, Martin, 156n
Fly About the House, 92
Fools of Fortune, 53, 54
Ford, John, 87
  The Quiet Man

Foucault, Michel, 106, 107, 108, 113
Fowler, Roger, 94
Frameworks, 83, 84, 86, 88
Freadman, Anne, 35
Frears, Stephen, 12, 129–42
  The Snapper
Friese-Greene: close-up of an inventor, 75n
Friese-Greene, William, 74
From *An Evil Cradling*, 80, 86

Gaffney, Cathal, 79, 83
Galway Film Fleadh, 82
Gender and sexuality in modern Ireland, 143n
Gentile, Mary C., 153n
Gerald McBoingBoing, 82
Gerow, Aaron, 39, 43, 46
Gerrard, Lisa, 146n
Gibbons, Luke, 69, 129, 130, 131, 142
Gibson, Mel, 48, 49, 54, 55
  Braveheart
Gifford, Denis, 77n
Gifford, Douglas, 52n
Ging, Debbie, 84n
Give Up Yer Aul' Sins, 79
Gladiator, 85n
The glass eye: artists and television, 85n
Gleeson, Brendan, 134
Goldberg, Whoopi, 150
Grace, Helen, 33n
Greengrass, Paul, 13, 154–64
  Bloody Sunday
Griffith, R., 93n
Grossberg, Lawrence, 28n
Guo huo zi zhi ren zai jiang hu, 26n, see
  Young and Dangerous

Halas and Batchelor, 90–6
  Animal Farm
  Charley's Black Magic
  Charley's Junior School Days
  Charley's March of Time
  Diphtheria Immunisation
  Fly About the House
  A Mortal Shock
  The Shoemaker and the Hatter
  Train Trouble
Halas, John, 11, 90–6,
Hallström, Lasse, 109
  My Life as a Dog

The Hand, 88, 89
Harkin, Margo, 12, 112, 113, 129, 131,
  133–6, 139–41
  Hush-a-Bye Baby
Harvey, Sylvia, 81, 84
Hayes, Joanne, 130n
HEA, *see* Higher Education Authority's
  North South Programme for
  Collaborative Research
Hedd Wyn, 49
Hell's Kitchen, 156
Henry V, 47
Herbert, Stephen, 75n
Hess, Harry, 82
Hickey, Aidan, 82
Hickey, James, 106
Hickey, Kieran, 83n
Higher education: a policy discussion paper,
  20n
Higher education: a policy statement, 20n
Higher Education Authority's North
  South Programme for Collaborative
  Research, 9
Higher education in Hong Kong, 20–1
Higson, Andrew, 47–8, 49, 52, 54, 55, 56
Hill, John, 53, 54, 154
Hillen, Sean, 87
Hinde, John, 87
Hinds, Richard, 18n
HKSAR, *see* Hong Kong Special
  Administrative Region
Hogan, Paul, 23
Hollindale, Peter, 106, 107, 108, 109, 111,
  113
Hollywood cinema, 144n
*Hong Kong connections: transnational
  imagination in action cinema*, 26n
Hong Kong Special Administrative
  Region, 9–10, 19
Hong Kong University Grants Committee,
  19–20
Hooper, James, 35n
Hoover, Michael, 26n
Horgan, Cashell, 81n, 82
Horgan, James, 82
Horne, Donald, 19
Hotel Hibiscus, 39, 41–2, 43
Hounsou, Djimon, 145, 149, 150
How to Play Polo, 92

Hungarian Bauhaus, *see* Mühely Academy
Hush-a-Bye Baby, 12, 112, 113, 129, 131,
 133–6, 139–41
Huston, John, 49
 The Dead
Huxley, Aldous, 61

I Went Down, 109n
IDA, *see* Industrial Development
 Authority
The idea of Africa, 143n
The Iliad, 69
Imamura, Shohei, 38n
Imitation of Life, 150
In America, 12–13, 143–53
*In the kingdom of the shadows: a companion
 to early cinema*, 70n
In the Name of the Father, 13
Industrial Development Authority, 81, 82
*Infinite varieties: Dan Lowrey's Music Hall,
 1879–97*, 70n–71n
The invention of solitude, 62
IRA, 101, 105, 154, 157
The IRA in the twilight years, 1923–1948,
 101n
Ireland 1848, 83
Irish Animation Festival, 82
*Irish contraception and crisis pregnancy
 (ICCP) study: a survey of the general
 population*, 141n
Irish Film Archive, 82n
Irish Film Board, 79, 80, 83, 84n, 86, 87,
 156
Irish Film Institute, 82
*Irish film: the emergence of a contemporary
 cinema*, 80n, 109n, 111n, 154n
Irish Flash, 83
Irish national cinema, 48n, 53n, 54n, 80n,
 85n, 86n
Irish Postgraduate Film Research Seminar,
 9, 13
Irish Republican Army, *see* IRA
Irish Research Council for the Humanities
 and Social Sciences, 69n
Irish Tourist Board, 48, 82
Islands of discontent, 39n
ITV, 154, 156

J. Walter Thompson advertising agency, 91
James, Charles Augustus, 74

James, Kevin, 106
Jesus Christ, 112, 113
Jim Sheridan: framing the nation, 143n
Johnston, Claire, 153n
Jordan, Neil, 50, 85, 86, 87, 105, 109, 110,
 111, 112n, 113
 The Butcher Boy
 Michael Collins
Joseph, Claudia, 161n
Joyce, Giorgio, 122, 124, 125, 126
Joyce, James, 12, 64, 81, 86, 117–28
Joyce, Lucia, 122, 126
Joyce, Nora, *see* Nora Barnacle
Joyce, Stanislaus, 122, 124
JWT, *see* J. Walter Thompson advertising
 agency

Kamigami no hukaki yokubo, 38n
Kaplan, E. Ann, 152
Kapur, Shekhar, 48
 Elizabeth
Kavaleer Films, 88
Kavanagh, Andrew, 79, 80, 86, 88, 89
 The Depository
 From *An Evil Cradling*
 The Milliner
Keane, Dolores, 139
Keating, David, 109n
 Last of the High Kings
Keenan, Brian, 80, 86
Keeping it real: Irish film and television, 80n
Kellegher, Tina, 131
Kelly, Daragh, 122
Kelly, John, 87
Kerr, Aphra, 80n
Kiely, Richard, 53n
Klimowski, Andrzej, 88
Knights, Robert, 53
 The Dawning
Ko, Mika, 10, 13
Korea, 11, 86, 87, 97–105
Kraicer, Shelly, 24n, 27n
Kulezic-Wilson, Danijela, 10
Kung Fu, 23

La Jétee, 83n
Laffan, Pat, 134
Landsberg, Alison, 162, 163
The language of George Orwell, 94n

Larminie, William, 69n
Last of the High Kings, 109n
Lau, Andrew Wai-keung, 9, 24–32, 36
 Young and Dangerous IV: 97
Lau, Jeff, 26
Layden, Dervila, 12, 132n
Lean, David, 49
 Ryan's Daughter
Lee, Bruce, 23
Lefebvre, Henri, 18
Lehane, Dennis, 23
Leitch, Luke, 156n
Lemass, Sean, 110
Lévi-Strauss, Claude, 59, 60, 62
Liebmann, Michael, 135
Lillington, Karlin, 79n
Linehan, Hugh, 107
Lingnan University, 19, 32, 34
Linnecar, Vera, 91
Literary ideals in Ireland, 69n
Lloyd, David, 123
Lloyd, Genevieve, 57n
The location of culture, 157n
*Looking for the Other: feminism, film and
 the imperial gaze*, 152n
A Love Divided, 119
Love's Love, 43–5, see *Tsuru-Henry*
Lovett, Ann, 112, 130n
Lowrey, Dan, 70
Lye, Len, 93
Lynch, David, 54, 55
 Blue Velvet
Lynch, Susan, 118

Macbeth, 49
McCabe, Ruth, 133
Macartney, Syd, 119
 A Love Divided
McCourt, Emer, 113, 133
McCourt, Frank, 124
McCrone, David, 53n, 55
MacDonald, Peter, 122
McElhinney, Ian, 112
McGahern, John, 97, 97n, 102
McGovern, Jimmy, 13, 154–8, 160–4
 Sunday
McGregor, Ewan, 118
McGuigan, Bernie, 160, 161, 163
Macintyre, Dr. John, 77

McKendrick, Alexander, 91
McKernan, Luke, 75n
MacKinnon, Gillies, 49, 130, 131
 The Playboys
 Regeneration
McLoone, Martin, 49, 80n, 109, 111, 154,
 156, 163
The Macquarie dictionary, 17, 28
Mad Max, 55
Madden, John, 49
 Mrs Brown
Maddox, Brenda, 117, 125
Maeve, 12, 117, 118, 120
Magdalene Laundries, 130n
Magma, 82
Magnolia, 10, 57–65 (esp 58, 60, 61–5)
Maley, Willy, 52, 55n
Maltby, Richard, 144n
Man, Alex, 30
Manchevski, Milcho, 60
 Before the Rain
Mann, Aimee, 62, 63, 64, 65
Manovich, Lev, 83, 84n
Marker, Chris, 83n
 La Jétee
Marshall Plan, 93
Massey, Doreen, 28
The Matrix films, 88
Meaney, Colm, 132
Meaney, Gerardine, 118n, 119, 121, 123,
 125n, 128, 153
Melrose Place, 23
Memento, 60, 61
Memoires for Paul de Man, 164n
Memory and popular film, 162n
Meteor Garden, 23
Michael Collins, 85, 105
Miller, George, 55
 Mad Max
The Milliner, 88, 89
Ministry of Information, 92
Mrs. Brown, 49
Mister Magoo, 82
Mitt Liv som Hund, see *My Life as a
 Dog*
Modern Times, 92
Mok, Karen Man-wai, 31
Molony, Fiona, 98
Monarch of the Glen, 49

Monger, Christopher, 49
  The Englishman who went up a hill but came down a mountain
Monster, 82
Monty Python, 63
Morris, Angela, 53n
Morris, Meaghan, 9–10, 19n, 21n, 22n
Morris-Suzuki, Tessa, 38
Morrison, Toni, 152n
A Mortal Shock, 92
Morton, Samantha, 145
Morvern Callar, 54–5
Mountjoy Gaol, 98, 100
Moving Still Productions, 80, 86, 87, 88, 89
  From *An Evil Cradling*
  Ship of Fools
  Sir Gawain and the Green Knight
Mudimbe, V.Y., 143n
Mugen Ryukyu Tsuru-Henry, see *Tsuru-Henry*
Mühely Academy, 90
Muir, Edwin, 52
Murai, Osamu, 37
Murakami Wolf, 81
Murphy, Fionnuala, 134
Murphy, Kathleen, 91
Murphy, Pat, 12, 117–28
  Anne Devlin
  Maeve
  Nora
Murphy, R., 49n
Murray, James, 72n, 75n, 78n
Murtagh, Matthew, 70n
Music and the mind, 57n
The Music Man, 91
My Left Foot, 13, 50, 143
My Life as a Dog, 109
Myths to live by, 63–4

Nabi no koi, 39–41, 42, 43
Nabi's Love, see *Nabi no koi*
Nakae, Yuji, 39–43
  Nabi no koi/Nabi's Love
  Hotel Hibiscus
Nanto ideorogi no hassei, 37n
Narration in the fiction film, 58n
Narrative comprehension and film, 122n
National cinema and beyond: studies in Irish Film 1, 9, 50n, 132n
National College of Art and Design, 82
National Film Institute of Ireland, see Irish Film Institute
National Trust (British), 47
Neely, Sarah, 10, 11, 50n, 55n
Neighbours, 23
Neil Jordan: exploring boundaries, 54n, 79n
Nesbitt, James, 157
Newhall, Beth, 12–13, 143n, 145n
Newmark, Kevin, 132n
97 Wise Guys No War Cannot Be Won, 27, see *Young and Dangerous IV: 97*
Nolan, Christopher, 60, 61
  Memento
Nora (Gerardine Meaney, 2004), 118n, 119n, 121n, 123n, 125n, 126n, 128n
Nora (Pat Murphy, 2000), 12, 117–28
Nora: the real life of Molly Bloom, 117, 125
North South Programme for Collaborative Research, 9
Northern Ireland Arts Council, 87
The novel and the nation: studies in the new Irish fiction, 52n
NRL premiership, 35
Number 96, 23

O Briain, Art, 87 [Art]
O'Brien, Eugene, 79n
O'Brien, Harvey, 106n, 124
O'Brien, Paul, 80, 81n
O'Byrne, Joe, 97, 110
  Pete's Meteor
The O.C., 23
O'Connell, Dióg, 12
O'Connor, Hugh, 106
O'Connor, Pat, 49, 53, 54
  Circle of Friends
  Fools of Fortune
O'Connor, Sinead, 112n, 113n
O'Donnell, Damian, 109n
  Thirty-Five a Side
O'Flynn, Sunniva, 82n
O'Sullivan, Thaddeus, 49, 130, 131
  December Bride
Odham Stokes, Lisa, 26n
The Odyssey, 69, 87
Of grammatology, 163n, 164n

Okinawa – nexus of borders: Ryukyu reflections, 38
Olivier, Laurence, 47
Once upon a time in China: a guide to Hong Kong, Taiwanese and Mainland Chinese cinema, 26n
Orientalism, 144n
Orpheus, 80
Orwell, George, 90, 93–5
Orwell: the authorised biography, 94n
The Oscars, 79, 143
Our Boys, 112
Overtones and undertones, 60n

Pal, George, 90, 91
Paley, William, 75
Parker, Alan, 50
 Angela's Ashes
Pasolini, Pier Paolo, 160, 161
Paul, Robert, 71
Pearl Harbour, 85n
Perry, John, 63
Pete's Meteor, 110
Peter Pan, 92
Petrie, Duncan, 48n
Pettitt, Lance, 80n, 130
Pidduck, Julianne, 50n
Pieperhoff, Edith, 80
 An Bonnán Buí
 Orpheus
Pieterse, Jan, 151n, 153n
Pine, Emilie, 11, 12
Planet Hong Kong: popular cinema and the art of entertainment, 26n
The Playboys, 130, 131
Point counter point, 61
Point of view in the cinema: a theory of narration and subjectivity in classical film, 51n
Poitier, Sidney, 150
Ports of call: Central European and North American culture/s in motion, 23n
Powrie, Phil, 49, 50, 53, 56
The practice of everyday life, 18n
Prezioso, Roberto, 120, 123, 126
Profane mythology: the savage mind of cinema, 61n
The profound desire of the Gods, 38n
The Promise of Barty O'Brien, 98n

Proust, 57
The public culture: the triumph of industrialism, 19n
Pulp Fiction, 27

The Quiet Man, 87
Quinn, Paul, 109n
 This Is My Father

Radio Telefis Éireann, 79n, 82, 85, 86, 119n
RAE, *see* Research Assessment Exercise
Ramsay, Lynne, 50, 54–5
 Morvern Callar
 Ratcatcher
Rankin, Ian, 23
Ratcatcher, 50
Rattlebag, 119n
The raw and the cooked: introduction to the science of mythology, 59n
RDS, *see* Royal Dublin Society
A reader in Animation Studies, 84n
Rebel, see *Brendan and the Book of Kells*
Recherche du temps perdu, 57
Redfern, Jasper, 75
Reefer and the Model, 12, 129, 131, 139
Regeneration, 49
Reichs, Kathy, 23
Reiniger, Lotte, 82
Reinventing Ireland: culture and the Celtic Tiger, 84n
Reisenleitner, Markus, 23n
Research Assessment Exercise, 21
The rise of the cinema in Great Britain: Jubilee Year 1897, 77n
Road, S., 93n
Rob Roy, 54
Robinson, Ruairí, 79
Rockett, Emer, 54
Rockett, Kevin, 54, 84, 86n, 98n
Ronell, Avital, 162, 164n
Röntgen, Wilhelm, 70n, 72, 73, 74, 75, 76, 77, 78
Rose of Tralee festival, 86
Rosemary's Baby, 140
Rotha, Paul, 93
Royal College of Science, 76
Royal Dublin Society, 70
RTÉ, *see* Radio Telefis Éireann

Rundle, Kay, 141n
Russell, George, 69n
Ryan's Daughter, 49
Ryukyu University, 39

Said, Edward, 144
Salvioni, Professor, 77
Sands, Bobby, 80
Saunders, F.S., 94n
Saville Inquiry, 156
Saving Private Ryan, 85n
Schwartz, Dennis, 152n
*Scotland – the brand: the making of Scottish
   heritage*, 53–54n
Scott and Scotland, 52n
Scott, Andrew, 97
Scott, Sir Walter, 49
Scottish history: the power of the past, 55n
*Screening Ireland: film and television
   representation*, 80n, 130n
Screening Scotland, 48n
Sellar, Ian, 50
   Venus Peter
Shakespeare, William, 108
Shannon, Alan, 79
Shaw, Cecil, 75, 76
Shelden, Michael, 94
Sheridan, Jim, 12, 13, 50, 119, 143–53,
   156
   In America
   In the Name of the Father
   My Left Foot
Ship of Fools, 87, 88, 89
The Shoemaker and the Hatter, 93
Shohat, Ella, 13, 143, 150–152, 153n
Short Shorts, 83, 86
Signs of childness in children's books, 107
Sino-British Joint Declaration (1984), 26
Sir Gawain and the Green Knight, 80
Sit, Margaret Tsui, 30n
Smith, G.A., 77
Smith, Murray, 54
Smyth, Gerry, 52
The Snapper, 12, 129–42
Song For a Raggy Boy, 112
The Sopranos, 23
Space, place and gender, 28n
Stalin, Josef, 94, 96
Stam, Robert, 13, 143, 150–2, 153n

Star Theatre of Varieties, 70, 76
Stembridge, Gerald, 119
   About Adam
Stevenson, Robert Louis, 49
Storr, Anthony, 57
The story of Halas and Batchelor, 91n, 92n
Street Kids Violence, 26n
*Studies in Scottish fiction: 1945 to the
   present*, 52n
*Subversion and scurrility: popular discourse
   in Europe from 1500 to the present*, 52n
Sullivan Bluth, 81
Sunday, 13, 154–8, 160–4
Sutherland, Stewart R., 20, 21
Sweeney, Ellen E., 10, 13

Takamine, Go, 10, 39, 43–6
   Tsuru-Henry
Tanaka, Yasuhiro, 37, 38, 42, 43
*Ten years after: the Irish Film Board,
   1993–2003*, 84n, 86n
Terraglyph, 80, 82
   Wilde Stories
Thatcher, Margaret, 20, 47
Thirty-Five a Side, 109n
This Is My Father, 109n
Thought Lines: an anthology of research 6,
   81n
Tornatore, Giuseppe, 109
   Cinema Paradiso
Train Trouble, 91
Trainspotting, 54, 55
Trajectories: inter-Asia cultural studies, 22n
Trauma: explorations in memory, 132n
Trinity College Dublin, 9, 143n
Trnka, Jiri, 88, 89
   The Hand
Tse, Michael, 25
Tsui, Hark, 26
Tsuru-Henry, 10, 39, 43–6
Tung Chee-hwa, 31–2
Turner, Graeme, 34
Turner, Paul, 49
   Hedd Wyn
Tushingham, Rita, 106

Ulster Amateur Photographic Society,
   75
Ulys, 86, 87

Ulysses, 81, 86
Under the Lion Rock, 23
Understanding animation, 88n
University of Edinburgh, 20
University of Limerick, 161n
University of Ulster, 9, 118
*Unthinking Eurocentrism: multiculturalism
and the media*, 143, 150, 151n, 152n
UPA, 82

Venus Peter, 50
Virgin Mary, 112–13, 135–6, 139
VisitScotland, 48
*Visual digital culture: surface play and
spectacle in new media*, 84n
The voice in cinema, 51n
Volta Cinema, 122, 126
Von Trier, Lars, 125
  Breaking the Waves

Wagner, Richard, 59
Wales Screen Commission, 49
Walker, Alexander, 156n
Wallace, William, 55
Walsh, Kieron J., 119
  When Brendan met Trudy
Walsh, Professor Dermot, 161n
Ward, Paul, 83
Waters, Lindsay, 34n
Watford Technical School, 90
Watters, Eugene, 70n
*Waving the flag: constructing a national
cinema in Britain*, 49n
Way of the Dragon, 23
Weinstein, Wendy, 147n
Wells, Paul, 88n
Westal, Bob, 149
When Brendan met Trudy, 119
Who Am I?, 23
*Who paid the piper? The CIA and the
cultural Cold War*, 94n
*Who's Who of Victorian cinema: a
worldwide survey*, 75n

Whyte, Pádraic, 10, 11, 12
Widgery Inquiry, 154, 157, 160, 161, 162,
  163
Widgery, Lord, see Widgery Inquiry
Wilde, Oscar, 80
Wilde Stories, 80
Wilford, Colonel, 159
Wilson, Robert, 156
Window, 80
The Winter's Tale, 107
Wolf, Günter, 82, *see also* Murakami Wolf
Wong, Jing 24n
Wong, Kar-wai, 26
  Ashes of Time
Wong, Manfred, 25
Woo, John, 26, 27
Woodley, Karen, 134
Woods, Steve, 80, 81n, 82, 83
  Ireland 1848
  Window
World's Fair Waxworks, 74
Wuzburg University, 72

X-Ray Cinematography of Frog's Legs, 77
The X-Ray Fiend, 77

Yamagata International Documentary Film
  Festival, 38
Yanagida, Kunio, 37
Yang, Jeff, 26n
Yeats, William Butler, 69
Yellow Submarine, 93
YIDF, *see* Yamagata International
  Documentary Film Festival
Yokota Einosuke, 75
Young and Dangerous IV: 97, 9, 17–36
  (esp. 24–32, 34)
Young and Dangerous series, 24, 26–8, 30,
  34
Yuen, Corey, 26
Yuen, Woo-ping, 26

Zagreb Studio, 93